WHEN BRAVE MEN SHUDDER
The Scottish origins of Dracula

MIKE SHEPHERD

A Wild Wolf Publication

Published by Wild Wolf Publishing in 2018
Copyright © 2018 Michael Shepherd

ISBN: 978-1-907954-69-6
Also available as an ebook

www.wildwolfpublishing.com

INTRODUCTION BY DACRE STOKER

Dracula scholarship has been around since the 1960s when the novel was deemed a classic by academics at Oxford University. Bernard Davies, Elizabeth Miller, Sir Christopher Frayling, Radu Florescu, Raymond McNally, and Richard Dalby, as well as four early biographers, Ludlam, Belford, Farson and Murray, led the charge in revealing connections and putting forth theories about Bram's motivations and inspirations for writing *Dracula*. There were precious few pieces of source material to base their theories on; their evidence was mainly provided by Bram Stoker's notes for *Dracula*, the preface to the Icelandic edition and the *Dracula* typescript.

More recently, three researchers have added new information. Hans De Roos interpreted Bram's notes to lay claim to the actual location of the fictional Castle Dracula. David Pybus, the curator of the Whitby Museum, pieced together evidence of Bram's movements and contacts during his Whitby holiday in 1890. John Edgar Browning discovered a slew of reviews of *Dracula* published world-wide which refutes the long-standing claim that *Dracula* only met with mixed reviews while Bram was alive.

Now Mike Shepherd has made a most significant discovery of his own. He has found numerous pieces of evidence that point to Bram spending at least twelve or thirteen of his summer holidays in Cruden Bay (then called Port Erroll) and nearby Whinnyfold. While Bram was there he most likely wrote *Dracula*. He also wrote two other novels based in Cruden Bay - *The Watter's Mou'* and *The Mystery of the Sea*.

Mike is the first to investigate Bram Stoker's time in Cruden Bay in detail. The Aberdeenshire village in the north of Scotland is perhaps too remote for most; that is, except for Mike - he lives there. This helps, as he is intimately familiar with the localities associated with Bram Stoker and has access to unpublished local archive material.

3

Mike's findings take nothing away from Whitby, where Bram did a significant amount of research and found the name Dracula in a book by William Wilkinson in the Whitby Subscription Library. He chose to set the action of chapters six, seven, and parts of eight of *Dracula* in Whitby, the town resting in the shadow of Whitby Abbey and St Mary's Church. This provided the perfect gothic backdrop and a very realistic setting for the arrival of the vampire count into England.

But it was in Port Erroll (Cruden Bay) that Bram did the actual writing. I can imagine him arriving at the Kilmarnock Arms Hotel or one of the nearby cottages in later years, opening his trunk and unpacking his booklet of notes along with his research books. Once he had set up a writing desk, he would allow his imagination to put everything together. Bram Stoker was a part-time author for most of his life, and his monthly holidays to Cruden Bay provided the largest slice of time to write his books after 1893. He returned to Aberdeenshire year after year. His new writing regime, starting at the age of 45, provided a regular slot for writing books. I also wonder if Bram managed to find time to write while on his many Atlantic crossings back and forth to America.

I visited Cruden Bay in 2017, and the memory of Bram Stoker's time there is strong, even though it's over a hundred years since his last trip north. I talked to a woman whose neighbour told her in the 1970s that she would look over and see Bram Stoker writing his books in her front garden. I met another woman whose great aunt was my great grand-uncle's landlady. She told me she remembered her 'Aunt Isy' as a young girl.

When Brave Men Shudder aims to understand Bram Stoker using source material from those who knew him. The villagers saw him as a cheery Irishman full of jokes and not the dark, haunted soul some have made him out to be. It is important to make a distinction between the man himself and his professional interest in gothic horror. It is almost as if Bram needed to transform himself from being the full time theatre manager in London to a part-time writer on his perfect stage of Cruden Bay.

This lovely and quaint Scottish village was Bram's chosen holiday location. It was suitably far away from the hustle and bustle of London and the stress of managing Sir Henry Irving and the Lyceum Theatre. He would walk up and down the beach and trample along the cliffs thinking out the stories for his novels. It was here that he was able to be at his creative best. As a part-time writer myself, it is important to find an escape from the pressures of one's other life before starting to construct great stories. Not only must one have the presence of a stimulating environment, but also an environment involving an absence of interruptions and pressures. I believe that Bram was at one with Cruden Bay. Mike points out a very interesting connection between the writings of Walt Whitman about his love and connection to the natural world, and the undertones of some of Bram's writings, even in *Dracula*.

It is interesting for me to note that Bram frequently 'sought' uncluttered spaces away from the hustle and bustle of city life to clear his head and allow his creative juices to flow freely. These places usually involved the ocean. I feel that Bram was drawn to the ocean for the relaxed atmosphere, away from the Lyceum Theatre, but it also provided the right setting for the adventure of travel and the unknown that goes with it. He was bought up in Clontarf, outside Dublin. It is possible that in the early part of his life the ocean near Clontarf provided a sense of solitude. Once he moved into Dublin proper he would ride the train out to Greystones, a small beach community south of Dublin. It is here that he wrote an entry into his 'Lost Journal' entitled Night Fishing in 1871.

Bram seemed like a very personable man. It is obvious from research by Mike in Cruden Bay and David Pybus in Whitby that Bram sought out the local fishermen as well as members of the local coastguard to pick up the local lore. Some of it made its way into his novels. Bram was a story teller. He seemed to gravitate to other storytellers to get an insight into local drama. The inclusion of local lore into his stories brought a sense of realism to them.

Bram Stoker professed 'great love for this part of Scotland' (1904: Peterhead Flower Show). This explains why someone who gave dinner parties to the rich and famous of London society chose to take his annual holiday in a remote fishing village. Apart from the peace to write his books, the beautiful coastline around Cruden Bay reconnected him to nature and a mystical sense of the universe at large. Perhaps it was this that stimulated his mid-life creative explosion.

Furthermore, Mike has pointed out the locally-known connection between a specific octagonal room in Slains Castle and a description of the same room in Bram's fictional castle in *Dracula*: 'The Count halted, putting down my bags, closed the door, and crossing the room, opened another door which led into a small octagonal room lit by a single lamp, and seemingly without a window of any sort.' Visitors to this day can visit Slains Castle and get a glimpse of this odd shaped room, although it now lacks a roof and the elaborate panelling and upholstery that would have been around when Bram saw the room more than one hundred years ago.

Mike Shepherd now joins a short list of Bram Stoker *Dracula* enthusiasts who have fairly recently made significant contributions to the research and understanding of Bram Stoker's life and writing.

Dacre Stoker, South Carolina. May 2018.

[Dacre's great-grandfather was Bram Stoker's youngest brother. He is Canadian by birth, the family having moved to Canada at the time of the First World War. He now writes and lectures full time about his famous ancestor. His new novel, in conjunction with J.D. Barker, is *Dracul*, a prequel to Dracula. It has been optioned for a film by Paramount film studios.]

Dacre Stoker and Elsie Watt. The great-grandnephew of Bram Stoker with the grandniece of Isy Cay, Bram Stoker's landlady at the Crookit Lum Cottage. November 2017. Copyright Mike Shepherd.

PROLOGUE: THE DEAD UN-DEAD

Bram Stoker walked along Cruden Bay beach agonising over the next chapter of his book. His hands behind his back, and head stooped in thought, he stepped over the shallow stream called the Bleedy Burn. Viking hordes had long ago fought the Scots on the sandhills behind the beach, and when the crimson sun went down that evening, the stream, gashing deep as it exited the dunes to the sea, disgorged blood across the flesh-coloured sand. Cruden Bay is a place stained forever by the horror of that moment: the name *Cruden*, it's said, means slaughter of the Danes.[1]

Where the sandhills edge out is the Hawklaw, a low grassy hillock. A bird of prey with hooded eyes hovers over the summit. Its sharp beak points down and claws spread out in anticipation of the kill to come. Seabirds, crows and jackdaws flee in terror from the sight.

At the far end of the beach sharp rocks pierce out of the sea - Bram saw them as fangs. The granite on the surface of the rocks has weathered to a dark red-brown colour with the texture of encrusted gore. The waves lick up around and drench them in white foam.

Reaching the mid-point of the beach he looked up at the two-mile stretch of foreshore as it curved around him. 'If Cruden Bay is to be taken figuratively as a mouth, with the sand hills for soft palate, and the green Hawklaw as the tongue, the rocks which work the extremities are its teeth,' he once wrote. Not many would see Cruden Bay beach as a mouth with teeth, Bram Stoker did.

Back in the year 1895 the part-time author was on holiday in the remote Scottish village of Port Erroll; his job as a business manager of a London theatre left well behind. However, this was no ordinary holiday - he was writing *Dracula*. It proved anything but a relaxing break for Bram Stoker or his family. His wife and son had been appalled by his behaviour – the Irishman had entered into the spirit of the novel with manic zest. Gripped by a demon of creative intensity he withdrew emotionally from his family, grumbling at any interruption to his work.

But at least he was writing the book. It had taken him a long time to get this far - five years since he conceived the idea. Early on, the working title for his novel had been *The Un-Dead* or alternatively *The Dead Un-Dead*. Yet for the next few years the project wasn't so much un-dead, it was in deep slumber. The author tinkered with the plot outline, added another detail to the character notes, and read more books about the supernatural, but somehow couldn't bring himself to start writing it. Bram Stoker didn't normally mess around in life: he worked with relentless energy, and most of his books were written very quickly. This one was the exception.

Dracula had now risen from the page. Just as the dust in the moonbeams coalesced into voluptuous maiden vampires, the words finally melded together and the famous story came to life. His discovery of Port Erroll and Cruden Bay had prodded him into action. What he found there brought *Dracula* into the world.

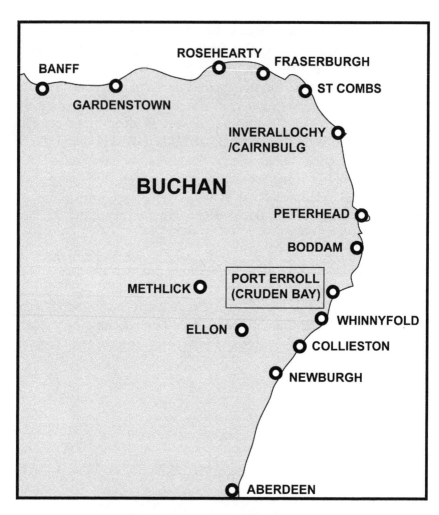

NORTH EAST SCOTLAND

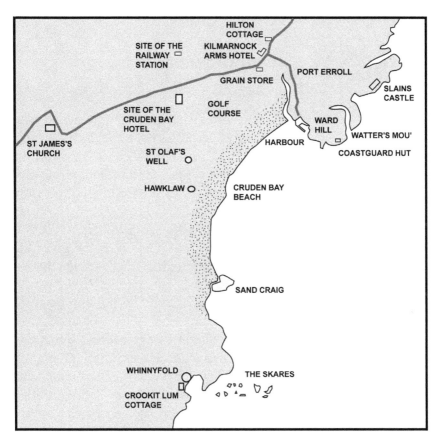

BRAM STOKER'S CRUDEN BAY

1
THE ROAD TO DRACULA

What was Bram Stoker like? Let's find out from someone who had met him: 'He was one of the nicest men I ever knew, a big, cheery, handsome Irishman,' said Mrs Cruickshank, who ran the Port Erroll Post Office. 'Bram had a fine sense of humour always joking about something. He had such a strong and pleasant personality.'[2]

Could this possibly be the man who wrote *Dracula*? Yes, is the answer. An American reporter wrote years later that given the gory nature of the novel everyone found it 'remarkable' that 'it had been written by a mild, gentle Irishman and man of the world, who went about his way peacefully, never raising his voice in argument.'[3]

Yet in modern times, Bram Stoker has gained the reputation as a dark haunted soul because many academics, although not all, assume he must have been like that to have written the book. The idea that Bram sought release from his demons by writing gothic horror tales helps to add lurid content to papers in literary journals. If their authors had taken the pains to look beyond the subject matter of *Dracula* and examined the evidence, they would have found this view to be utter nonsense: Bram Stoker was a nice guy and, judging him by how he behaved to others, he acted like he was a nice guy.

So we have to ask: how did a reasonably normal person come to write *Dracula*? And what was in the mind of the man who wrote it? My book sets out to address both these questions. The answers are surprising, and they will not disappoint *Dracula* fans. The chapters that follow tell the story of how Bram Stoker discovered the supernatural, became immersed in it, and how this guided the writing of his gothic novels.

Bram Stoker was born near Dublin in 1847. He was brought up the third child of seven with four brothers and two sisters. It was a close family, and made so by his loving and affectionate parents

Abraham and Charlotte Stoker. This left its mark. Bram went through life seeking out cosy relationships, perhaps in an attempt to recreate the family warmth he experienced back then. He would go on to have a family of his own with one child, a son Noel. This was a man who had been granted with the gift of loving closeness. The adult Bram Stoker was friendly with everybody no matter what their station in life, and he doesn't appear to have been in the least bit self-important.

For the first seven years of his life Bram suffered from a mystery illness that has never been fully explained although, as his relative Dacre Stoker explained to me, it was probably an asthma-related ailment common within the family. 'In my earlier years I had known much illness,' Bram would write later. 'Certainly till I was about seven years old I never knew what it was to stand upright. This early weakness, however, passed away in time and I grew into a strong boy.' Adding that: 'I was naturally thoughtful and the leisure of long illness gave rise to many thoughts which were fruitful according to their kind in later years.'[4]

As he recovered from his long illness, Bram grew stronger and stronger. His childhood experiences would now shape the man; his love of books and the theatre came about at this time. Although the Stoker family were not especially well off, their one luxury was to keep a well-stocked library. The father spent his evenings at the fireplace reading, and it was a library that was also picked over by the son. On occasions, his father would put down his book to tell Bram stories of the Dublin theatre and about the performances of the great Irish actor Edmund Kean.[5]

Bram had been brought up to be honest, decent and honourable in his personal affairs. Both his parents were devout Protestants. He was given a Bible for his ninth birthday and read it thoroughly, underlining large sections of the text as he went along. A letter from father to son gives a sense of the moral code imparted to the family: 'Honesty is the same in every relation of life, and anything obtained by a different course cannot be right,' Bram was told. His father prayed every night such that he might be able to rear his children "in honesty and uprightness..."[6]

Because of his early illness Bram started school later than normal. His performance at school suffered. He was 'dull as to results' although 'secretly ambitious,' he would write later.[7]

Where was this ambition leading? A hint is to be found in Bram's work of non-fiction *Famous Imposters*. In describing John Law, the Scots-born eighteenth century banker and fraudster, he wrote that, 'Law did not enrich human life... or add to the sums of human well-being and happiness.'[8] The idea of making a positive contribution to society mattered to Bram. As a young man stepping into the adult world he sought personal and spiritual fulfilment. He intended to make a name for himself, and his leaning was towards an interest in books and the theatre.

The adult Bram Stoker was tall at six foot two inches with a sturdy build stemming from his athletic pursuits while at Trinity College in Dublin. He had blue eyes, brown hair and a full auburn beard. Photographs show a bulky brooding giant; these have led to uninformed comment on the internet that he was a gloomy soul. However, this is misleading. It wasn't the fashion in Victorian times to smile at the camera. Photography was in its early days, and the subjects copied the pose of sitters from paintings, although they didn't have to: the unfortunate souls enduring the torture of a painted portrait never smiled for the artist for the simple reason it was much too painful to keep a grin going for hours and hours.

He spoke with a high voice and a mild Irish accent except when he was in an argument; then his Irish accent became much stronger. Bram could be assertive when he needed to be, a quality essential for his professional life to come. His height and build added considerably to his authority.

Some of his associates described him as well-dressed - he was always turned out in a suit and tie - others saw him as scruffy. His friend Horace Wyndham sided with the latter view. 'He told me – and I quite credit it – that he always carried his dress suit in a small despatch case. From the concertina-like creases in them, I should have been fully prepared to believe that he rolled up the trousers and put them in his pocket.'[9]

Bram's life changed at the age of twenty-three when he discovered the writings of the American poet Walt Whitman. His quest for identity, a goal for many a young adult, landed here. Walt Whitman's other-worldly outlook took the place of Bram's Christian faith. The American wrote sensual poems that emphasized the positive aspects of life. They praised self-acceptance, the glory of nature and a spiritual enlightenment that lay in mystical realms well beyond the boundaries of orthodox religion. Bram had found here a philosophical basis for life that would take him into maturity.

The young Bram Stoker sent a fan letter to Walt Whitman describing himself 'as a pupil to his master'. In his 1855 introduction to his collection of poems *Leaves of Grass*, Whitman had told his readers how the aspiring poet should live; he advised adopting what was essentially the lifestyle of a saint: 'This is what you shall do: Love the earth and sun and the animals, despise riches, give alms to everyone that asks, stand up for the stupid and crazy, devote your income and labour to others, hate tyrants, argue not concerning God, have patience and indulgence toward the people, take off your hat to nothing known or unknown or to any man or number of men, go freely with powerful uneducated persons and with the young and with the mothers of families, read these leaves in the open air every season of every year of your life, re examine all you have been told at school or church or in any book, dismiss whatever insults your own soul...' Should you do this, 'your very flesh shall be a great poem.'[10]

It was inspirational material for an acutely sensitive young man with a literary outlook. Bram took the advice to the core of his being; his soul now firmly anchored in Walt Whitman's world view. Yet Bram could only go so far with the poet's advice for the good life. Walt Whitman had written in his poem *Whoever you are holding me now in hand*, 'You would have to give up all else, I alone would expect to be your sole and exclusive standard.' Bram told Whitman in his letter that he wasn't willing to 'give up all else' by going all the way to slavishly copy his hero's saint-like demeanour. He could not abandon his worldly ambitions. Bram still held firm to the attitude that men should stamp their mark on the world. 'An individual who is not in any way distinguishable from his fellows is but a poor creature,' he would write in his late 50s, adding that they are 'not held of much account by anybody.'[11] Bram knew what he was about and faced the world with certainty; he had established a goal in life and that was to establish his name amongst his fellows.

Bram would, nevertheless, commit himself to the ideals expressed in the poetry and abandon his prejudices. The evidence is that Bram Stoker carried out Whitman's advice to the end of his life. He appeared to accept everyone for who they were and made no judgments about them. Bram was also tolerant of the religious beliefs of others in an age when anything other than Christianity was generally sniffed at.

A sense of Bram's other social attitudes comes across from his novels. They are very much the mind-set of the time, although not necessarily those of modern liberal thought. For instance, he held a Victorian attitude to women as the weaker sex and believed that men were responsible for defending them. Nevertheless, he had become aware that women were starting to assert themselves in society and that a spirit of feminine independence was emerging. He even discussed this in *Dracula*, acknowledging the arrival of what was called the new woman, albeit in somewhat patronising terms. Some day the new woman might even take the initiative in proposing marriage to men: 'And a nice job she will make of it too!'

His father had spent his life as a junior clerk in the Irish Civil Service; Bram now followed him there, and for 13 years he too served as a clerk. His first book was written as part of his government duties - its title as boring as a doorknob - *The Duties of Clerks of Petty Sessions in Ireland*. The author is listed as Bram Stoker, M.A., Inspector of Petty Sessions. His job entailed visiting the Irish courts to monitor the less serious civil and criminal cases, ensuring that they ran efficiently. An excerpt from the first page of the book demonstrates why it has never rivalled *Dracula* in the best-seller stakes: 'Such subjects as the advisability of uniform filing of papers or folding of returns, of using dots instead of 0's in money columns, or of forwarding returns at the earliest instead of the latest date allowable, may seem too trivial to treat of; yet every Clerk would do well to remember that a rigid adherence to the advice on such matters which I have given would facilitate the audit of the returns...'[12]

Bram had originally intended to be a full-time author. The urge to write had been present from an early age. He listened to the old Irish tales his mother told him as a child and tried writing some stories himself. Early success came when his short stories were serialised in the periodicals *London Society* and *Shamrock*. The lure of word-craft had now bewitched his soul. While working as a civil servant, he wrote a long letter to his father announcing his intention to give up his job, move to London and become a writer. His father was appalled at the idea, suggesting that he stay on in Dublin. Only when he was sure of success as a writer should he consider quitting a career job. Bram took the advice and writing became a part-time occupation for most of his life.

He also dabbled with art, and was one of twelve founding members of the Dublin Painting and Sketching Club when it started up in 1874. His interest in art extended to sketching, demonstrating a high standard in the drawings he produced.[13] Dacre Stoker sees his ancestor as very-much inclined to the visual, someone who took a painterly approach to descriptive writing. Bram was hyper-sensitive to the mood of a place, Dacre told me, an aspect that shows up to great effect in the books.

Bram Stoker's main soul-saving distraction from his civil service duties was as an unpaid drama critic reviewing plays for the local Dublin newspapers. He first met Henry Irving face to face in 1876 when the famous actor played Hamlet at the Theatre Royal in Dublin. Bram had favourably reviewed the first night performance and Irving asked to be introduced to him. Something clicked. Irving was much impressed by the qualities he saw in the young Bram Stoker, and two years later offered him the post as business manager for the Lyceum Theatre in London.

But first of all, Bram had to attend to another matter; on the 4th December 1878 he got married. His new wife, Florence, would be admired as one of the most beautiful women in London society. That first meeting took place in Dublin; she was 18, he was 29 years old. Bram took one look at her and decided that this was the woman for him. He had been entranced by her tall graceful features, fine brown hair, and an exquisitely beautiful face, oval in shape with grey-blue eyes. Behind them lay intelligence and an eagerness to expand her knowledge of the outside world.[14]

When Bram met her, Florence was being courted by Oscar Wilde, who in his early days had dallied with women. Oscar and Florence went out together for two years. He wrote passionate love poems to her. These were followed by poems of hurt dejection when she married Bram without even telling him about it, witness for example *Silentium Amoris* (The Silence of Love):

But surely unto Thee mine eyes did show
Why I am silent, and my lute unstrung;
Else it were better we should part, and go,
Thou to some lips of sweeter melody,
And I to nurse the barren memory
Of unkissed kisses, and songs never sung.

He was genuinely distraught at the loss of Florence. In 1880 (and almost two years after her marriage to Bram) he sent the actress Ellen Terry some flowers for Florence to wear, mentioning in the accompanying letter that he is glad that anything of his would touch her. He went on to complain bitterly that she thinks he never loved her and had forgotten her.[15]

Oscar Wilde's biographers disagree about what went wrong with the relationship although nobody knows for sure. A difference in sexual chemistry is an obvious explanation given Oscar Wilde's homosexual tendencies. Alternatively, it's been suggested that Oscar spent too much time out of Dublin and had neglected Florence more than he should have done. Meanwhile, Bram jumped in to seize the prize.[16] Florence was a no-nonsense sort of woman, and wasn't going to hang around when there was a life to be lived. The marriage worked – the Stokers 'got on very well together.'[17] She called him Brammie and they worked as a team. Her husband read his stories to her as they were written: she gave him glowing approval in return.

Ten days after the wedding Bram started work in his new management job at the Lyceum Theatre. The role combined what today would be provided by a large team of managers. He coped with finance, personnel, logistics, and transport organisation for theatre company tours, acted as secretary for Henry Irving, and even wrote many of his speeches. He had yet another key function to carry out. The Lyceum Theatre was one of the select places visited by the elite for an evening out and Bram, in a palace of marble colonnades and velvet plush, was the person that greeted them at the top of the stairs.

Bram Stoker now mixed with London society, and he became part of the dinner-party set. The Stokers knew many people of consequence, not just in Great Britain but also in the United States where the theatre company frequently toured. It was a list that included Prime Ministers, US Presidents, famous writers, poets and artists. Their London house in fashionable Cheyne Walk, Chelsea, was located in a neighbourhood favoured by famous artists and men of letters. The artist James Whistler and the poet Gabriel Dante Rossetti lived nearby.

A friend wrote that the Stokers, 'knew everybody worth knowing, and were also exceedingly hospitable, one could always make sure of finding interesting people there.' W.S. Gilbert of Gilbert and Sullivan opera fame was a regular visitor to their home. On one occasion he was observed in a raging temper at the Stoker's Chelsea house; he had a tendency to bark at people if talked to, yet would sulk if ignored. Those who knew him could guess the reason for his vile mood: 'I fancy he must have overheard some tactless person praising Sullivan.'[18]

Bram was passionate about the theatre, and not because it exposed him to an exalted social circle. Hob-nobbing with the rich and famous doesn't seem to have mattered much to him. A character in one of his early novels was described as not 'in any way addicted to society life,' instead they longed 'for the wilderness.'[19]

And likewise, the author of these lines was a man who preferred to take his summer holidays in an Aberdeenshire fishing village rather than to be seen swanning about with the smart set on the boulevards of Paris. The stage meant far more to Bram than the means to mix with the upper class – it was a calling, a mission, a reason for being. A play should not be thought of as a play, he once wrote, it provides an 'education of the heart, the brain and the soul'. A person of 'pure imagination' could thus know themselves 'a little better' and by doing so, 'to better know the world and its dwellers.'[20]

Through his life in the theatre he had achieved the happy feeling that his work was meaningful and supremely worthwhile. Years later, while pursuing a side line as a freelance journalist, he was granted a rare interview with Winston Churchill, then a rising career politician in the British Cabinet. The interview contained words of wisdom which Bram could have uttered himself: 'It is only by following one's own bent that there can be the really harmonious life.' Churchill told him why: 'The great majority of human beings have to work the greater part of the day and then amuse themselves afterward – if they are not too tired. But the lucky few derive their keenest interest and enjoyment not from any contrast between business and idle hours – but from the work itself.'[21]

Once he took the post with Henry Irving in London, his managerial responsibilities left him little time for writing. He committed to the job with characteristic devotion and energy. 'Bram Stoker's capacity for work is the envy and despair of all his associates' an American journalist wrote. 'He never seems to show fatigue, and his only recreation seems to be a change of occupation. When he moves it is with extraordinary rapidity and apparently oblivious of all obstacles.'[22]

In his full time job at the Lyceum Theatre he dashed around with frenetic energy, forever muttering in his Irish accent that he was in a 'ma-artal [mortal] hurry.'[23] There was so much to do. Amongst countless other duties, he reckoned he wrote at least fifty letters a day on Lyceum business.

Years later he gave a tribute to Henry Irving: 'When a man with his full share of ambition is willing to yield it up to work with a friend whom he loves and honours, it is perhaps as well that in due season he may set out his reasons for so doing.' He saw Henry Irving as the supreme actor with superb stage technique, but more than that, the man was a force for the social good, an educator of the soul. In the final reckoning he had given to Henry Irving: 'All the gifts required of me.'[24]

Bram held to a firmly entrenched Victorian sense of duty. It's something which is difficult for us to understand in today's cynical times, yet it was well-rooted as part of the shared cultural attitudes of the time. This steadfast integrity served him through his adult life. 'He is one of the most kind and tender-hearted of men' wrote the actress Ellen Terry, who worked with Bram in the Lyceum Theatre. 'He filled a difficult position with great tact, and was not so universally abused as most business managers, because he was always straight with the company, and never took a mean advantage of them.'[25]

Bram Stoker always sought to do the right thing, as did the band of heroes intent on dispatching Count Dracula; their unquestioned task to save the world from evil. On one occasion he took civic duty to a heroic level. He was travelling on a ferry down the River Thames en route to London Bridge when an elderly man jumped over the rails in a suicide attempt. Bram threw off his coat, and without hesitation leapt into the river, grabbed hold of the drowning man, and dragged him back on board. He then took the man to his house in Chelsea, and his brother George, a doctor, was called in. It was too late, the man lay dead. The newspapers praised his courage the next day, and he later received a medal from the Royal Humane Society. Florence was reportedly very upset at the incident; the house was never the same for her after seeing a dead body there.

Bram's packed lifestyle still left him with a few odd moments of spare time to pursue his writing ambitions. Nevertheless, his commercial output up until 1890 had been somewhat limited - a book and several short stories. The book is a collection of children's stories with the title *Under the Sunset*. It was well reviewed but not exactly a best seller.

In 1890 Bram Stoker at forty-two years old had it all – but not quite. One shadow spread across his sun-lit path. Bram was living at the edge of his financial means even though Henry Irving paid him reasonably well. He rented a house in up-market Chelsea and regularly entertained guests at considerable expense. His writing provided a means to supplement his income from the Lyceum Theatre with the glorious upside that he might go on to make his fortune as a popular author. In a newspaper interview he hinted at his hopes of gaining success in the London literary scene: 'A writer will find a chance here if he is good for anything;

21

and recognition is only a matter of time.' And with that recognition, money will follow: 'Some men now-a-days are making ten thousand a year by their novels'.[26] That would be equivalent to just over £900,000 a year today.

Bram wanted fame, he wanted to enrich human life, he wanted money - his writing would serve that end. But before it could happen he first had to write a book that would get noticed.

2
TO KILL VAMPIRE DRIVE STAKE THROUGH CORPSE

Bram Stoker's working notes for *Dracula* survive. Some pages are dated and the earliest date is the 8th March 1890. About this time he wrote down four pages of excerpts from an article on Transylvanian superstitions.

The following note grabs your attention: 'Vampire, or nosferatu. To kill vampire drive stake through corpse or fire pistol shot into coffin or cut off head & replace in coffin with mouth full of garlic, or extract heart & burn it & strew ashes over grave.'[27] He would also have read this in the article, 'every person killed by a nosferatu becomes likewise a vampire after death, and will continue to suck the blood of other innocent people till the spirit has been exorcised,' and 'rubbing the body with garlic is a preservative against witchcraft and the pest.'[28]

Transylvanian Superstitions was written by Emily Gerard, a Scotswoman born in 1849, and published in the periodical *Nineteenth Century* in 1885. The first adventurous steps on the route from her family home in Airdrie to faraway Transylvania took Emily to a boarding school in Switzerland.

From there she moved to Venice, and in that dreamy city of canals and gothic edifices she met and married Miecislaus Laszowski, a cavalry officer in the Austro-Hungarian army. In 1883 her husband was posted for two years to Transylvania (now part of Romania), and she went with him.[29] What she found there intrigued her: 'Transylvania might well be termed the land of superstition,' she wrote. 'It would almost seem as though the whole species of demons, pixies, witches, and hobgoblins, driven from the rest of Europe by the wand of science, had taken refuge within this mountain rampart, well aware that here they would find secure lurking-places, whence they might defy their persecutors yet awhile.'

In an 1897 interview Bram cited the Gerard article as influential for *Dracula,* 'I learned a good deal,' he said, and mentions another key source. This was *The Book of Were-wolves* by the Reverend Sabine Baring-Gould, published in 1865.[30]

The Anglican pastor was a prolific writer of novels, non-fiction books and hymns. Apart from helping to inspire *Dracula*, he is best known for writing the words for the hymn *Onward Christian Soldiers*. Baring-Gould's book on werewolves provided some choice phrases that went into Bram's notebook: 'Canine teeth protruding over lower lip when mouth closed' and 'Werewolf has broad hands, short fingers & has some hairs in hollow of hand.'[31]

Bram Stoker now started thinking about the storyline for his new novel. The ideas came quickly in the first flurry of excitement. His early notes mention a Count, who is as yet unnamed. He lives in a castle and is described as an 'old dead man made alive.' There follows another page of notes, and at the top, written in bold letters and underlined, is the word **Vampire**. The start of a story is written down in outline. The Count intends to buy a property in England; a solicitor is sent to the castle, and before long is made: 'A prisoner for a time.' Some of the features used in the novel have already been identified at this stage. There are 'no looking glasses in Count's house', and another note is added, 'never can see him reflected in one – no shadow?'[32]

Although Bram Stoker wrote the most famous vampire story of them all, he wasn't the first to use the theme. He was aware of the vampire tale *Carmilla* written by Joseph Sheridan Le Fanu and published in 1872. Both authors lived in Dublin at the same time. It's likely that their social circles overlapped; they had probably met at soirees held by Oscar Wilde's parents.

Carmilla is a short novel about a young teenage girl who is befriended and subsequently preyed upon by a female vampire, Carmilla, or as she was in ages past Mircalla, Countess Karnstein. Towards the end of the story, the grave of the countess is located, opened up, and 'the face now disclosed to view. The features, though a hundred and fifty years had passed since her funeral, were tinted with the warmth of life. Her eyes were open; no cadaverous smell exhaled from the coffin.' These were signs of vampirism so remedial action was required: 'The body, therefore, in accordance with the ancient practice, was raised, and a sharp stake driven through the heart of the vampire, who uttered a piercing shriek...' [33]

Others had written about vampires in their novels even before *Carmilla* was published, and the public were familiar with them. Bram must have realised that something extraordinary was required for his vampire tale. It would have to be a new approach - one that would astound the reader. And like the glowing sun brilliantly lighting up a new dawn, Bram Stoker's train of thought melded into glorious inspiration. How about a king vampire, an evil boss intent on world domination? It would make for an epic tale.

The villain would be an ancient warlord from a remote land, full of the vigour and determination that had won him battles in a distant past. How could you then explain why he is still around today? Easily enough, he is a disciple of the Devil and he is un-dead!

And the inspiration kept coming. Every dragon needs its St George, so how about pitting a gang of fearless heroes against the master vampire? A promising story with a definite shape was emerging: evil has awoken / evil causes mayhem / evil is destroyed. It's a vampire novel, so it must include the classic gothic elements - a castle of course. It would preferably be somewhere remote enough to create a suitably exotic atmosphere, Transylvania will do.

Throw into the mix a pack of wolves, not ordinary wolves – they are were-wolves. These children of the night need somebody to terrify. Living around the castle are the superstitious peasantry who cower at the evil presence in their midst, their crucifixes held aloft in trembling hands.

This is an epic tale, so the focus of the action will be moved from Transylvania to England. By placing ancient evil in a modern setting the story will play off the utter ghastliness of the situation. Count Dracula terrorizes London, the great city of the empire where millions live! All are in danger: lovers, husbands, wives and children. This would not be a story about pale, listless bloodsuckers in a remote European forest whose eradication effectively amounts to a form of pest control. No, not at all.

It's possible that Bram's epic idea had been inspired by reading Henry Rider Haggard's 1886 novel *She*.[34] Set in Africa, the hero of the book encounters the mysterious white queen Ayesha. She is over 2,000 years old and her beauty has been preserved because she has bathed in the fire of the Pillar of Life. Ayesha - 'She who must be obeyed' - is all powerful and ambitious, very ambitious. Her intention is to move to London and take over from Queen Victoria on the throne.

The narrator, Horace Holly, shudders at 'the result of her arrival there. What her powers were I knew, and I could not doubt but that she would exercise them to the full. It might be possible to control her for a while, but her proud, ambitious spirit would be certain to break loose...' The result was inevitable: 'In the end she would, I had little doubt, assume absolute rule over the British dominions, and probably over the whole Earth...' Britain who had colonised large parts of the globe was now in danger of becoming a colony in turn. It wasn't to be. Ayesha met a ghastly end before this could happen, having rather unwisely entered into the fires of the Pillar of Life for a second time. She reverted to the hideous form of her true age and died shortly afterwards. Queen Victoria's continuing reign on the throne was not now at risk.

And like Ayesha in *She*, Count Dracula has the capacity to cause utter havoc in the capital city. All are vulnerable to the monster who can transform ordinary people into un-dead servitude. We are told by Professor Van Helsing:

"They cannot die, but must go on age after age adding new victims and multiplying the evils of the world. For all that die from the preying of the Undead become themselves Undead, and prey on their kind. And so the circle goes on ever widening, like as the ripples from a stone thrown in the water."

Later we would get King Kong in New York, Godzilla rampaging through Tokyo and the zombie apocalypse; nevertheless it was Bram Stoker who popularised the horror story as told on the epic scale.

This was a plot for a novel that frothed with commercial potential. Bram was on first-name terms with the literary set in London; he knew which books were eagerly bought by the public and those left unopened on dusty shelves.

Not only that, he helped with script selection for the plays staged at the Lyceum Theatre, receiving feedback from the receipts each play brought in. He was tuned into the popular tastes of the public, and was well aware they liked edgy thrills. In particular, dramas with supernatural themes drew in big crowds. More to the point, they filled the Lyceum bank account with money.

One such play, staged at the Lyceum Theatre and on tour, was *Faust*. In a script based on the dramatic poem by Goethe, Faust encounters the archdemon Mephistopheles. Mephistopheles makes a bargain to grant Faust's quest for knowledge of the essence of life in exchange for his soul. It was the 'drawing' play according to Henry Irving. Bram Stoker noting that:

> The educational effect of Faust was very great. Every edition of the play in England was soon sold out. Important heavy volumes, such as Anster's, which had grown dusty on the publisher's shelves were cleared off in no time. New editions were published and could hardly be printed quick enough. We knew of more than a hundred thousand copies of Goethe's dramatic poem being sold in the first season of its run.[35]

The play also caused a sensation when they toured the United States. It struck a chord with a deeply religious population. Bram records that: 'In Boston, where the old puritanical belief of a real devil still holds, we took in one evening four thousand eight hundred and fifty two dollars - more than a thousand pounds - the largest dramatic house up to then known in America.'

The theatre company came across a similar reception elsewhere on the tour: 'In Philadelphia, where are the descendants of the pious Quakers who followed Penn into the wilderness, the average receipts were even greater. Indeed at the matinee on Saturday, the crowd was so vast that the doors were carried by storm... They carried the outer door and the checktaker with it; and broke down by sheer weight of numbers the great inner doors of heavy mahogany and glass standing some eight feet high.'

The message was clear to Bram: tales of the diabolical sell. He probably envisaged *Dracula* as frivolous - a shilling shocker down there with the meanest of their type. It wasn't his usual sort of book. Bram had written his other novels to be taken seriously - many contain sections expressing his view of the universe; their intent to educate the soul.

Dracula is generally free of such messages. The novel was aimed at the popular end of the market - the busy end where big money could be made by providing chills and thrills to the teeming millions - people otherwise living drab lives in grimy streets. He was probably embarrassed when asked in a newspaper interview if *Dracula* held a 'purpose'. He seemed evasive: "I suppose that every book of the kind must contain some lesson," he replied, "but I prefer that readers should find it out for themselves."[36]

On the 14th March 1890, Bram Stoker wrote out an outline for his new novel on Lyceum Theatre notepaper. At this stage the plan was for four sections or 'books', each with seven chapters. The main events of each chapter are listed and the story is taking shape; it's not quite the final novel yet, although some of the key elements are in place. The count's trip from Transylvania to England is in part one. The stormy arrival by ship to Whitby is also mentioned. And for the final action of the story in part four we read: 'Bring in the Texan'. When *Dracula* was eventually written, the Count was dispatched in the last chapter by Quincey P. Morris, 'an American from Texas'.[37]

Three months later a conversation over dinner with Henry Irving gave glorious affirmation to Bram that his writing efforts were gaining attention. Henry Morton Stanley, the American reporter and explorer, had read his pamphlet *A Glimpse of America*.

This was the published text of a speech he had given to the London Institute in 1885 about the American way of life. It was based on material that Bram collected while travelling in the United States with Henry Irving's theatre company. Stanley became famous after searching for the Scottish missionary David Livingstone through 700 miles of tropical Africa; an encounter which when it happened after great hardship was reported to have led to his famous greeting, 'Dr. Livingstone, I presume.'

Bram wrote that: 'Stanley had evidently got hold of it, for one night when we were in Manchester, June 4th, 1890, I had

28

supper alone with Irving and he told me that the last time he had met him, Stanley had mentioned my little book on America as admirable. He had said that I had mistaken my vocation – that I should be a literary man! Of course such praise from such a man gave me a great pleasure.'[38]

A friend told him later that this was one of the few books Stanley took with him on his African expedition. He had said it held 'more information about America than any other book that had ever been written.'

Later that year, Bram Stoker's first novel *The Snake's Pass* was published. A romantic adventure story set in the west of Ireland, it's the story of a wealthy Englishmen, an extraordinarily beautiful peasant girl, buried treasure, and Black Murdock, an evil money lender. The reviews were mixed. According to *Punch*: 'The novel reader will do well not to pass by *The Snake's Pass*.' The *Athenaeum* review was much less impressive, 'so long, so good, and so dull is Mr. Bram Stoker's new novel.' This probably upset the author, so he would have been utterly delighted to receive praise for his book from an unexpected source. The Prime Minister William Gladstone on a visit to the Lyceum Theatre surprised Bram by reciting quotations from *The Snake's Pass*. One particular scene he described as 'very fine indeed!'

In late July 1890, Bram arrived in Whitby for a three-week holiday, Florence and Noel joining him a week later.[39] It was a suitably gothic place to bring Count Dracula ashore in England.

He describes the North Yorkshire fishing village in *Dracula* with its 'red-roofed' houses 'piled up one over the other.' On a cliff top looking over the town 'is the ruin of Whitby Abbey' which is 'a most noble ruin, of immense size.' It has a suitably spooky past, 'a girl was built up in the wall' a reference to a nun who broke her vows of chastity in Walter Scott's poem *Marmion*, and it's said that 'a white lady is seen in one of the windows.' Between the abbey and the town beneath is St Mary's Church 'with a big graveyard, all full of tombstones... It descends so steeply over the harbour that part of the bank has fallen away, and some of the graves have been destroyed.'

The action in Whitby takes place over three chapters in the novel. Count Dracula arrives there when the schooner *Demeter* is

29

beached during a storm, 'a shudder ran through all who saw her, for lashed to the helm was a corpse, with drooping head, which swung horribly to and fro at each motion of the ship.'

This was the unfortunate steersman. Count Dracula bounds off the ship in the guise of an 'immense dog', and runs up the cliff towards the graveyard where he disappears 'in the darkness.' The graveyard is where Lucy Westenra is later attacked vampire-style by the Count.

Bram made extensive notes as he walked around Whitby. He talked to the coastguard and was given a written description about an incident involving the 120 ton Russian schooner *Dimitry*. It had been bringing silver sand from the mouth of the Danube to Whitby in October 1885.

Caught up in a force eight gale, the ship made for the harbour, getting in, but became a wreck during the night on being pummelled by the gale. The crew managed to escape. He used this episode for *Dracula,* changing the name of the ship from *Dimitry* to *Demeter.*

Whitby inspired him: he wrote down conversations with the local fishermen and the coastguard, recorded inscriptions on the gravestones in St Mary's churchyard, almost a hundred of them, described the town, drew maps and noted the weather conditions. While he wandered around Whitby he thought about how he would use its landmarks for events in his novel. He wrote in his notes: 'When ship ran in to Collier's Hope, big dog jumped off bow & ran over pier – up Kiln Yard & church steps & into churchyard.'[40]

The defining moment which set him on the path to fame came in a rather unlikely spot. He entered the local subscription library and checked out the book *An Account of the Principalities of Wallachia and Moldavia with Various Political Observations Relating to Them*. It was written by William Wilkinson in 1820.

A footnote in the text caught Bram Stoker's attention and it's the first item in his notes taken from the book: 'DRACULA in Wallachian language means DEVIL. Wallachians were accustomed to give it as a surname to any person who rendered himself conspicuous by courage, cruel actions or cunning.'[41]

The Dracula referred to here was a real person commonly

known as Vlad the Impaler - a savage warlord living in fifteenth century Wallachia (now part of Romania). The nickname was appropriate because he impaled his enemies on wooden stakes in their thousands.

Such gruesome details passed Bram by; it was the name that got his attention. He wouldn't actually decide to use the name Dracula for his king vampire until close to the publication date in 1897. It was always a serious candidate though. The top of a page of notes from about this time is scribbled variously 'Count Dracula', 'Dracula', and then 'Dracula' again as if trying to get a sense of how the name appears on the page. One can imagine him repeating the word out loud to himself. Lower down the page he writes 'Count Wampyr' only to score out Wampyr and replace it with Dracula.[42]

He discovered another book in the Whitby Museum Library, *A Glossary of Words Used in the Neighbourhood of Whitby*.[43] He wrote down a long list of local dialect words into his notebook. He would eventually use these words when writing the dialogue of a Yorkshire fisherman as he talks to Mina Murray and Lucy Westenra. The young women probably would not have understood much of the conversation: "It be all fool-talk, lock, stock, and barrel, that's what it be and nowt else. These bans an' wafts an' boh-ghosts an' bar-guests an' bogles an' all anent them is only fit to set bairns an' dizzy women a'belderin'."

He returned from Whitby refreshed after all that salty sea air, and gave more thought to the novel. That thinking would continue for a very long time to come – a span of several years. The outline plot for the book was filled in at a glacial pace. Each chapter was given a separate page on which the highlights of the action were noted. By the time he reached section three (of four) the notes are dated 29th February 1892. This was almost two years after the first dated entry, and he still wasn't finished yet.

Included within the notes are copies of a commercial calendar printed on pale yellow paper with the lettering and lining in pink. It's a generic calendar with no year or dates given, these are left to be filled in. Bram has added dates and notes in pencil, and they provide a timeline for the events in the novel. The first event is a letter from Dracula to his English solicitor on Thursday

16th March. The last event is on Tuesday 31st October as the hunt for Count Dracula in his Transylvanian lair nears its dramatic conclusion. The dates are consistent with the action having taken place in 1893.

By this stage 1892, possibly 1893, Bram Stoker has a list of characters, a detailed plot, and a timeline; he also had a book to write. That still hadn't happened yet.

Why did he take so long to start writing *Dracula*? Nobody knows. It's curious that in the hundreds of books and articles written about *Dracula* there is little in the way of discussion as to why Bram took seven years to complete the novel. It bothers me though. The effort involved wasn't trivial; he wrote down pages of notes and went to the trouble of typing out some of them. Much of his holiday in Whitby was devoted into research for *Dracula*. And the notes were kept going year after year.

Maybe the delay came from a compulsion to get this novel exactly right and to take the time to make sure this happened. I doubt it. A modern writer tries to avoid such a long delay, keeping the development time for a novel to a minimum - no more than three months and often much shorter. An author has to make money to live and eat. For most authors that income is pitifully meagre; taking years over a commercial novel is an indulgence that few can afford. At least Bram had his wages from the Lyceum Theatre to pay the bills, although the extra income would surely have helped to subsidise his luxurious lifestyle.

I suspect he was mainly concerned about his professional and social standing; that the ghoulish subject matter in *Dracula* would hurt his reputation as the business manager of the Lyceum Theatre. Let's remind ourselves what he had to lose. According to his friend Horace Wyndam:

> To see Stoker in his element was to see him standing at the top of the theatre's stairs, surveying a "first-night" crowd trooping up them. There was no mistake about it – a Lyceum *première* did draw an audience that really was representative of the best of that period in the realms of art, literature, and society. Admittance was a very jealously guarded privilege. Stoker, indeed looked upon the stalls, dress circle, and boxes as if they were annexes

to the Royal Enclosure at Ascot, and one almost had to be proposed and seconded before the coveted ticket would be issued. The rag-tag-and-bobtail of the musical comedy, theatrical, stock exchange and theatrical worlds who foregather at a present-day *première* would certainly have been sent away with a flea in their ear.[44]

What reception would his gory novel get amongst the clientele of the Lyceum Theatre with their refined taste in culture? Perhaps the prime minister of the day wouldn't step out of the audience to congratulate him on this one.

Mind you, others had got away with outlandish horror stories, and were even seeing their books sell in large numbers. Robert Louis Stevenson's *Strange Case of Dr. Jekyll and Mr. Hyde* had been published in 1886 to great acclaim and what's more, commercial success.

Perhaps the problem was that few dared to test the limits of public taste at the time; that is, to find out what could be tolerated and what couldn't. As we now know from our modern perspective, public taste can be stretched an impressively long way. Bram realised that *Dracula* would take the novel to a new level; one more intense and grisly than had ever been attempted before.

The ratchet of horror was about to go up another notch - would he get away with it? He chatted with the elite of London at dinner parties and met them in the Lyceum Theatre. What would they think about the macabre aspects of the story? What if the writing style came across as unconvincing and silly? He would become a figure of fun - little whispers here and there as he walked about, stifled guffaws sounding out every now and again.

It is now 1893 - the project has stalled after three years. He somehow needs to jump over the daunting wall of scruple which blocks his path, and then having done so, to drip words of gore onto virgin white pages. Can he summon up the will to do it? What will get him going?

3
'WHEN I FIRST SAW THE PLACE
I FELL IN LOVE WITH IT'

Towards the end of July 1893 the Lyceum Theatre closed for a month. Every year at this time the upper classes that made up their usual audience deserted London. They either headed north for shooting holidays on the grouse moors of Scotland or crossed the Channel to 'take the waters' at fashionable spa resorts on the continent. There was no point in keeping the theatre open, and its business manager now had some free time to do whatever he wanted.

Friends had told Bram that the air on the Aberdeenshire coast in the north-east of Scotland is very bracing. He liked the thought of this, and set off on the long journey north to the port of Peterhead; his intention to explore the coastline. For the first part of his hike he tramped northwards along 16 miles of beach to the town of Fraserburgh, passing the fishing villages of St Combs, Inverallochy and Cairnbulg on the way.

For the second part Bram went south, taking in eight miles of rocky coastline, walking past Slains Castle standing aloof on the edge of the cliffs, before alighting on the village of Port Erroll. It lay next to the two-mile-long beach of Cruden Bay. Astonishing as it might seem, this little-known Aberdeenshire fishing village with a population of 500 was about to change his life forever.[45]

'When first I saw the place I fell in love with it,' he wrote in *The Mystery of the Sea*, one of two novels based in Port Erroll. The words are narrated by the main character Archibald Hunter, although they undoubtedly reflect the feelings of the author. And the result of this: 'The next year I came again, and the next, and the next.'[46]

Bram Stoker did indeed return to the Cruden Bay area for most of the years between 1893 and 1910. Documentary evidence shows that he came here for his summer break at least twelve or thirteen times, probably more.[1]

It was the scenery of the coast that attracted Bram. He appears to have felt a natural affinity for the sea, having been brought up within sight of Dublin Bay. Three of his earlier holidays had been to the seaside resorts of the Isle of Wight, Boscastle in Cornwall and Whitby in Yorkshire. Descriptions of the sea abound in his books.

The natural beauty of Buchan, the region at the north-east corner of Aberdeenshire, resides in its coastline rather than the adjacent countryside; the latter described as 'somewhat bare and uninviting'.[47] The inland scenery is rolling farmland: an extensive green desert of grass and cereal rather than the hills and heather traditionally regarded as characteristic of the north of Scotland. It's 'Treeless Buchan' according to some and this is almost true, although the occasional forest and small wood can be found here and there. Dr Samuel Johnson once joked that a tree in Scotland is as rare as a horse in Venice.[48]

The Aberdeenshire coast is mostly rocky; its line of cliffs between 100 and 200 feet in height interspersed with glorious stretches of beach. Cruden Bay beach is one of these: a two-mile-long crescent of golden sand bookended by rocky headlands to the north and south.

'The curved shore of Cruden Bay, Aberdeenshire, is backed by a waste of sandhills in whose hollows seagrass and moss and wild violets, together with the pretty "grass of Parnassus" form a green carpet,' Bram wrote. The high dunes along the western margin of the beach provide a pleasing display on windy days, the 'bentgrass' that covers them 'is eternally shifting as the wind takes the fine sand and drifts it to and fro.' In a strong wind, 'the tall bentgrass' will tilt over, 'showing the paler green of its under side; the blue-green, metallic shimmer which marks it, and which painters find it so hard to reproduce...'

The village of Port Erroll, as it was called in 1893, forms a line of houses clasped to the shore of the northern headland. Here

---

1

See Appendix 1.

the estuary of the Water of Cruden, no more than a stream, emerges into the sea. The headland struts out from beyond the village and where 'the rocks of red granite rise jagged and broken,' according to Bram.[49]

At the other end of the beach, the southern headland is marked by a curving cliff line. A short distance beyond, and near the village of Whinnyfold with its 21 houses, a broad low-lying reef of numerous isolated rocks extends offshore for almost half a mile. It's as if a bored giant had thrown dozens of enormous slabs into the sea for the want of something more interesting to do.

These are the Skares and pronounced the 'Scaurs', a word derived from the Gaelic for a rock in the sea - *sgeir*. Bram was known to have stood for hours on the headland overlooking the treacherous reefs of the Skares, the site of many a shipwreck over the centuries. He seems to have become morbidly fascinated by the disasters that had happened there: 'Did the sea hold its dead where they fell, its floor around the Skares would be whitened with their bones, and new islands could build themselves with the piling wreckage.'[50] What was in his mind as he looked at the Skares for hours on end? There is a hint in *Dracula*: 'it needed but little effort of imagination to think that the spirits of those lost at sea were touching their living brethren with the clammy hands of death...'

Bram's short story *Crooken Sands*, first published in 1894, gives a clue as to why he returned to Port Erroll year after year. The main character in the story, Mr Markam, is heading towards Cruden Bay beach for a late evening walk:

> The moon was up and he easily followed the path through the sand-hills, and shortly struck the shore. The tide was out and the beach firm as a rock, so he strolled southwards to nearly the end of the bay. Here he was attracted by two isolated rocks some little way out from the edge of the dunes, so he strolled towards them. When he reached the nearest one he climbed it, and, sitting there elevated some fifteen or twenty feet over the waste of sand, enjoyed the lovely, peaceful prospect.

The rock that Mr Markam sat on can be identified from the description. It's a grassy knoll with a stony cairn on top called the

Sand Craig. It is accessible at low to moderate tides.

> For a good while Mr. Markam sat and looked at the rising moon and the growing area of light which followed its rise. Then he turned and faced eastwards, and sat with his chin in his hand looking seawards, and revelling in the peace and beauty and freedom of the scene. The roar of London - the darkness and the strife and weariness of London life seemed to have passed quite away, and he lived at the moment a freer and higher life.

The view is spectacular: 'The full moon was behind him and its light lit up the bay so that its fringe of foam, the dark outline of the headland, and the stakes of the salmon-nets were all emphasised.'

He could see in 'the brilliant yellow glow' the lights in the windows of Port Erroll and 'those of the distant castle of the laird trembled like stars through the sky'. It made a lasting impression: 'For a long time he sat and drank in the beauty of the scene, and his soul seemed to feel a peace that it had not known for many days.'[51]

You can look out from the Sand Craig today and see this view more or less exactly as written. The lights of 'the distant castle of the laird' were those of Slains Castle, the residence of the Earl of Erroll and his family. The only difference is that Slains Castle is now a ruin, whereas it had been inhabited in Bram Stoker's time. If anything the desolate remains of the castle looks more gothic today by comparison to photographs from the 1890s which show it to have been an oversize mansion house tacked onto a sixteenth century tower.

This was the start of Bram's long association with Port Erroll and the Cruden Bay area; a place where he could relax after the stressful pace of London life. How did he spend his time while on holiday there?

Apart from writing, he went walking mainly. He also liked to cycle, riding a distinctive and rather unusual–looking bicycle on the roads around the village. He also took it along the beach. The bicycle was described by local resident Sandy Cruickshank as having 'stays all over the place and an upright saddle shaped like a hammock'.

The journalist and cycling enthusiast Gordon Casely, who interviewed Sandy in 1966, recognised the make as a Dursley Pedersen with its distinctive cantilever frame and hammock-style saddle.[52] The design made it easier to ride over the bumpy roads of the time.

Every day at seven o'clock, and before breakfast, Bram walked across Cruden Bay beach and back. Mrs Cruickshank, who worked at the Port Erroll Post Office, described his appearance while out and about. Dressed in tweeds and with a round beret on his head, 'he became a familiar figure with his stout walking-stick as he strolled along the sands and the cliffs'.[54]

Another resident remembers him as wearing a long cape and a wide-brimmed hat. His pose was highly distinctive; Bram walked along the beach with his hands behind his back, head down with a slight stoop and with the air of someone completely absorbed in intense thought.[55]

At other times Bram would take Florence along with him to the village of Whinnyfold just beyond the headland at the far end of the beach. Mrs Cruickshank would wave to them both as they passed the post office on the way out. Not much is known about how Florence spent her time while on holiday. Other than walking out with her husband on the beach, she played golf. The first part of a new golf course was available to play at Port Erroll from 1897, and there is evidence that an earlier course existed up until then, that is until a new railway line cut it in two.

Her presence on the golf course caught the admiring glances of the locals, and she was said to be one of the prettiest women who ever played the fairways there.[56] I would guess that Florence must also have had several friends to chat to in Port Erroll. She was known to the villagers as 'Mrs Bram'.

Bram Stoker's holidays in Port Erroll gave him a month out of every year to devote exclusively to writing. He also wrote outside this holiday period, although it was a struggle to find those spare moments given the intense demands of both his work and social life in London. He worked six days a week, with only a break in the afternoon before returning to the Lyceum Theatre in the early evening for what was usually a very late night. Sunday was a rest day, although it was often spent with the family, or taken up with socialising.[57]

Bram probably managed to squeeze some time in for writing when he was on tour with the theatre company, particularly on transit by ocean liner to the United States, and on the long train journeys once he got there. Nevertheless, Port Erroll appears to have given him the largest share of time for his efforts. As an American newspaper reported in 1902: 'It is a mystery to most people to know when he gets time to write his books but the secret is that this is his principal amusement during his holiday.'[58]

Bram's holidays boosted his writing career from a gentle amble to a full-throttle thrash. His month-long trips to Scotland provided a regular allocation of time for his literary work and disciplined him into the writing habit.

Up until this point his life had focussed on supporting Henry Irving and the theatre. He now had a month every year that he could devote to his own activities; the other eleven months were given over to Henry Irving. It certainly helped that London and the Lyceum Theatre were over 500 miles distant. Henry Irving still sent him letters and telegrams on company business to Port Erroll Post Office but not to an overwhelming extent. The results of this regular writing stint were spectacular. At the age of 45 in 1893, Bram Stoker would now go on to add ten novels, a collection of short stories and two non-fiction books to his published works.

The area gave him the peace and quiet to think about his books. The task was much easier here by comparison to his life in London where, even if he did manage to find the odd moment when he could think about his books, he was probably too tired to concentrate on the task properly. Mrs Cruickshank from the post office confirmed this, 'he got all his ideas for his stories when he was on holiday in Cruden Bay, walking the sands to Whinnyfold or scrambling over the rocks...'[59]

The morning walk may have formed part of his writing routine. Many a writer likes to go for a walk to limber up, clear their head, and to think through the issues that bother them about their current writing project. Often it's more than that.

The creative part of writing can be a daunting task; it's not like turning on a tap. The ideas either come or they don't, and every writer worries that today could be the day when the flow comes to a halt and the creative juice dries up. Such anxiety leads to demotivation and is at worst self-sustaining once that kicks in. Rather than starting the day hopelessly staring at a blank page that stays blank, the author first takes a long walk and freshens up. It acts as a springboard for the task to come.

Cruden Bay beach is a great place to think things out; you can walk along the shoreline with no-one else around to disturb you. The lapping waves on a calm day make a soothing rhythmic noise that relaxes you and helps to focus your thoughts. That thinking time was all important for Bram. Novels require to be planned; the plot assembled and then populated with the main characters and all their quirks.

Something else happened here that would invigorate Bram Stoker and give him the added drive to write his books. The coastal scenery around Cruden Bay reconnected Bram to a spiritual sense of nature. I'll try and give an idea as to what his impressions might have been as he walked along the shore.

My qualification to do so is appropriate. Cruden Bay beach is 200 yards from my house in what is now the Port Erroll Conservation Area within the village of Cruden Bay. I walk along Cruden Bay beach early every morning just as Bram Stoker once did. It's common at that time to have the beach all to yourself. The local area is sparsely populated; visitors to Scotland tend to travel up the west coast rather than the east. An early attempt was made at the end of the nineteenth century to transform Port Erroll into a tourist resort. It failed, although the golf course has survived as an attraction.

I am alone and close to nature as I walk along. The only human anyway; a variety of seabirds, jackdaws and crows congregate on the shore. The beach is backed by the long curving amphitheatre of the sand dunes; the edge facing the sea forming a low, continuous wall about 50 to 60 feet high with all but the base covered in lime-green marram grass.

It feels like an intimate space, a theatre perhaps. And if I am the audience in that theatre, the main act is the sea and the roar of the waves as they crash onto the sand.

Some of the locals, perhaps beguiled by the intimacy of walking along Cruden Bay beach, talk as if the sea is alive. One resident even believed it. An old woman, who owned a house in Harbour Street facing the bay, would sit at an upstairs window watching the sea for hours while sipping her glass of whisky. "The sea is in an angry mood today" she would say to her visitors and she meant it. It's a special form of eccentricity that is easy to slip into around Cruden Bay.

The beach shoals gently towards the dunes with a large flat-lying expanse of sand exposed at low tide 'as smooth and firm as the floor of a cathedral'.[60] The waves travel a long distance up the beach before falling back again. As they do so, a wide strand of wet sand is left behind which reflects the colour of the sky. I call it the moody beach because the colours mirrored in the wet sand are variously blue, grey, white, gold at sunrise, and oranges and intense yellows at sunset.

I can walk along the edge of the sea, hearing the white noise of the waves and the call of the birds. The sea brings in the detritus of the deep, seaweed, mussel and razor shells, the occasional crab, jellyfish and sea urchins. I have two miles of beach to walk back and forth with nobody to disturb my thoughts, thoughts made in a scene of great beauty. Who would not feel as one with nature here?

The mood changes from day to day. I've seen the beach on a windy day at low tide. The wet sand is a rustic brown shade whereas a strip of silver-coloured dry sand borders the dunes at the high-tide mark. A flurry of wind will of a moment bring flowing trains of dry sand over the darker wet sand in its wake.

These 'dust devils' resemble ghostly snakes as they speed and writhe across the beach for a second or two. Once the wind dies down, the lighter sand comes to rest and forms patterns that resemble pictures of dancing ghosts. I often wonder if they inspired those famous scenes in *Dracula* when the three vampire sisters appear before Jonathan Harker:

> Something made me start up, a low, piteous howling of dogs somewhere far below in the valley, which was hidden from my sight. Louder it seemed to ring in my ears, and the floating moats of dust to take new shapes to

the sound as they danced in the moonlight... Quicker and quicker danced the dust. The moonbeams seemed to quiver as they went by me into the mass of gloom beyond. More and more they gathered till they seemed to take dim phantom shapes... The phantom shapes, which were becoming gradually materialised from the moonbeams, were those three ghostly women to whom I was doomed.

Bram Stoker picked up on the sights and sounds provided by nature. They made him feel part of the scene; not just there but connected to it. He seemed less concerned with individual plants and animals. You get the impression that they merely blended into the overall picture and they weren't that important to him.

He mentions the rabbits on the sand dunes bounding Cruden Bay and that's about it. That and certain flowers; violets and the Grass of Parnassus, a beautiful yet tiny flower with five white petals shot through with delicate green veins that is said to be found in the wetter patches of ground along the coast.

Port Erroll was responsible for prompting a major mid-life change for Bram Stoker. At the age of 45 he had found an area of natural beauty and tranquillity; somewhere that would provide a base for channelling his creative energy into writing novels. It became his special place.

4
PORT ERROLL

Bram Stoker returned to Port Erroll in 1894 and booked into the Kilmarnock Arms Hotel. With him were Florence, Noel, and a friend, George Vaughan Hart, Professor of Law at Trinity College, Dublin. Bram also brought along a special consignment, a trunk full of booze.

It would remain the abiding memory of the hotel staff down the years, and one still talked about in the 1950s. Even though the hotel ran a strict alcohol-free policy, nothing seems to have been said.[61] The guest book from this period still survives and records that the Stoker family stayed between the 2nd and 29th August 1894. Bram wrote in it: 'Second visit to Port Erroll. Delighted with everything & everybody & hope to come again to the Kilmarnock Arms.'

The Kilmarnock Arms Hotel had been built by the 19th Earl of Erroll in 1877, and the name celebrates the day when his father first sat in the House of Lords as Baron Kilmarnock. Its site had been chosen to make an impact on the visitor when they cross the little bridge over the Water of Cruden. The first impression: a solid and confident frontage. Built out of flesh-coloured granite, the hotel is two storeys high and laid out in an L-shaped plan. The shorter arm faces onto Bridge Street with three bay windows, the longer side with five bay windows looks over the front lawn and the Water of Cruden. The small stream is still lined by 'a fringe of willows protecting its sunk garden'.

An 1896 advertisement sets out what the visitor could expect by staying there:

THIS HOTEL contains 12 Bedrooms, 2 Bathrooms (hot and cold water), Sitting Rooms, Dining Hall, etc; and is admirably adapted for small parties or families. Excellent Bathing Beach within seven minutes' walk; Bathing Houses for use of Visitors. All Visitors may have Trout Fishing in Cruden Water free of charge. There is good sea Fishing, and boats may be had for hire; also a good Golf Course. The proprietor is Lessee of over 6000 acres of Shooting (well stocked with low ground Game, which includes a small Grouse shooting). Gentlemen residing at the Hotel may have Shooting by previous arrangement, with use of dogs, etc, on reasonable terms. Horses and Machines [carriages] kept for hire. Postal and Telegraph Office in the Hotel.

JAS. CRUICKSHANK, Proprietor.

The housing of the post office in the hotel proved to be a great convenience for Bram Stoker. The post arrived daily by the horse-drawn mail gig from the nearby town of Ellon at 11 a.m., and he would check in at noon to see if there was any business letters or telegrams from Henry Irving. The gig passed back through the village at 3 p.m., collecting mail on the return journey.[62]

The Kilmarnock Arms was frequently referred to in Bram's time as the Temperance Hotel because the sale of alcohol was banned at the insistence of the earl. Anyone turning up and asking for a bottle of beer was told that only non-alcoholic ginger beer was available; a reply that didn't always please.

A zealous fervour of anti-drink campaigning had gripped Britain in late Victorian times in response to the drunken excesses of an earlier age. Just how bad the situation had become nationwide can be seen from a letter written by Reverend Sidney Smith in 1830: 'Everybody is drunk. Those who are not singing are sprawling. The sovereign people are in a beastly state.'

The Kilmarnock Arms would stay dry until as late as 1942. The change of heart took place in the middle of the Second World War when it was felt that the soldiers stationed in the village deserved to drink beer. It was only fair - they were about to risk their lives to save their country. The hotel has continued to sell alcohol since then.

The rallying cry of the temperance movement can still be heard in Aberdeenshire. Temperance marches are held in the Aberdeenshire coastal villages of St. Combs, Inverallochy and Cairnbulg between Christmas and the first week of the New Year.

44

The villagers march around the houses playing flutes, often striding through snow and driving sleet to do so.

The local schools teach flute-playing to their pupils to keep the tradition going, and a tradition is what it is now. The villages aren't entirely alcohol-free these days. Nevertheless, the marches provide jolly occasions on bleak winter days in the north of Scotland, even if the original message isn't exactly heeded.

The proprietor of the Kilmarnock Arms was James Cruickshank, a remarkable man. He had taken over the management of the hotel in August 1892 when his father George died. George had originally been a farmer, but had sold up with considerable debts after a series of bad seasons and low prices. James would go on to manage the hotel for over 40 years, selling it in 1938. His friend John Adam Lillie has left a pen portrait of the man:

> James Cruickshank took exceptional care of his guests:
> He was mine host *par excellence* and dined with them and was the central figure with his cigar in the billiard room after dinner when he discoursed on Buchan and Buchan people. He took his male guests on Sunday afternoons over his farms and discoursed on things agricultural. Short, vigorous, vivacious and friendly, he naturally ruled every company he was in.[63]

Bram was undoubtedly given the same hail-fellow-well-met treatment when he arrived at the Kilmarnock Arms in August 1894. A photograph of the man who stepped out to meet him hangs in the lobby of the hotel today. On shaking James Cruickshank's hand in greeting, Bram would have seen the long face with its enormous forehead rising well above narrow eyes.

The first impression, this man is exceptionally intelligent. The second impression, he has a kindly, genial look. Above his wide mouth is a bushy moustache, the 'mouser' common amongst the men of rural Aberdeenshire at the time.

James Cruickshank was naturally curious about everything. He was described as 'an authority on the Buchan countryside and a most racy reporter of its humours and the character of the people.'[64] He was a resourceful man and the type of person that Bram would have greatly admired.

James Cruickshank had a head for business, and was able to quickly pay off his father's debts when he took over. Before long, not only was he managing the hotel, he took charge of several farms, ran the post office and was a director of the local store of the Aberdeen Lime Company. The latter provided the farmers with manure, feedstock and shipped coal by sea from Aberdeen.

But most remarkable of all, James Cruickshank was a self-made expert on agricultural science. This went much further than a passing familiarity with existing methods. He came up with new techniques which he then applied on his farms to great success. This was his crusade; he wrote papers on agricultural matters, popularised his new methods in the north of Scotland, and was even invited to Cambridge University to talk about them.

John Boyd Orr, the director of the Rowett Research Institute in Aberdeen which specialises in agriculture, valued his practical skills. When the institute set up an experimental farm for research purposes, Boyd Orr sought advice for it from an expert panel of the 'five farmers whom I regarded as the most experienced and successful' in North East Scotland. James Cruickshank was amongst them.[65] Boyd Orr was later awarded the 1949 Nobel Peace Prize for his research into agriculture and nutrition.

Bram became a close friend, and would go on to send James first-edition copies of his books inscribed to 'my dear Cruickshank'. Some of these were still in the village until recently.

James Cruickshank was instrumental in connecting Bram Stoker to Port Erroll. He encouraged his hotel guests to get to know the villagers, often through social events. This had two consequences. First of all, by talking to the locals Bram uncovered new material that he would use for his novels. Secondly, it bonded him to the people of Port Erroll, a place where he now felt welcome: part of the community even.

When the journalist Gordon Casely visited the village in the 1960s to interview those who knew Bram Stoker, it was clear that Bram was well liked. Not only that, they told Gordon that they were immensely proud that Bram had chosen their village to write his books.[66]

By meeting James Cruickshank, Bram had gained a highly-intelligent guide to local life and customs in Port Erroll. And the author of *Dracula* would go on to find much of interest in the village.

Shortly before he arrived there in 1894, a gang of workmen who had been opening up a trench for a new water pipe made a ghoulish discovery. While digging at a depth of 12 to 14 feet they came across about a hundred human skeletons. The location of the remains is a sandy knoll only a few hundred yards south of the Kilmarnock Arms Hotel. Members of the Buchan Field Club, a local history and natural science group, arrived to examine the find.

The workmen's picks had shattered most of the skulls, although a few were intact. These were well preserved; in particular the teeth were in excellent condition and showed no sign of decay. The well-drained sandy soil, entombing the bones, had kept them from crumbling away.

This was the site of St Olave's Chapel, known to have stood on the sandy knoll. The chapel was said to have been built following the battle in 1012 between the Vikings and the Scots Army in Cruden Bay. Tradition has it that the battle-weary Viking survivors, intent on returning home, had asked for their dead to be buried locally.

The members of the Field Club now stood over the age-old bones, speculating that these were the human remains from the battle.[67] It's possible. Various relicts such as battle-axes, mortuary urns and neck chains had previously been recovered for several miles around the site of the old church.[68]

Bram Stoker's four-week stay allowed him to explore the village and the surrounding coast. Here's how he described Port Erroll:

> The village, squatted beside the emboucher of the Water of Cruden at the northern side of the bay is simple enough, a few rows of fishermen's cottages, two or three great red-tiled drying sheds nestled in the sand-heap behind the fishers' houses. For the rest of the place as it was when first I saw it, a little lookout beside a tall flagstaff on the northern cliff, a few scattered farms over the inland prospect, one little hotel down on the western

47

bank of the Water of Cruden...[70]

The population of Port Erroll was 487 people back then. About 300 of them were fishermen and their families; the rest worked in a variety of occupations. Most of the buildings in the village lay along the road which followed the course of the Water of Cruden between the Kilmarnock Arms Hotel and Port Erroll Harbour, a distance of about a mile. Although there were only 97 houses in Port Erroll, two separate communities lived here. The upper village, closest to the hotel, was where the tradespeople and their families lived; the lower village, closest to the harbour, was where the fisherfolk had their houses and sheds.

From the hotel, the road runs straight for half a mile past a row of terraced two-story houses on the left-hand side. They present a continuous facade of salmon-coloured granite and white-washed buildings overlooking the grassy bank of the Water of Cruden. For this reason this part of the road was named The Terrace (today it's Main Street). This is the upper village. The trades-people who lived here when Bram Stoker first arrived, included three shoemakers, two carpenters, several carters, a grocer, a slater, a tailor, a blacksmith, a cooper, a butcher and a baker.

The road bends as it turns to track the Water of Cruden, and the houses start up again as the stream straightens out. A small stretch called The New Block quickly gives way to the long row of terraced houses forming Harbour Street. Together with the four small side roads of Hay Street, Ward Street, Green Street, and Hill Street, This is the lower village. It is where the fisherfolk lived and it's the oldest part. Bram Stoker knew it well.

The lower village was often called 'the Ward' from its former name, the Ward of Cruden. The trades-people and the fisherfolk didn't mix much socially, referring to themselves as the 'up the streeters' and the 'down the streeters'. Their children fought in the street and the adults tended to regard each other with haughty disdain.

The houses in the fishing village are of two types. The bigger houses are on two storeys with white-painted dormer windows. Less common are the older single-story houses built with two rooms only, and which were known as 'but and bens'.

The 'but' was the kitchen and living room; the 'ben' was the inner room and the best room in the house with its fancy cabinets and china ornaments - the children were not allowed to play there. A small middle room, the 'orra room', lay in between for storage.

The lower village was crowded in Victorian times. It was not uncommon to find eight, nine or ten individuals housed in the two rooms of the single-storey cottages. The two rooms of the single storey house at 5 Harbour Street held eleven members of the Summers family according to the 1891 census. It was said that in the smaller houses there was scarcely enough space to breath in bed. The stench of the bodies living in such close proximity must have been overpowering.

At the far end of Harbour Street Cruden Bay beach comes into full view on the right hand side. Here too is the estuary of the Water of Cruden, 'it runs to the sea over a stony bottom' wrote Bram. 'The estuary has in its wash some dangerous outcropping granite rocks, nearly covered at high tide, and the mouth opens between the most northerly end of the sandhills and the village street...'[71]

The road bends in response to a short dogleg in the ancient cliff line that lies behind the houses. At this point the slope is gentle enough to carry a rough track up to the grassy area beyond known as Ward Hill.

A small house once overlooked the cliff here, and a bit further on is where a tiny coastguard lookout station was located. Bram Stoker spent many hours chatting to the coastguards on duty at the hut, hearing much about the village in turn.[72] We know the coastguard's names from the 1891 census; Frederick Dyson from Leeds and Walter Heron listed as having been born in England. The coastguard hut no longer stands; although you can still see its foundations. Bram mentions that it had windows and a door which locked. The wooden flagstaff, which stood next to the hut and which was used to make signals, survived until recently. Some kids visited the spot for a midnight party and chopped it up for their bonfire.

Round the far side of the bend in the road are a small cluster of buildings: the Salmon Bothy and ice house on the right hand side and the single-story building of the Rocket House on the left-hand side. The Board of Trade life-saving apparatus was stored in the Rocket House; hefty rockets which could be fired towards stranded ships; a rope trailing in their smoky wake. Once the rope was secured onboard a marooned vessel, a steel hawser and a breeches buoy was dragged across from the shore, essentially a cradle and harness, and it was used to pull the men to the safe reaches of solid land.

Further on is the harbour. It was described by Bram:

The harbour of Port Erroll is a tiny haven of refuge won from the jagged rocks that bound the eastern side of Cruden Bay. It is sheltered on the northern side by the cliff which runs as far as the Watter's Mou', and separated from the mouth of the Water of Cruden, with its waste of shifting sands by a high wall of concrete. The harbour faces east, and its first basin is the smaller of the two, the larger opening sharply to the left a little way in. At the best of times it is not an easy matter to gain the harbour, for only when the tide has fairly risen is it available at all, and the rapid tide which runs up from the Scaurs makes in itself a difficulty at such times.[73]

The fishermen hanging around the harbour were instantly recognisable. Their faces were covered in grizzly beards and a tenaciously held clay pipe drooped out of their mouths for most of the time.

Onshore they wore short jackets and buttoned-up dark waistcoats or 'ganseys' - thick woollen jerseys. Flat caps or bonnets covered their heads, and it was rare to see a fisherman bare-headed. Bram describes an Aberdeenshire fisherman: 'His pilot-cloth trousers, spangled all over with silver herring scales, were tucked into great, bucket-boots. He wore a heavy blue jersey and a cap of weazel skin.'[74]

At sea they used what Bram refers to as 'great thigh-boots' made of leather.[75] Their thick jerseys and overclothes were treated with linseed oil. It was important to keep as warm and dry as possible as they would spend hours out in the open sea, and were often exposed to the wildest of weather.[76] They carried out a specialised job showing the skills of boat-craft and navigation in addition to fishing know-how. It was a dangerous life and the men lived with that danger on a daily basis.

Every morning brought with it a question whose answer could mean the difference between life and death – should they go to sea? They only had their barometers and their vast experience of reading the weather signs to help judge an answer. Bram refers to the 'fisherfolk and sea folk of all kinds whose weather instincts are keener than is given to the inland born'.[77]

Their job was highly risky, although its unpredictable nature helped to create the sense that every fishing expedition was an adventure. And somehow they would cope; the fishermen were proud of their competence in handling anything that came their way. Behind that competence lay a set of skills that had been passed down through the generations. Sons followed their fathers into fishing; nobody else could do it.

The small harbour at Port Erroll is tidal and almost empties of water at low tide; because of this it could only be used by boats for part of the time. It was too small to be used as a regular base for the larger herring boats, although some herring boats were sheltered there at the end of the season.

The local fishermen migrated to Peterhead for the summer herring-fishing season, and returned in September when they would carry out line-fishing near to the shore. 'Sma' lines' (small lines) were used by the Port Erroll fishermen to catch inshore fish such as haddock, the most popular fish eaten in Scotland. Whiting was also caught.[78]

The lines were prepared onshore, an operation that was labour intensive and took hours to complete. They were at least 300 foot long and held 100 or more small hooks at intervals of three feet. Once the bait was attached, the lines were laid out to avoid them getting entangled, and then coiled within a scoop-shaped basket called a scull for transfer to the fishing boat.[79] They were taken out to the fishing grounds the next morning, cast in the water, and retrieved later in the day.

Having caught the fish, the next job was to process the catch and then sell it. Fresh fish was not easy to transport to the large population centres back then because there were no easily available facilities for refrigeration. The fish were therefore preserved by smoking, drying or salting, and this is how fish were usually eaten in the cities and towns of Scotland in the nineteenth century. A character in one of Bram's novels eats smoked haddock in the dining room of the Kilmarnock Arms Hotel. There may not have been too much variety on the menu. Speldings were a speciality in the Cruden Bay area, and made by slicing open, gutting and cleaning a haddock. It was then hung on a fence to dry in the sun. A strong fish smell must have been permeated the village on the days when the sun's warm rays could be felt.

The salmon fishing was run as a separate operation. The conventional fishermen of the village and the salmon fishers tended to avoid each other's company; they were cliquey that way. The salmon fishermen mainly worked on the beach. Stake nets were strung on posts near low tide which acted to deflect the salmon into bag nets where they were trapped.

Bram mentions seeing the fishermen drawing in their nets at the ebbing tide. He adds that they also operated in the lee of the cliffs further north, although they would have had to watch out for the strong tidal conditions there. 'I had often tossed on that swell when I had been out with the salmon fishers, when they had been drawing their deep floating nets'.[80]

The fishermen and women of Aberdeenshire kept much to themselves and married only within the fishing community. In his book *Salt in the Blood*, a history of the fishing industry in Scotland, James Miller describes the necessity of intermarriage amongst the fisherfolk as a means of preserving their way of life. No woman outside the fishing community would ever want to get involved; it was a demanding and onerous lifestyle.

When the boats returned with the catch, it was the woman's job to sell the fish, typically walking up to twenty miles a day with heavy creels (baskets) on their backs. They sold the fish for cash in the towns and bartered for milk, butter, eggs and cheese in the country districts.[81]

The women also carried out their domestic duties. A fishing cottage had earth floors bare of carpet and linoleum. A generous layer of sand was sprinkled across the earth floor every day. Sometimes quicklime would be added to take away the smell of any bait that had fallen on the floor. It was an early morning job for the fisherwives to sweep up the previous day's sand, dumping it on the beach, and then gathering a fresh supply of sand for the day to come.

Bram neglects to mention in his writings that Port Erroll was once an exceptionally smelly place. The reason for this may have been straight-forward. Lingering odours of the foul kind were normal in Victorian towns and villages, and not a fact considered worthy of note. Unswept horse manure littered the roads and sewage disposal in rural districts was not always effective.

The minutes of the Ellon District Council committee for 1891 described the situation in Port Erroll:

> There are a good many imperfect ash pits in this place with stagnant water causing very bad smells. There is also a slaughter-house here which ought to be removed to a greater distance from the village, as it is too close to the houses and not at all well kept....
>
> In regard to this place the Medical Officer's remarks are, first - the condition of the ash pits. These are I think in the worst condition of any I have as yet seen. Every ash pit in the upper village was nothing but a reeking cesspool. All the privies are directly connected with them. A condition of things more detrimental to health, especially for children, or more calculated to originate or intensify disease can scarcely be imagined.

What's not mentioned here is that the sanitation problem was worse for the upper village than in the lower village. The fisherfolk resorted to a more convenient means of waste disposal, although it wasn't ideal. It was the job of the fisherman's wife to empty the contents of the chamber pots into a sanitation bucket every morning and to then dispose of the contents into the sea nearby. For the larger households this may have involved several trips.

No running water was available in the houses, and water had to be collected in buckets from three cast iron pumps located around the village. The 1891 committee report discusses the water supply:

> This is, for the lower village, very deficient, especially when the fishermen are all at home. This deficiency has

53

led on one or two occasions to water riots. - On one of these the fishermen cut off the supply to the upper village, being determined that their neighbours should not enjoy a supply which left them in scarcity. The supply for the lower village is apparently about 2160 gallons per day, giving to the population, which is over 300, a supply of about 7 gallons per head a day. I expect at times the supply is very considerably under this.

Given the filthy nature of the work carried out by the fisherfolk the shortage of water in the village proved to be a major problem. This might explain the following comment made by a more than attentive visitor to Port Erroll in 1901:

It was a new world to some of us to see the natives each busy *in* his or her own way, *either in* front of their houses, or at the miniature harbour - a people apart from the visitors; just as though one had crossed the North Sea. Look at that stately girl, no daughter of the soil is she; born on the edge of the sea, she will doubtless marry there and so *in* good time will her daughter as did her mother.

It is not forbidden to admire beauty, even bare-legged beauty; but we envied not the fisher lad his sturdy bride, for, alas, a second look revealed the fact that her limbs were not on too intimate terms with soap.[82]

No fishermen worked on Sunday. They were deeply religious with a choice of three churches for worship in the Cruden Bay area.

Only one, the Port Erroll Congregational Church, was actually located in the village itself. The Episcopalian Church of St James lay about a mile to the south, and the parish church a similar distance to the west.

Some of the fishermen belonged to a religious cult known as the Plymouth Brethren, or the Brethren for short. A revival movement had gripped Scotland in 1859. The leader of the movement in Aberdeenshire was a Peterhead cooper called James Turner, and he was responsible for converting thousands of followers along the Buchan coast (the Brethren are still around today in fishing villages in Aberdeenshire).

The Brethren don't believe in ministers and take everything in the Bible as read and infallible. They believe that the second coming of Christ is nigh, an event they anticipate with great excitement. In the absence of ministers, individuals from within the Brethren preached to each other at their meetings.

In Bram's time, the fishermen and their families would gather in Harbour Street on a Sunday evening. The women sat in stools in front of the houses, square cloths covering their heads; the men stood in their best suits on the other side of the road with the Water of Cruden estuary at their backs, 'and in the centre of the street a huge fisherman pouring out his soul in a fervent proclamation of the Gospel.'[83] Sometimes the excitement would get too much; the Brethren meetings on Easter Friday were referred to by outsiders as the 'passion storm'.[84]

The 'evangelical hysteria' became a talking point in the village. The following conversation was overheard - it took place in 1900 between the clerk of Cruden Parish Church and his deputy:

"What's coming over your folk about the Ward? If they go on like this, the whole village will be in the asylum."

"Oh just your damned religion. The Salutation captain comes out of Peterhead, and works up the poor wretches about their souls, till off they go."[85]

Disharmony was evident between the various religious groups in the area. The Episcopalian Church had been losing members to the Congregational Church, and the Brethren were forever aggressive in trying to recruit new members.

It hadn't helped that the 20th Earl Charles Gore was showing much less interest in attending church services than his predecessor William Harry, who had died in 1891. On one of the few occasions he turned up, he was told off by the minister, "Sir, your father's path to the kirk is growing green.'[86]

Throw into the mix Bram Stoker. It is curious to note that in his two novels set in Port Erroll, Bram doesn't mention any of the churches, although they are all prominent landmarks in and around the village. One of his rare mentions of the local ministry is made in *The Mystery of the Sea*. The main character, Archibald Hunter, wants to know something of the traditions surrounding the time of year known as Lammastide (1st August):

> Doubtless I could have found out all I wanted from some of the ministers of the various houses of religion which hold in Cruden; but I was not wishful to make public, even so far, the mystery which was closing around me. My feeling was partly a saving sense of humour, or the fear of ridicule, and partly a genuine repugnance to enter upon the subject with any one who might not take it as seriously as I could wish.

It's not merely that he doesn't want to talk to the ministers; the idea fills him with 'repugnance'. Village gossip has left no hint of any tension between Bram Stoker and the local clergy, none that I know about anyway. Nevertheless, one senses that not all is right here. Let's enter into speculation.

Bram Stoker was known to like drinking alcohol in a village that was largely abstemious. He was probably seen working on a Sunday in a community which was somewhat pious and would strongly disapprove of such behaviour. But worst of all, this was the man who would go on to write *Dracula*, an entertainment about the evil activities of an undead monster who resorts to black magic and all sorts of devilish goings on.

Not only that, Count Dracula's nemesis, Abraham Van Helsing, is a Roman Catholic, and he uses the idolatrous tools of silver crucifixes and sacred wafers to subdue the evil foe. Much of this novel had been written in the village. The ministers wouldn't have liked that – no, not at all.

5

THE WATTERS' MOU'

Bram Stoker marked his discovery of Port Erroll by producing both a short story and a novel set there. The short story, which I've already referred to, is *The Crooken Sands*, and it was published in the Christmas 1894 edition of the *Illustrated Sporting and Dramatic News*. Arthur Fernlee Markam, a London merchant, arrives on holiday with his family and stays at the Red House.

He wears the full regalia of kilt, sporran and Glengarry hat complete with an immense eagle feather which he fancies makes him look like a highland chieftain. However, he is totally out of place in Port Erroll where nobody else dresses like this; or to be exact, not since the 19th Earl, William Harry died in 1891. As Bram would have known, he walked around the village in a similar outfit.

The Crooken Sands is a strange tale about a doppelganger, the double of a living person. Arthur Markam's double wears the same costume, and who the double might be is revealed at the dramatic end of the story.

Bram mentions actual places and actual people in Port Erroll. The Red House is on the west side of Aulton Road and is used today as a guest house. A real-life person from the village gets a part. Known locally as Supple Sandy, he was a simple soul, having been employed as a servant by the 19th earl in an act of charity.[87] Not that his fellow servants in Slains Castle were that charitable, they took advantage of his dim-witted nature by playing practical jokes on him. Bram renamed Supple Sandy as Saft Tammie in the short story; 'saft' is the local dialect word for soft as in 'soft in the head'.

The 20th earl, and the one Bram Stoker knew, bundled Saft Tammie out from the castle during the day. Bram mentions:

His sole occupation seemed to be to wait at the window of the post-office from eight o'clock in the morning till the arrival of the mail at one, when he carried the letter-bag to a neighbouring baronial castle.

The remainder of his day was spent on a seat in a draughty part of the port where the offal of fish, the refuse of the bait, and the house rubbish was thrown, and where the ducks were accustomed to hold high revel.[88]

The Watters' Mou' is a short novel about a fishing family involved in smuggling. It revolves around the agonised conflict of a woman caught between her duty to her family and to her lover, one of the local coastguards. The woman is Maggie MacWhirter, the daughter of an old fisherman who lives in Port Erroll; the coastguard is William Barrow, otherwise known as Sailor Willie.

The villain is straight out of pantomime, he's a criminal involved in smuggling activities. Behold a cunning and grasping elderly Jew by the name of Solomon Mendoza, and recognisable by his 'bald head, keen eyes, a ragged grey beard, a hooked nose and an evil smile.'[89]

Maggie's father is short of money and has mortgaged his boat the *Sea Gull* with Mendoza. His financial plight has become so desperate he is close to losing possession of the boat and his livelihood with it. The situation has been exploited mercilessly by the evil Mendoza. He has persuaded the father to bring in a consignment of smuggled spirits and tobacco for him.

These were picked up from Cuxhaven in Germany and loaded onboard the *Sea Gull*. They are on their way back across the North Sea to Port Erroll at the start of the novel. However, the scheme has been rumbled. The authorities have somehow been told that the smuggled goods are on the way, although they don't know exactly where the boat will land. Sailor Willie has been informed about this by telegram. Its terse message: "Keep careful watch tonight; run expected; spare no efforts; most important."

That night Sailor Willie attends a wedding in the village. He notices some of the guests behaving rather strangely; not only that, he also spots a large number of carts lined up outside, some of which he knows belong to characters of dubious reputation.

This raises a suspicion in his mind that the smuggling run is about to be made into Port Erroll and that the wedding celebration is an elaborate ruse to get him out of the way. He immediately

58

takes off from the festivities to keep watch from his coastguard hut for any suspicious boats coming in to the coast. On getting there he is met by his fiancée Maggie, who knows about the telegram, 'I saw Bella Cruickshank hand ye the telegram as ye went by the post office,' she tells him.

Maggie more or less confesses to the smuggling operation, and tells Willie that her father is involved. She pleads with him to keep quiet about this. This puts her coastguard lover in great difficulty because he has his duty to perform; one that he is professionally obliged to carry out. Maggie knows this only too well; the Victorian state of mind was locked into the idea of 'duty' and the readers would have understood this.

Maggie points out that the *Sea Gull* could return to the Watter's Mou' (the Water's Mouth). It's a feature of the local landscape that exists for real, a deep cleft in the rock where the Back Burn enters the sea to the south of Slains Castle.

However, the wind is rising and a storm is imminent. Sailor Willie tells Maggie that the Watter's Mou' is hazardous for a boat during a storm:

"To try and get in there in this wind would be to court sudden death. Why, lass, it would take a man all he knew just to get out from there, let alone get in, in this weather! And then the chances would be ten to one that he'd be dashed to pieces on the rocks beyond."

Willie 'pointed to where a line of sharp rocks rose between the billows on the south side of the inlet. Truly, it was a fearful-looking place to be dashed on, for the great waves broke on the rocks with a loud roaring, and even in the semi-darkness they could see the white lines as the waters poured down to leeward in the wake of the heaving wave. The white cluster of rocks looked like a ghostly mouth opened to swallow whatever might come in touch.[90]

The entrance to the inlet does indeed resemble a mouth. I can confirm that at high tide, sharp pyramids of granite rock are seen just above the water level at the entrance on the southern side of the inlet. There are about ten 'teeth' altogether, similar in size and evenly set. During stormy weather the waves surge out revealing the rocks and then surge in again covering them. This creates the impression of a pair of teeth gnashing in and out at the southern entrance of the Watter's Mou'. It's uncanny.

An alternative course of action is available to Maggie. A small boat is moored in the Watter's Mou'. Ignoring Sailor Willie's judgment and taking great risk, Maggie takes the boat and sails from the Watter's Mou' during the storm. Evading the rocks, she intercepts her father's boat out to sea. On being told that the operation has been discovered by the authorities, her father dumps the contraband goods overboard, and returns to Port Erroll Harbour empty-handed.

Maggie, meanwhile, sails back in the little boat to avoid any suspicion that she has warned her father. The boat is wrecked during the storm, and what's left of it together with Maggie's dead body are washed up into the Watter's Mou' by the waves. Sailor Willie finds the body and attempts to retrieve it. He is none too successful, drowning in the process. The book finishes on a sombre note:

> There, on the very spot whence the boat had set sail on its warning errand, lay its wreckage, and tangled in it the body of the noble girl who had steered it – her brown hair floating wide and twined around the neck of Sailor Willy, who held her tight in his dead arms.
>
> The requiem of the twain was the roar of the breaking waves and the scream of the white birds that circled round the Watter's Mou'.

It's a desperately sad end for the two lovers.

On the face of it *The Watter's Mou'* is pure melodrama, yet it's likely that Bram intended a deeper supernatural meaning to the story. The journal from his younger years has recently been published together with a commentary provided by the editors, Elizabeth Miller and Dacre Stoker. It's a commonplace book full of anecdotes, jokes and ideas for stories. Item forty-one, written in 1881, is the plot for a story with the title *The Angry Waters* – which 'wishes ill to person & kills them then murmurs sorrowfully for ever'. Bram's hand-writing is underneath with the word [Written]. The editors' footnote suggests that this is probably a reference to *The Watter's Mou'*[91]

The implication is that the sea in *The Watter's Mou'* is a supernatural entity prone to powerful emotions. The mouth of the Watter's Mou', with its rocks resembling teeth, has swallowed up the two lovers in a fit of anger and left them dead.

Much of the dialogue in *The Watters' Mou'* is written in the local Buchan dialect or 'Doric' as it is commonly called. Here's the heroine Maggie McWhirter talking to her lover: 'O Willy, Willy! I'm in sic sair trouble, and there's nane that I can speak to. Nae! Not ane in the wide warld.' ['O Willy, Willy! I'm in such sore trouble, and there's none that I can speak to. No! Not one in the wide world.'] This accurately captures the sounds and rhythm of the local dialect, the vowel shifts such as sore to 'sair' and none to 'nane'; although perhaps not in a way that's accessible to many beyond Aberdeenshire.

Doric can be impenetrable to outsiders. It includes many dialect words such as *loon* for a boy and *quine* for a girl. A familiar experience for students arriving at Aberdeen University from England and elsewhere is to be utterly baffled when they hear students from rural Aberdeenshire talking to them in a strong Doric dialect. It will sound vaguely like the English language but not in any recognisable form. In my opinion, Bram had done exceptionally well to tune into the Doric dialect so quickly, and to the extent that he could use it to write dialogue after only his second visit. It demonstrates that he frequently talked to the locals.

Modern novelists tend to avoid the use of excessive dialect in their fiction because it acts as a barrier to the reader. Bram Stoker often lapsed into long sections of dialect in his novels, be it Doric, Yorkshire or Irish.

There's a curious scene in *Dracula* whereby an old Yorkshire fisherman speaks in his local dialect at length. The author slips in a phrase in Doric – 'I wouldn't fash masel' (I wouldn't trouble myself). It's one of the commonest phrases heard in the Doric dialect even today. Fash is derived from the French word for angry – fâché. It's also a dialect word in the north of England; yet it's the word masel' that reveals the phrase as Doric with its vowel shift and the missing f at the end.

This phrase was not amongst the notes on Yorkshire dialect

words Bram Stoker wrote down from the book he found in the Whitby Museum library. It's possible he could have heard phrases from the Doric dialect spoken in Yorkshire; the fishermen travelled up and down the coastline and could have picked up the dialect on visiting ports in Buchan. Dacre Stoker is of the opinion that the Doric phrase was deliberately inserted into the text of *Dracula* as a tribute to the people of Port Erroll.[92] Alternatively, Bram may have made a mistake.

The Watters' Mou' describes real places and the minor characters are real people including James Cruickshank, proprietor of the Kilmarnock Arms Hotel, and Bella Cruickshank from the post office.[93] The Earl of Erroll also gets a speaking part and is treated with much deference.

Maggie was described as 'a favourite with the ladies of the Castle'. The earl shows much generosity in appointing her father to the post as Harbourmaster at Port Erroll Harbour after Maggie's death, even though he has just been exposed as a smuggler.

The wedding in *The Watters' Mou'* is held in the grain store (which is now the Aulton Garage). The guests are real people from the village: William McPherson and James Beagrie the shoemakers, David Mitchell from the salmon fishery, the fisherman Andrew Masson (misspelling his name as Andrew Mason), John Reid who ran the grocery store and Hugh McKay the butcher. They are listed in censuses and valuation rolls from the time.

Ann Findlay, one of my neighbours in the village, recalls: 'In my mother's day there was a cobbler in Main Street. Jimmy Beagrie kept a small monkey tied outside his shop. She told me that you had to watch out as it would go for the girls' long hair.' Bram Stoker gave a signed copy of *The Mystery of the Sea* to James Beagrie. He acted as his groom when he required a horse and trap to get around.[94]

Bram had based the wedding in the grain store on a real event. On Saturday 25th August 1894 he attended a bazaar which was organised to raise funds to build a public hall in the village. Florence and Noel also attended. The event was opened by the Earl of Erroll and it was probably the first time Bram met him.

The bare granite walls inside the grain store were garlanded with flags borrowed from the coastguard for the occasion, and brightly-coloured Chinese lanterns hung from the rafters. A flower stall, china stall, toy stall and a 'gentleman's stall' was set up on the top floor. Other attractions included a display of art, a wheel of fortune and a shooting gallery under the watchful eye of Sergeant-Instructor Thomson.

Music was provided later that afternoon by a string band and a pianoforte. The entrance fee was one shilling up to 2 p.m., sixpence to 6 p.m. and threepence after 6 p.m. The bazaar was crowded out from the beginning and altogether the day's events brought in £157, 14 shillings and 9 pence. This was a substantial contribution, and it meant that the hall could be built two years later.[96] *The Buchan Observer*, reporting on the day's events, mentioned the names of some of the villagers attending the bazaar. Amongst them were James Beagrie, William McPherson and David Mitchell, all guests at the fictional wedding in *The Watter's Mou'*.[97]

The plot of *The Watters' Mou'*, revolving as it does around the smuggling activities of the locals, is contrived. Although smuggling had been widespread in the area in the late eighteenth century and the early part of the nineteenth century, it died out 50 years before Bram Stoker turned up in Port Erroll.

The creation of free trade policies by the British Parliament in the 1840s reduced the tariffs on goods from overseas. This eliminated the large profits to be made from smuggling, and it came to a halt. The Port Erroll fishermen of 1894 were honest law-abiding citizens, the activity of smuggling now a distant memory.

The Scottish educationalist RF Mackenzie writes about how during the time of the First World War his uncle from Whinnyfold told him tales about smugglers: 'The storyteller didn't put dates on his stories and I don't know how many generations back he was talking about.'[98] Bram spoke to the locals in Port Erroll and would have heard much the same anecdotes.

Smuggling had been on the rise in Scotland ever since the Acts of the Union in 1707. Most of the tax duties in Great Britain were made common throughout the newly-formed kingdom. For instance, the introduction of a tax on salt in Scotland made a major impact on the economics of fishing operations because salt was necessary for preserving fish. However, the tax rise which caused the greatest distress for the population was the introduction of a malt tax in 1725. The price of beer rose as a result and this led to riots in the Scottish towns.[99]

The customs and excise duties increased even further over the years in order to pay for the costly wars that were being waged at the time. There was now a big difference in commodity prices between Europe and Great Britain. Tea could be bought on the continent at seven pence a pound weight (3p) and sold for five shillings (25p) at home – a massive price difference. A tub of gin or brandy costing £1 could be sold for £4 in Great Britain. Diluting the gin before selling it made for an even bigger margin. It created the circumstances whereby a huge profit could be made from smuggling, and because of this it became the most profitable activity in coastal towns and villages.

Barrels of gin are mentioned in the local smugglers tales. Tobacco, rum, brandy, silk and laces were also traded according to Bram. These were brought in from the continent and landed on the remote shoreline of Aberdeenshire, in particular between the villages of Collieston, seven miles to the south of Port Erroll, and Boddam, five miles to the north.

Bram notes that the coastline, 'broken up by every convulsion of nature, and worn by the strain and toil of ages into every conceivable form of rock beauty, offers an endless variety of narrow creeks and bays where the daring, to whom the rocks and the currents and the tides are known, may find secret entrance and speedy exit for their craft.'[100]

The locals did not see smuggling as wrong. Reverend John Pratt recorded that, 'so little was the feeling of disgrace attached to this demoralising traffic, that there was scarcely a family along the coast... that was not more or less embarked in it'.[101]

Smuggling was described as 'free trading'. Indeed some regarded it as a political act against the established monarchy. The ruling House of Hanover was highly unpopular in Aberdeenshire, particularly amongst the Jacobite sympathisers who claimed the Stuart royal lineage to be the rightful claimants to the throne. George 1st, who became the first Hanoverian king in 1714, was reputed not to speak English. In Scotland he was commonly referred to as 'the German-speaking laddie' and none too respectfully at that.

The government was well aware of the local smuggling activities, and sent out revenue officers, known as gaugers, to track down the smugglers. First-hand accounts from the time suggest that the locals saw avoiding the activities of the gaugers as a low-risk activity. The penalties for being caught were not particularly harsh and there was little personal risk involved in breaking the law. There were not enough gaugers to cover the long rocky coastline of Aberdeenshire, and many smuggling operations got through.

The Crookit Mary was the most famous smuggling boat in the area. Once it arrived on the Buchan coast laden with contraband, the crew sent out a pre-arranged signal to watchers onshore to confirm that the goods were onboard.

A return signal from land gave the assurance that the 'coast was clear'. *The Crookit Mary* would then move offshore just within sight of land, waiting until everyone onshore was ready to take the goods. A frenzied burst of activity then ensued. The word spread around, furtively passed in coded messages from village to village and from house to house.

Extreme caution was required, the gaugers employed secret informers amongst the population, and the smugglers could never be too sure who could be trusted and who couldn't. As night fell, the boat approached the coast again. The contraband would either be landed onshore at the darkest hour or transferred to a fishing boat out to sea which could then slip into harbour without raising any untoward attention.

The next stage was to find a suitable hiding place. The simplest ruse was to conceal the goods in the caves found up and down the coast. These proved too obvious a choice becoming well known to the authorities, so somewhat more subtle hiding places were sought. Underground bunkers were built using bricks or planks of wood, the sand dunes were eminently suitable sites for these. The bunkers could hold up to 300 barrels of gin.

The roof was positioned at depths greater than six feet below the surface, because this was the length of the spears the gaugers used to probe for contraband when searching in the sand dunes. The ideal location was near a hollow in the ground where the barrels could be stacked out of sight ready for concealment. Ideally a recognisable landmark or feature should be nearby to help locate the site during the dark. Only the select few would be allowed to know the hiding place.

Once a 'run' was put in operation and the fisherwomen and farm servants turned up to receive the smuggled goods, the lair was opened by digging into it from the side. Two pieces of sail cloth were laid out next to the opening. Dry sand was deposited on one and wet sand on the other. When the lair was sealed up, the wet sand was thrown in first and the dry sand went on top. Any footprints in the vicinity were swept over.

The fisherwomen were ideal agents for moving the kegs of gin inland. They wandered the countryside in large numbers carrying their load of smoked fish in their creels for barter or for sale. A keg of gin could fit just as easily into a creel.

They had to be careful, because the gaugers were well aware of what they might be up to. The gaugers were wary of searching the fisherwomen in their native villages. The men were known to carry concealed carriage wheel spokes and attacked anyone harassing their womenfolk. The safest strategy was to accost the women inland. Even then, the fisherwomen would not necessarily give in meekly. These were strong lassies used to carrying heavy loads. They had been known to get the better of the tussle, binding the gauger's feet and hands, and leaving him suitably out of the way until their business was complete. Later they would send a small boy to 'accidentally' find the gauger and set him free. The boy would be sixpence richer for his good deed.

The cat chased the mice and the mice fooled the cat. Tales of how the gaugers were distracted or duped out of seizing the contraband provided an endless source of entertainment for the locals. And these were some of the anecdotes that Bram Stoker would hear many years later.

Reverend William Low tells of how *The Crookit Mary* had been spotted off the coast and the gaugers had also seen the boat.

The hunt was on and they searched everywhere for the smuggled goods. One of the gaugers spotted a fisherwoman walking northwards along the coast road her shoulders straining to carry a creel which looked to be unusually heavy. The fisherwoman ran off taking refuge in a wayside cottage. She shouted to the women who lived there, 'for any sake, take this out of my creel and hide it, for the gauger is at my heels.'

In an instant the keg was thrown into a child's cradle, rolled up in a blanket, and the woman's apron was thrown over the head of the cradle to shield the 'child's' eyes from the sunshine. The official arrived shortly afterwards, searched the creel lying there only to find two pairs of smoked haddock.

Unconvinced, he then searched the whole of the house without finding the keg. Meanwhile, the resident of the cottage was rocking the cradle and singing, trying to sooth the sleeping infant upset by all the noise the gauger was making as he frantically made his search. He had never thought of looking in the cradle – the real infant had been taken away by the woman's sister to a neighbour's house.[102]

A smuggling operation near the village of Collieston ended in tragedy, and it's mentioned by Bram in *The Watter's Mou'*: 'It was many a long year since Philip Kennedy met his death at Kirkton at the hands of the exciseman Anderson.'

The date was 18th December 1798. A boat had landed its contraband onshore only for the gaugers to find out about the operation from an informant. The carts carrying the contraband were expected to pass along the road to the Kirk of Slains.

Three gaugers lay in waiting about a quarter of a mile north of the church. Before long they observed the smugglers' carts approaching with an advanced guard of several men walking some distance in front. A struggle ensued, and one of the advanced guard of smugglers, a big powerful man called Philip Kennedy, grabbed two of the gaugers, holding on to them while imploring his companions to grab the third.

They ignored him, ran as far as they could, and then hid amongst the gorse bushes. The gauger left standing, exciseman Anderson, then attacked Kennedy with his sword, striking his head repeatedly and inflicting severe wounds. Kennedy still held firm.

The gauger then held up the blade of his sword to the moonlight searching for its sharp edge. The final blow, flashing downwards, cut open Kennedy's skull and blood gushed out in torrents. He staggered a quarter of a mile to a nearby farm, where sitting on a wooden bench, he uttered his last words, reportedly: 'If all had been as true as I was, the goods would have been safe, and I should not have been bleeding to death.'[103]

The excisemen were tried for murder at the High Court in Edinburgh, but were let go by the jury with a not guilty verdict. Phillip Kennedy is buried in Slains churchyard where his grave can be seen today next to the church. It bears the inscription: 'In memory of Philip Kennedy, who lived sometime in Ward of Slains, who died the 19th December, 1798. Aged 38 years.' The wooden bench he died on still survives.

The historical business of smuggling was an obvious topic for a novel. Somehow, Bram had to contrive an up-to-date narrative that accounts for why smuggling was still taking place at a late date and to avoid blackening the name of his new-found friends within the village. Hence a modern-day Shylock was introduced to the story in the form of Solomon Mendoza.

The Watter's Mou' was published in 1895, two years before *Dracula* appeared. It was dedicated: 'To my Dear Mother in her loneliness'. The novel came out as a companion piece to *The Parasite* by Arthur Conan Doyle. The review in *Punch* was ecstatic:

> Says the Baron, "What I who have read Mr. BRAM STOKER's latest romance could tell you about *The Watter's Mou'* would make your mou' watter with longing desire to devour it. It is excellent: first because it is short; secondly because the excitement is kept up from first page to the last; and thirdly, because it is admirably written throughout; the scenic description portion being as entrancing as the dramatic.[104]

The review in the *Athenaeum* magazine was more circumspect noting 'a tendency to melodramatic and stagey writing in some of the speeches and situations'. For instance, a typical scene, 'seems more adapted for the Adelphi stage than for a discussion between two Scotch lovers:

"What is it that you would make of me? Not only a smuggler, but a perjurer and a traitor too. God! Am I mistaken?"

But in spite of a certain air of unreality about the whole tale, it has interest and movement enough to arouse and sustain the attention.'[105]

This was useful criticism for Bram to think about if he wanted his writing skills to improve.

The Watter's Mou' was quickly followed by a third novel, *The Shoulder of Shasta.* It was probably written following his second visit to Port Erroll in 1894. The main character is a teenage girl named Esse, and the novel is about her coming of age as she develops into a woman.

Esse becomes involved with two men, Grizzly Dick, an adventurer based on the real-life person of William Cody, better known as Buffalo Bill, and later with Reginald Hampden, an English painter. The early action takes place in the lee of Mount Shasta, a mountain in the Cascade Range of California which Bram Stoker had seen while on tour with the theatre company in the United States.

What's of interest today is that parts of the novel appear to be autobiographical. Bram invested his characters with what are plausibly his own thoughts and attitudes. In particular, Esse is described as a pantheist.

Pantheism is the idea that everything in the universe is 'God' or a unity of some sort. And because all is 'God', it includes everything in nature including human beings. This is a belief that lies closer to eastern religious thought than it does to the idea of a Christian God.

It was the pantheism expressed by Bram's guiding light Walt Whitman in his poem *On the Beach at Night Alone*:

A vast similitude interlocks all,

All spheres, grown, ungrown, small, large, suns, moons, planets, comets, asteroids,

All distances, however wide,

All distances of time - all inanimate forms,

All Souls - all living bodies, though they be ever so
different, or in different worlds,
All gaseous, watery, vegetable, mineral processes - the
fishes, the brutes,
All men and women - me also,
All nations, colours, barbarisms, civilizations, languages,
All identities that have existed, or may exist, on this
globe or any globe,
All lives and deaths - all of past, present and future,
This vast similitude spans them, and always has
spanned, and shall forever span them, and compactly
hold them.

Esse's pantheism was inspired by nature. One morning in a
'mood of semi-religious, semi-emotional exaltation', she wakes
up to find that, 'the full chorus of Nature proclaimed that the day
had come.'

Echoing a line from a Walt Whitman poem, 'a thousand
things impressed themselves on her mind,' she had discovered
pantheism, and what she saw in the natural landscape were 'items
of a vast mutually dependent whole.'

Now the realisation came that 'the whole scheme of Nature
was one deep underlying purpose in which each thing was merely
a factor; that she herself was but a unit with her own place set,
and the narrow circle of her life appointed for her...'

So nature is seen as having a purpose and the individual is
part of it. What exactly is this purpose? It's not exactly clear,
although there is an overpowering sense that one exists:

'It might be destiny, it might be fate, it might be simply the
accomplishment of a natural purpose; but whatever it might be,
she would yield herself to the Great Scheme, and let her feet lead
her where instinct took them.' This is because 'the deep,
underlying forces of her being were making for some tangible
result which would complete her life.'[106]

Esse's thoughts appear to reflect Bram's spiritual outlook in
1894 at the age of 46. If this was the case, they differ from those
of his childhood when he had been brought up within the
Protestant faith. His spiritual outlook probably changed on
discovering the writings of Walt Whitman when he was 23 years

old.

A 'mood of semi-religious, semi-emotional exaltation' plausibly reflects how he felt as he walked along the Cruden Bay shore. The pantheistic views expressed in his books, like those of Walt Whitman, focus on an appreciation of nature and the outdoors; a sensitivity that would now be greatly heightened during his holidays in Port Erroll.

Bram Stoker envisaged nature as somewhat more than the living world of animals and plants; it was closer to how Walt Whitman saw it, and encompassed the entire natural environment: It was 'the land and sea, the animals fishes and birds, the sky of heaven and the orbs, the forests mountains and rivers.'[107]

Let's speculate further. Bram's reawakened spirituality gave him something more, indeed much more. He now had a renewed sense of mission in life. It seems he didn't quite know what it was, but he sensed it. The nature he saw around him had a 'deep underlying purpose' and he felt part of it. And like Esse in *The Shoulder of Shasta* he would let himself go and 'yield' to the 'Great Scheme', his instincts taking him forward. That purpose in Port Erroll was to write books and to establish his name as a man of letters.

Disillusion came with the review of *The Shoulder of Shasta* in the *Athenaeum*. The adventures of Grizzly Dick and Esse Elstree in the Californian wilderness were not appreciated, 'the book bears the stamp of being roughly and carelessly put together. Mr. Stoker can probably do much better work than this; so perhaps the less said about *The Shoulder of Shasta* the better for everyone concerned.'[108]

Must try harder is the message. And I suspect that the author was crushed by such a merciless review - who wouldn't be? Nevertheless, one of the short stories Bram Stoker wrote at the time is an absolute cracker, and he must have been supremely proud of it. It's a horror story called *The Squaw* and it came out in *The Illustrated Sporting and Dramatic News* in December 1893. It's his best-known short story appearing repeatedly in anthologies ever since.

The Squaw is set in Nuremberg. A married couple on their honeymoon in the German city meet up with a brash American called Elias P. Hutcheson. Together they visit the Burg, a castle sitting on a prominent rock. They come to the top of a deep moat on the northern side with a tea garden at its base, fifty to sixty feet below. Looking down they see a cat with her kitten. On a whim the American drops a big pebble to give them both a surprise; instead it accidentally kills the kitten. The mother is enraged and wants revenge. She now stalks the American with relentless intent.

The cat's revenge comes when the American visits the Torture Tower and spots an Iron Virgin, better known today as an Iron Maiden. This is an execution device consisting of a large body-shaped cabinet with a hinged door. It's big enough to contain a human being, and when the door is shut, sharpened iron spikes swing towards the doomed victim piercing with a squish through their eyes, heart and vital organs. Elias P. Hutcheson sees the opportunity for a thrill, the heightened buzz that a near-death experience will bring. He bribes the custodian to allow him to enter the device. The custodian ties a rope to the door, playing it out short of the door shutting completely. At this point the cat pounces on the custodian, claws his face, and as he jumps back in terror he drops the rope... The result is gruesome:

As the door closed I caught a glimpse of our poor companion's face. He seemed frozen with terror. His eyes stared with a horrible anguish as if dazed, and no sound came from his lips.

And then the spikes did their work. Happily the end was quick, for when I wrenched open the door they had pierced so deep that they had locked in the bones of the skull through which they had crushed, and actually tore him out of his iron prison till, bound as he was, he fell at full length with a sickly thud upon the floor, the face turning up as he fell.

Now that's much more like it. Bram Stoker could write gothic horror far better than love stories and perhaps he knew it.

Our author still has a task on his hands and he hasn't got there yet - he requires a breakthrough novel to establish his reputation. The lesson from *The Shoulder of Shasta* is clear. It will only come about with care, attention and a bit more effort

72

than normal. Something is needed that will grab the attention of the public... How about dusting off that vampire plot?

6

FROM THE PAGAN WORLD OF OLD

Bram Stoker was spellbound by the old smuggling tales he heard in Port Erroll. But as he got to know the locals better he would have found out something far more interesting about them. The villagers, particularly the fishermen, held numerous superstitions that were pagan in origin. These were ancient superstitions which had survived the arrival of Christianity in sixth century Aberdeenshire.

Before we go any further, let's take care of that word 'pagan'. It was used in Victorian times for any system of belief that didn't belong to the main religions, in particular folk religions where multiple gods or spirits were worshipped. This is how Bram Stoker would have understood it. The academics don't like the word 'pagan' much because it has all too often been used down the years with a sneer, as if to say 'my religion is superior to your peasant beliefs'.

Today the word pagan is often associated in a popular sense with the worship of nature as practiced by the ancient Celts on the western fringes of Europe, including Scotland. This is how I've used it in this chapter.

The superstitions surviving from the pagan past had long since become detached from the worship of nature; their spiritual significance all but gone. The Port Erroll fishermen were Christians, their devotions focussed entirely on Jesus Christ and the Christian God. They would have been greatly offended should anyone have suggested otherwise. Bram picks up on this in his Port Erroll novel *The Mystery of the Sea*. The old crone Gormala is insulted when it's suggested to her that she might not be a Christian, even though it has been made clear earlier that many of her beliefs derive 'from some of the old pagan mythologies'. Orthodox religion and pagan superstition survived side by side as part of the individual mindset of the fishermen without in any way appearing incongruous to them. As the historian Henry Graham wrote, they were 'like flowers and weeds springing up in an unkempt garden.'[110]

So what then was the background to the local superstitions and traditions that Bram Stoker encountered in Port Erroll? The area around the village had been a hot spot of spirituality and the supernatural ever since humans first settled there. The early farmers built stone circles on the hills and fields of Aberdeenshire, and these are between 4,000 and 5,000 years old. The most common are the recumbent stone circles. The two largest pillars in one of these circles face to the south-west and an enormous flat-lying slab lies between them – the recumbent stone that gives the circles their name.[111]

Let's paint a fanciful scene of an ancient ceremony back then. The farmers have lit their bonfires and vast quantities of heather ale have been drunk. The full moon rises in the sky; tattooed hands thrust up in exultation as it reaches the mid-point between the two pillars. The milky moonlight shines onto the recumbent slab where an ox has just been sacrificed; its dripping blood appears strangely black against the stone.

Scattered on the ground are broken lumps of milky-white quartz reflecting the light and dazzling the eye. Everyone dances in joyous abandon circling in the direction of the moon's graceful path through the luminous sky. They are chanting and cheering in great ecstasy - the great spirit of the night has bathed them in life-infusing moon glow.

Perhaps the spirits of the stones linger. In 1831 a tenant farmer removed seven or eight upright stones which had formed a stone circle about a mile and a half to the west of the Cruden Parish Church. This deed was carried out in the name of improving the land. When the stones were hauled out, 'he came upon a whole colony of lizards, *lacerta vulgaris* [smooth newts], living in holes at the bases of the stones, at a time when lizards were unknown in that part of the country; it being left to a vivid imagination to conjecture that these were of the stock which had flourished there under Druidical patronage...'[112]

Many generations later the tribesmen in the region have been given a name by the Romans; they are now known as the Picts, the painted people. They speak a Celtic language that sounds to the ear more like Welsh rather than the Gaelic spoken on the west coast of Scotland. The worship of nature is abandoned when the Picts were converted to Christianity in the sixth century. One almighty God replaced the spirits in the trees, flowing water and the whistling wind. The Picts themselves eventually disappear as a tribal entity, merging into the greater Scots kingdom after 843 AD. The old language goes too. English started to take over as the common tongue in Aberdeenshire during the twelfth century, although most of the original place names of Pictish or Gaelic origin survive.

Christian worship in Scotland soon came under the influence of the established Catholic Church, and this lasted until the Reformation in 1560. The white-frocked priests of the Catholic Church were then banished forthwith and replaced by black-coated ministers of the Protestant Church.

The newly-formed Church had assumed they would inherit the land and revenues of the ousted Catholics. However, their hopes were dashed when the nobles seized everything and kept hold of a large share. It's the reason why they had supported the religious revolt in the first place. The lack of money explains the wretched state of the church buildings in the countryside up until the early nineteenth century.[113] These were long, narrow buildings, their roofs thatched with heather, and they leaked water.

A church service could be a grim affair: 'The floors were earthen, and in some older kirks in the North the bodies of many generations had been buried beneath them, to the detriment of health, decency, and comfort; for sometimes the bones of the dead so strewed the floor that they were kicked by the worshippers, whose noses were afflicted by the "corrupt unripe corps" disturbed to make room for new tenants.'[114] Wooden pews came later. In the meantime the people brought their own stools to sit on. They had to endure sermons which could last up to seven hours.

The rural church officials were tyrannical and took control of the private life of everyone in the neighbourhood. It was impossible to escape their judgments; your business was their business. Attendance at the Sunday service was compulsory, and should anyone dare not to turn up, the church elders would storm out and get them. Fines were handed out for anything that incurred the wrath of the church; for instance, idly staring out of a window on the Sabbath day. A typical punishment for such lapses was a fine of £4 in Scots money and to be stood up on a stool in front of the congregation wearing sackcloth. Wrongdoers, both men and women, often had their hair shaved off on one side of the head. The men would also have the beard on one side of the face removed.[115]

Church officials acted as both a moral authority and the local police force. Any moral lapse was rebuked and not just the sin of fornication. This might include profanity of speech or gossiping. The church elders operated a nightly curfew going through the streets and entering the local inns to send the occupants home. They also dealt with any public disorder such as brawling. The consequences of disobeying the rule of the church were severe. For a serious offence, a parishioner could be excommunicated, their property seized and condemned as outlaws. Even if they moved elsewhere, their reputation followed them.

The Church of Scotland wasn't only concerned with keeping the public under control at a local level; they had a national crusade in mind. According to Reverend James Rust in his book *Druidism Exhumed*, the Church created a commission in 1649 with the task of stamping out the pagan traditions still surviving in Scotland (and over 1,000 years after the arrival of Christianity). A large number of church ministers were appointed to the commission, together with judges, lawyers and doctors. 'They directed their attention to the Remains of Druidical Superstition and Sorcery practised at the old places of worship,' Reverend Rust informs us. These were 'dedicated not only to the greater, but to the lesser gods, the familiar spirits, the household divinities, or demigods of the ancients, who, as was supposed, could be consulted, and could grant charming powers to their votaries...'

An all too visible tradition was in their sights, 'the Druidical customs observed at the fires of Beltane, Midsummer, Halloween, and Yule. All these fires were ordered to be abolished.'[116] Two major pagan festivals were held during the year; Beltane which is equivalent to our May Day, and Halloween, sometimes called

77

Samhain (and pronounced Savin), which was held in the first week of November. They marked major events in the agricultural year; grazing farm animals were put out onto summer pastures at Beltane and returned to the home fold after Halloween. Both festivals were celebrated by lighting bonfires on prominent hillsides with large crowds marching around them holding blazing torches. Fire held a great fascination in pre-Christian folk beliefs. It was a mysterious entity endowed with the powers of destruction and subsequent renewal.

Fires were also lit to celebrate Midsummer Day and Yuletide at the New Year, although these were less obviously pagan in origin. The latter festival was celebrated as a holiday, although the Church of Scotland disapproved of what they saw as a popish tradition, insisting that their congregation worked over this period. The Church in England was less harsh, allowing the Christmas and New Year holiday to be celebrated.

The Beltane fires at May time were intended to purge the evil powers of darkness lingering from the previous winter. In particular, livestock and crops now had a chance to thrive in the summer season as a result of the destruction of evil influences caught up by the purifying flames. It was believed that witches were consumed with the fire:

> The younger portion danced round the fire or ran through the smoke shouting, "Fire! blaze and burn the witches, Fire! Fire!" The ashes were scattered far and wide, scaring the powers of evil and fertilising the fields. The whole company continued till dark to run through the ashes, crying "Fire! Burn the witches."[117]

The flame used to light the fire was special. It had to be newly sparked into existence and by doing so it was deemed conjured up from the spirit world; no other source of flame could possibly be used. This was 'needfire'; fire produced by the friction of a pointed wooden rod twirled rapidly by hand onto an underlying stick. The creation of virginal fire for the celebratory bonfires was an event of great importance to the community. All the hearth fires in the houses within sight of the bonfire were extinguished. A large pile of peat clods were put into the bonfire and everyone picked up a flaming lump to take home so that their hearth fire could be re-lit with the new source of flames. It was kept burning continuously over the year to come.[118]

A Beltane fire festival held in Perthshire in 1769 has been described by Thomas Pennant. A pot or cauldron was hung above the bonfire and a caudle, an ancient version of eggnog, was heated up. It was made from eggs, butter, oatmeal, milk, beer and whisky. The ceremony started by spilling some of the caudle onto the ground as an offering to the spirits. Then everyone took a specially baked oatmeal cake with nine square knobs raised on its surface. The oatcake was broken up and each fragment containing a knob was thrown in turn over one shoulder. Each bit was tossed to the words: 'This to thee, protect my cattle: This to thee, O fox, spare my sheep: This to thee, O eagle: This to thee, O hooded crow, save my lambs,' and so on.[119] Then the caudle was drunk. As Henry Graham wryly notes, 'next day, probably, these idolaters were sitting in their pews in orthodoxy, most demure.'[120]

The Halloween fires were held as winter closed in. Each village would celebrate the festival, and fires were also lit on high spots around Aberdeenshire farms. The intent was to destroy the evil spirits and to ensure the fertility of their crops and animals in the year to come. On the farms, the adults, servants and their children slowly marched around the boundary of their fields carrying blazing torches. They always headed in the direction that the sun travelled in the sky (to walk 'widdershins', that is in a counter-clockwise direction, was considered to bring exceptionally bad luck). The farmland was now purified of the evil influence of the witches which up until now had been gathering in ever-increasing numbers as the nights got longer.

The pagan fire festivals continued as a tradition until well into the nineteenth century. Reverend Pratt, minister at St James's Church near Port Erroll, wrote in 1858 that Halloween fires were still being lit in Aberdeenshire and that they 'present a singular and animated spectacle - from sixty to eighty being frequently seen from one point.'[121]

Flowing water was also believed to be a mysterious quantity and was worshipped as one of nature's spirits. Water nourished humans, the animals and the crops of the field. Whereas fire provided the spark, it's water that sustains. For the pagan worshippers the well was a living thing. Springs that arose out of the ground were held with particular reverence and became known as holy wells. They were holy to the pagans and most certainly not to the Protestant Church. Some of the wells in medieval times had become associated with the cult of individual saints within the pre-Reformation Catholic Church. The priests had expediently taken over a pagan tradition from an earlier time and adopted it as one of their own.[122] St Olaf's Well, now within the perimeter of Cruden Bay Golf Course and mentioned by Bram Stoker in one of his novels, is a holy well.

Holy wells were believed to hold special properties for treating illness or curing infertility in women. On the evidence of a rhyme traditionally attached to St Olaf's Well - 'St Olave's Well, low by the sea, where pest nor plague shall ever be' - its waters were sought after as a cure for infectious diseases and the plague. St Olaf was the King of Norway in the eleventh century and canonised as a saint, having been said to have converted the Norwegians to Christianity. He was later made the patron saint of Norway. Historical lore places King Olaf at Cruden Bay where he is said to have led the Vikings against the Scots army.

There are many holy wells around Aberdeenshire and they were visited regularly up until the nineteenth century. The Protestant Church vehemently discouraged their use; in 1579 they prohibited any pilgrimages to the wells. This proved ineffective. According to James McPherson, 'the task of weaning peer and peasant from recourse to the holy well in time of distress was one of the most difficult the Church had undertaken, and one of the last to yield to her strong arm.'[123]

The pilgrimages continued despite the strident efforts of the Church to stop them. On reaching a well, the supplicant approached it barefoot and barelegged. A rag or a piece of clothing was dipped in the water, rubbed on the affected part of the body and then tied to a nearby bush or tree. A prayer was said. The disease had thus been removed and transferred to the rag by the cleansing powers of the well's water. A holy well could be recognised by the large number of cloths tied to nearby bushes. A small coin might also be thrown into the well. It was intended as a personal sacrifice to the spirit that lived there in return for the services rendered.

The wells were busier at the times of year when they were considered to be at their most potent. These were the first Sundays of February, May, August and November. Large crowds attended in May and August when better weather could be expected. The August pilgrimage took place on a weekend close to Lammas on August 1st, traditionally the first day of the harvest. Great crowds converged on the holy wells arriving at midnight on the Saturday. It was said that whoever drank the first draught of the water would get the maximum benefit. This tradition was the source of a popular tale that whoever in a new marriage first drank of water from a holy well would be master of the house. One newly-wed husband ran to the well as soon as the marriage service was over. He was too late. His bride had already taken a bottle of water into the church before the ceremony, drinking it as he rushed off out the door.

Any source of flowing water was deemed to hold spiritual significance for the pagan worshippers. Rivers were living things, and the river spirit commonly appeared in the form of a horse known as a kelpie. This was a black horse with mad staring eyes which haunted the fords of rivers in flood. On no account should anyone climb onto the back of a kelpie to help them get across the river. At first the beast would prove cooperative enough, but then once in mid-stream the rider was bodily thrown off and left to drown in the water.[124]

The residents of rural Aberdeenshire also firmly believed in the existence of fairies. The church didn't approve of this at all; the Synod (provincial assembly) of Aberdeen issued a decree in 1669 warning the population not to communicate with fairies.[125] It's a decree that's astonishing to us from a modern point of view; we consider fairies to be the stuff of children's fantasy books. Yet from a pagan point of view, fairies were the spirits that lived in the earth. They were considered to be distinct from witches; although fairies were troublesome and extremely annoying at times, they couldn't be called upon by humans to cause evil.

Fairies are 'that obliging, humorous, kindly, sometimes tricky and mischievous, diminutive, aerial class of beings, who sometimes assumed the human form.' They didn't like being called fairies, and out of deference to their feelings the locals referred to them as 'the fair folks' or the 'good neighbours'.[126] They were believed to be household demigods inhabiting palaces within the bowels of the earth. The fairies came out at night, carousing in merry revelry in the pale moonlight. Amongst them were good fairies and bad fairies. Good fairies could show kindness by helping out the impoverished farmer by providing assistance; giving him bread or seed corn for instance. Bad fairies caused all sorts of trouble. They were notorious thieves and any mislaid object was routinely blamed on them.

Fairies made their home in rounded green knolls dotted around the landscape. A fairy knoll could always be recognised because the grass covering it is richer and greener than the immediate surroundings. Farmers avoided cultivating them because it wasn't worth the trouble of angering the inhabitants. One can still find fairy knolls named on the maps of Scotland.

Pagan superstitions were also attached to a feature known as the Goodman's Croft or Fold, a small isolated area of rough land deliberately left untilled. 'Goodman' is a Scots word for landowner, and the Goodman referred to was a spiritual entity believed to live on the land. Many a Goodman's Croft had survived as a legacy from pagan days when a Great Spirit was worshipped there; others were created in more recent times. Church records mention some of the superstitious rites associated with a Goodman's Croft. For instance, farmers wishing their cattle to keep healthy, or if disease had affected them and they wanted respite, would lay out and dedicate a small patch of ground to a supernatural demon, uttering promises to leave it uncultivated. The deal was sealed by throw stones into the newly made lair.[127]

The established Church proscribed these areas of land because in their view they were consecrated to the Devil. Goodman's Crofts were not to be tolerated, and it actively campaigned to have them destroyed. The directive met with stubborn resistance; there was a great unwillingness to plough them over because nobody wanted to find out that they had indeed enraged the malignant spirits whose homes they had just destroyed. The Church resorted to threats of punishment to get them removed, although many survived despite their best efforts. Goodman's Crofts were a persisting feature of the Aberdeenshire landscape for hundreds of years until they mostly disappeared around the start of the nineteenth century. As the old superstitions weakened, an increased demand for land resulted in most of them being ploughed over.

And then there were the witches. Bram Stoker would have found only the faint aroma of smoke lingering from the witches' cauldrons around the Cruden Bay area. Any belief in witches had largely gone by the end of the eighteenth century, although the folklore survived. It was the Aberdeenshire residents of old that had believed in witches, and they were well aware that devil worship was taking place within the county. There were even reports from back then that the Devil had been sighted in Aberdeenshire. According to one account: 'He would be a decent enough chap, if he hadn't had a terrible head of horns and fearful long hairy legs with great cloven feet, but Lord, he had a terrible smell of brimstone.'[128]

It was commonly believed that the Devil could change his form to anything he wanted; typically a hare, a black cat or a dog. Joseph McPherson notes:

> He appeared as a branded dog to Jonet Coupar at the Brig of Brechin in 1650. Nine witnesses saw the dog accost her there. Jonet was burned. On one occasion a little black dog followed the Reverend John Mill of Dunrossness and his man Hector, whose mind was filled with fears. The venerable minister spoke words of cheer: "it is me, he wants, not thee." It was a common belief in the North that the Devil assumed the disguise of a dog.[129]

When Count Dracula landed at Whitby he bounded onshore in what was described by a newspaper cutting in Mina Murray's journal as an immense dog; it was later identified as a wolf by Professor Van Helsing. The root of the word Dracula, 'Drac' is the Romanian word for devil. The association is made more explicit when the Count, wishing to disguise his tracks, signs a letter as Mr de Ville. He is not the Devil however, but one of his disciples. At one point we are told by Professor Van Helsing that the Dracula family of old were believed to have had dealings with the Evil One. They had learned their dark secrets in the Scholomance, which according to Emily Gerard in her article *Transylvanian Superstitions* is a, 'school supposed to exist somewhere in the heart of the mountains, and where all the secrets of nature, the language of animals, and all imaginable magic spells and charms are taught by the devil in person.' [130]

Witches and warlords in Aberdeenshire were believed to have made their accord with the Devil and by doing so, practised both black and white magic. It's plausible that some of these witches were impoverished widows of no secure means who sold charms and incantations to eke out a living when otherwise they would have starved. Perhaps they also operated a protection racket along the lines of 'bribe me or your cattle will come to harm'.

A potent weapon in the armoury of the witch was the evil eye. This was not necessarily an attribute unique to witches. The phenomenon was believed to arise naturally whenever someone looked covetously at another's good fortune and became consumed with intense envy. An evil eye is injurious to whatever it falls on, be it human, animal or object. Mysterious ailments were believed to result, potentially leading to a general dwindling of the spirit and eventual death. It was considered prudent to avoid provoking the feelings in others that could bring on the evil eye. Just one glance by a witch could cause malevolence to anyone who had upset her or had bought her services to wreak harm on their enemies. Those thought to be particularly vulnerable to the evil eye were unbaptised children, cattle, poultry and fish. The witch didn't even have to look directly at the object of her evil intent; often just a glance at an item of clothing or an object belonging to the intended victim such as shorn hair or nail clippings would suffice.

The witches didn't have it all their own way. The rowan tree or 'mountain ash' with its distinctive red berries was considered effective as a deterrent to witches. Red, the colour of fire, protected against evil. Many a rowan tree was deliberately planted next to farms and houses in Scotland because of this. Rowan tree twigs and branches were gathered off the trees to hang in the home at Beltane time. These were placed above doors and windows, and also in barns, stables and even over the household refuse dump.

The rowan tree (mountain ash) makes it into *Dracula* as a protective charm against evil spirits. Jonathan Harker is in Castle Dracula and ponders over his journey there: 'How was it that all the people at Bistritz and on the coach had some terrible fear for me? What meant the giving of the crucifix, of the garlic, of the wild rose, of the mountain ash?' He will soon find out!

Recognition as a witch in the late sixteenth and early seventeenth centuries was a deadly affair. A witchcraft act was passed in Scotland in 1563, whereby witchcraft, sorcery and necromancy were decried as pagan, popish and erroneous superstition. In consequence anybody caught practising witchcraft could be subject to the death penalty. Trials were held, and a key piece of evidence was held to be the confession of a witch, often obtained under torture. The suspect was commonly deprived of sleep, essentially a form of torture. Hallucinations often resulted, and the ravings were faithfully recorded for use as 'evidence'.

Accusations of witchcraft were sometimes made by a neighbour; perhaps the children kept coming down with numerous illnesses and that cantankerous old woman next door had obviously cast the evil eye towards their house. Or an unfortunate individual discovered to their horror that their name had been blurted out during the interrogation of a suspected witch, and they too were dragged in for questioning. Once a suspect was in custody, a feature looked for was 'the devil's mark' - a blemish or an insensitive part of the skin. The latter was detected by pricking with pins. Witch-prickers were employed for the purpose; about ten are known to have operated in Scotland.[131] The suspect witch was doomed should the devil's mark be found on them.

At a very rough estimate, some 2,000 witches were executed in Scotland during the late sixteenth and early seventeenth century.[132] The preferred method of execution was strangling by garrotte; a metal collar which could be tightened around the victim's neck. Only once dead or unconscious was the body of the witch then burnt. A small number of witches were burned alive, although this didn't happen too often. To burn the body of a witch required 16 loads of peat and sometimes a small amount of wood and coal to get the flames going. The alternative was to burn the body in a tar barrel.[133] The witch burnings were open to public view and brought in large crowds.

A witch panic engulfed Aberdeenshire between January and May 1597 with 26 recorded executions. The first stirring of this was in the Slains area immediately to the south of the Cruden Parish.[134] Here, the Earl of Erroll formed a 'Commission of Justiciary' employing his officials for the purpose. The intent was to find witches and bring them to trial. It's possible that having recently returned from exile, he was aiming to show diligence in the eyes of King James VI. The King had written a book on the black arts with the title *Daemonologie* which was published in 1597. It starts as follows:

> The fearful abounding at this time in this country, of these detestable slaves of the Devil, the Witches or enchanters, hath moved me (beloved reader) to dispatch in post, this following treatise of mine... to resolve the doubting hearts of many; both that such assaults of Satan are most certainly practised, and that the instruments thereof, merits most severely to be punished...

Details about the witches of Slains parish are scanty; the trial documents have not survived, and they are known about only when mentioned in court cases from elsewhere. Helen Gray was tried in Slains and convicted on the 29th January, but underwent a stay of execution and was kept in prison. She was retried in Aberdeen later in April, found guilty, and was executed the next day.[135] One other name from the Slains witch hunt was mentioned during a trial held in Aberdeen. The accused was Katherine Gerard, and we are informed by the court records that her mother, who was described by her diabolical nickname of Hellie Pennie, had previously been burnt at Slains.[136] Also in the records is the name of Gilbert Fiddler, who had made a pair of shoes for the Countess of Erroll some ten years previously. She considered them to be bewitched although we are not told why. He was tried for witchcraft, acquitted and let free. That a woman was furious about her shoes was not considered sufficient grounds for executing someone, not even back then.

A louring cloud of fear hung over Aberdeenshire in 1597. The normal neighbourly feuds that abound in small communities spilled over into gossip and denunciation of the darkest sort. It became highly dangerous for anyone to be openly talked about as having dealt in the black arts. Aberdeenshire church records give accounts of several cases of slander being brought before the authorities. For instance, Janet Davidson from the farm of Leask near Port Erroll made complaints that she had been slandered as a witch. The outcome is not known as the original document has fragmented. What remains of it contains witness accounts of her alleged evil influence; a neighbour claimed that their affairs failed to prosper after she moved in nearby; another declared that she could influence whether a sick child lived or died. Janet and others like her had no choice but to take such actions; no one could allow a reputation for witchcraft to stand unchallenged and expect to live.[137]

The last case of witchcraft in the local church records was from 1709, when Alex Simpson from the Aberdeenshire village of Methlick was accused of charming away the headache of a George Ogilvie. The case was not proven.[138]

The Witchcraft Act was eventually repealed in 1736. There were a number of reasons for this. One was that the legality of proving witchcraft by gaining confessions under torture and pricking for the devil's mark had come under disrepute.[139] Another was that the western world was becoming more liberal in its attitudes, and it was at about this time that the Scottish Enlightenment took hold. The emphasis was now on science, reason and intellectual pursuit.

Before Bram Stoker discovered Port Erroll, he would have associated North East Scotland with one topic only; Shakespeare's play *Macbeth*. It was a favourite at the Lyceum Theatre. *Macbeth* is the supernatural play complete with witches, ghosts and dark forebodings of the future to come. When Henry Irving and the actress Ellen Terry arrived in North East Scotland on a working holiday in the summer of 1887 they visited locations associated with the play.[140] These included Cawdor Castle and the remaining vestiges in the east of Nairnshire reputed to have been the source of Shakespeare's inspiration for the 'blasted heath'. The three witches meet here at the start of *Macbeth*. On arriving at the moorland, Henry Irving asked his driver whether any witches were still around, only to be given the mysterious answer that they had disappeared 'at the time of the flood.' The confusion was cleared when it was established that the driver had been referring to the great Moray Flood of 1829 rather than the biblical event.[141] Ellen Terry mentioned the day in her diary and was vastly underwhelmed: 'Visited the "Blasted Heath". Behold a flourishing potato-field! A smooth softness everywhere.' The Lyceum Theatre could improve on this: 'We must blast our heath when we do *Macbeth*.'

Bram Stoker was thinking about his vampire project again, the book that would become *Dracula*. Something revitalised his interest; some spark got him going. Yes, he had found somewhere congenial to think about his books and to get them written - Port Erroll and the stunning coastal scenery around Cruden Bay proved ideal. But more than that, much more – it was a place deeply embedded within the supernatural; a place where mortal human beings confronted the demonic and had done so for thousands of years past.

7
'PAWNS ON THE CHESSBOARD OF EARTH'

The rural residents of Aberdeenshire past went from birth to death restricted by an enormous number of superstitions. They believed that the circumstances governing their lives were largely outside their control and in the hands of invisible and powerful agencies. These were part religious and part pagan. God and the Devil were seen as in confrontation over the fate of humans on earth; fairies, ghosts and witches also exerted their influence.

Men and women looked on as their lives were pulled hither and thither. Storm, disease, calamity and good fortune were not accepted as chance events, they were instigated by unseen forces. Good or bad luck were the outcomes of a joust between the agents of virtue and evil, each trying to get the upper hand. Mere mortals saw themselves as 'pawns on the chessboard of earth, moved by invisible opponents, who are trying to checkmate each other'.[142]

It was a view that had arisen with the origin of human consciousness; it came from a dawning awareness of the storm and fury of nature. The elements showed passions much like humans do, but with far more power than they could ever muster. The conclusion was clear. Behind these awesome forces lay supernatural influences which, at a whim, could overwhelm feeble human attempts to eke out a living. All anyone could do was to try and ward off disaster by adhering to the long-established traditions and rituals. If the elements at large couldn't be appeased, well at least you could avoid annoying them by scrupulously following the rules for appropriate behaviour.

This is what Bram Stoker would have discovered after talking to the villagers of Port Erroll. The idea that Christianity and pagan superstition could coexist within a community was not new to him. He would have encountered something similar in the rural villages of his native Ireland. He also came across the idea when he read Emily Gerard's article *Transylvanian Superstitions*. She had written that in rural Transylvania:

'Many old Pagan ceremonies are still clearly to be distinguished through the flimsy shrouding of a later period, and their origin unmistakable even through the surface-varnish of Christianity which was thought necessary to adapt them to newer circumstances, and like a clumsily remodelled garment the original cut frequently asserts itself, despite the fashionable trimmings which now adorn it.'[143]

In contrast to the peasants of Transylvania, the residents of Port Erroll didn't believe in vampires and had probably never seen a bulb of cultivated garlic. Nevertheless, the similarities between the two widely separated cultures were evident. The discovery of pagan superstitions and traditions in Port Erroll must have excited Bram enormously. His reaction may have mirrored that of Professor Van Helsing in *Dracula*: 'A year ago which of us would have received such a possibility, in the midst of our scientific, sceptical, matter-of-fact nineteenth century?'

Bram took the old pagan beliefs seriously. He wrote in one of his non-fiction books that 'in times when primitivity holds sway, we are most in touch with the loftiest things we are capable of understanding...'[144] And in *Dracula* Van Helsing asks, "Is there fate amongst us still, sent down from the pagan world of old...?'

The main guides to the superstitions of Aberdeenshire are Reverend Walter Gregor's 1881 book *Notes on the Folk-Lore of the North-East of Scotland* and Reverend Joseph McPherson's book *Primitive Beliefs in the North-East of Scotland* published in 1929. Bram may have read the earlier book because it was published in his life time. Nevertheless, he would have discovered many of the superstitions at first hand by talking to individuals in Port Erroll. Folk memories of the old superstitions survive today; my neighbours confirmed some of these during my research.

Day-to-day existence was problematic for the fisherfolk on the Aberdeenshire coast. The nature of a fisherman's work led to many superstitions. Much in his life lay in the realms of pure chance, and that included the state of the weather and the amount of fish caught during the day. The work was dangerous - a fisherman's boat was slung low, leaving no safety margin against falling overboard. This was of necessity because much of his routine work involved transferring fishing lines, nets and equipment over the side of the boat. If the fisherman fell into the sea this was likely to be fatal on account of the long and heavy sea boots he wore. Few fishermen bothered to learn to swim as it would probably make no difference anyway. Their water-logged boots would drag them to the bottom of the sea before they could do anything about it.

Even the simple task of getting to a boat for the day's work confronted the fisherman with numerous obstacles. He would not have wanted to cross the path of animals such as rabbits, foxes, and worst of all, hares. Horrors of horrors, a witch could transform into a hare. Pigs were another taboo animal; the mere mention of a pig brought gasps of revulsion from everyone within hearing range. In some villages the sight of a dog en route was most unwelcome.

Many a fisherman would not want to meet a woman on his way to the boat, not even his wife. In Port Erroll the sight of a woman dressed in red was considered ominous. The fisherman might also not want to meet someone with an unlucky name; one surname in particular caused distress – Ross. Indeed someone called Ross could not have their surname pronounced without risking bad luck. If the name was mentioned inadvertently, the careless person would immediately follow up by spitting on the ground – or 'spitting out a bad name' as it was said. If it was necessary to refer to someone with an unlucky name, circumlocutions could be found such as calling attention to 'the lad that lives in such and such a place' or using their nickname. One wouldn't want to lodge with someone called Ross because misfortune would inevitably result. The surnames Coull and Whyte were also considered unlucky.[145] At some time long past there would have been worthy explanations as to why these surnames were deemed to bring bad fortune, but they had long since been forgotten.

A most curious superstition was this: if a fisherman met a church minister on the way to his boat, it was considered an exceptionally bad omen. In Port Erroll he would return home even if it meant losing out on a day's income. The fishermen would show great respect for a minister onshore, but anything to do with the sea, that was different. It has never been the custom for a church minister to launch a new boat or even to be asked to say prayers during the ceremony. While at sea it was considered unlucky to mention certain words associated with religion, a church for instance. This could pose practical problems during the day because the tall spire of a church often made for a prominent landmark while out in a boat. The fisherman could get around the difficulty by being allusive – referring to the church as a bell-house - and the meaning would be clear to all onboard. Likewise church ministers were not mentioned at sea – and should the need arise to talk about a minister he was described as 'the man with the black coat.'[146]

Peter Anson, who wrote extensively on the lives and traditions of fishermen, reckoned that these were age-old superstitions throughout Europe, and they may have arisen during the early days of Christianity. It appears that the Christian religion was faithfully adhered to onshore, but the long-established awe and respect for the power of the sea prevailed offshore.[147]

On the west coast of Scotland, the Gaels were said to have retained their name for the sea spirit - Shoney (Gaelic: Seonaid and the equivalent of the English name Johnny). According to Reverend Walter Gregor the pagan belief in sea gods and demons survived in the Hebrides, whereas their names had long since been forgotten on the east coast of Scotland. Nevertheless, the east-coast fisherfolk appear to have sensed an awesome presence within the sea which was not Christian in origin.

Asking a fisherman who was about to put to sea where he was going to cast his lines or nets was taboo. It was a question that would bring bad luck to the day's work. On the other hand, there were ways of creating good luck. At New Year, the fishermen raced to the fishing grounds with the intent of beating their fellows in catching the first fish. This was the first blood of the year and it was sought as a lucky omen to ensure bountiful catches in the coming year. Should the weather be much too wild to go out fishing on New Year Day, the fisherman grabbed a gun and walked along the shore before dawn looking for the first living thing that he could wound or kill. He must have his first blood as a sacrifice to the power residing in the sea.

Fishermen avoided whistling as this invited trouble. Whistling is the sound that the wind makes; it's the noise of the sea-spirit. To imitate the spirit might insult them. This taboo is almost universal amongst fishermen in Europe. It was also considered exceptionally bad luck to point a finger at a boat or to count boats at sea or people onshore. Visitors to fishing villages sometimes fell into this trap unwarily, and having done so, were then astonished when an enraged fishwife threw a fish at them.

Fishermen held strong taboos about disaster at sea. Any boat that had been involved in a fatality would be strictly avoided by the fishermen in the village; they wouldn't even set foot in it. The Aberdeenshire fisherwife, Christian Watt, describes in her memoirs how her husband had been killed in an accident at sea when a loose sail whipped him overboard. With the loss of the main earner this left her and her family in dire financial straits. Yet nobody in the village would take over as skipper of the boat, and it was left unused on the shore. She eventually managed to hire it out to a fisherman from Aberdeen.[148]

Sometimes a boat was deemed to be possessed by evil spirits; perhaps someone with the evil eye had looked at the boat and by doing so had given it the power to 'glower' off the fish. A way of removing the evil was to put the boat 'through the halyards': the halyard is the long rope used for raising and lowering a sail or a flag on the mast. A noose was made out of the halyard which was wide enough to pass around the entire boat. Once the boat had passed through this magic circle, the evil spirits were deemed removed. Similarly, if a fisherman thought that one of his nets had been contaminated with evil he would burn it.

Ways were found to keep the evil spirits at bay. In pagan style, rowan tree twigs were tied to the fishing lines or the tholes, the pins on the side of the boat through which the oars pivoted. It was also common practice to nail a horseshoe to the mast. Iron was extremely useful to have around in a fishing boat because iron drives out evil. If a member of the crew mentioned a taboo word, those in hearing would shout out 'cauld iron!' (cold iron), and everyone immediately grasped hold of the nearest bit of the metal. This prevented a bad spell from being cast on the boat. The fishing boats and harbour area of Port Erroll resounded with the phrase at every slip.

This reverence for iron was pagan in origin, perhaps even a throwback to the beginning of the Bronze Age when the first metal implement would have been regarded with awe. The spirit in the stones had yielded up a mysterious substance all hard and cold to the touch. Once iron had been discovered, the strange property whereby two bits attracted each other by magnetism would have been noted. The explanation was clear, living spirits inhabit the metal.

Aberdeenshire started to change towards the end of the eighteenth century. Up until then the terrible condition of the roads made communications within and beyond the county extremely difficult. The local economy, in common with much of Scotland at the time, was based on subsistence agriculture; the population eking out a living close to starvation levels. The diet was largely oatmeal and dairy produce, with some fish.

As the eighteenth century came to a close, the roads improved, the Industrial Revolution took hold, and the economy boomed. Even rural Aberdeenshire felt the impact of this. Land rents, which had been static for most of the century, started to increase severalfold. It also helped that the introduction of good farming practice had improved yields. North East Scotland, long isolated from outside influence, was now being thrust into the modern world with poverty and starvation a distant memory. This was the first stage in the gradual loss of the old traditions and superstitions. The process accelerated once the railways came as Walter Gregor pointed out in 1881:

> The North, with its hills, and vales, and woods, and rocks, and streams, and lochs, and sea – with its fairies, and waterkelpies, and ghosts, and superstitions – with its dialect, and customs, and manners, has become part of myself. Everything is changing, and changing faster than ever. The scream of the railway whistle is scaring away the witch, and the fairy, and the waterkelpie and the

ghost. To give an account of the olden time in the North, as seen by myself, and as related to me by the aged, is the task I have set before me. It is true some of what is related has not yet passed away.

Yet these traditions didn't totally disappear. Many of the old superstitions still hold sway amongst fishermen in Scottish fishing ports. A friend of mine, Fiona-Jane Brown, completed her PhD thesis at the University of Aberdeen on the subject of beliefs and traditions in Scottish fishing communities. She comes from a Peterhead fishing family, and was able to gain the trust of those she interviewed in a way that might not have happened with an outsider. By doing so, she collected more than a hundred individual oral histories. Fiona-Jane referred to these as demonstrating the 'dualistic' beliefs of the fishermen. They are devoutly Christian, yet many of their traditions are pre-Christian in origin; even today.

Fiona-Jane quotes an example of this. Some of today's fishermen still keep to the tradition of turning out of the harbour entrance in the direction of the sun in the sky, that is, to the right. According to tradition it ensures success at the fishing. She was told by one Shetlander, only in his twenties: "When you leave the pier, and when you're turning, you always turn in the direction the sun goes. I'm no really superstitious, but I always turn wi the sun! Yes, I do that."[149] Turning in the direction of the sun is a tradition that has survived for millennia and is older than Jesus Christ, probably much older. For instance, it was recorded by the Romans in the first century BC that the people of Gaul turned in a right-hand direction when they worshipped their gods.[150]

Bram Stoker first visited Port Erroll with only four years to go before the railway arrived there in 1897. He would have caught the tail end of the old way of thinking in what was then a relatively isolated village. Up until he encountered Port Erroll, his professional attitude to the supernatural would have focussed primarily on what it had to offer for the stage: it provided a lively theme for the spookier plays staged in the Lyceum Theatre and guaranteed thrills for the audience. He had now found a place where the supernatural was taken much more seriously than that. It governed everything that happened.

8
DEATH IN ABERDEENSHIRE

The greatest superstitions will surround anything to do with death. 'Death has always been deemed the greatest evil that afflicts humanity,' wrote the folklorist J.G. Campbell 'and the terrors and awe which its advent inspires have given superstition its amplest scope.'[151] A death will bring out the strongest of feelings within a small close-knit community where the sparseness of numbers makes it an infrequent event.

The residents of Aberdeenshire held many superstitions about death. It could be foretold, they believed, with signs that a death was nigh. Some were ominous sounds that might be heard at any time, although they were usually experienced at night when it was quiet. One such omen was to hear three knocks spaced one to two minutes apart; they could come from anywhere within the house, in the rafters, on the entrance door, or on a table. The knocks had a distinctive dull and heavy sound to them. For the less superstitious, an earthly explanation could be found for the noise - this was the tap-tap mating call of the deathwatch beetle, commonly found on the wooden rafters of old houses.

Alternatively, one might hear the 'dead drop', which resembles the sound of the slow but regular drip of water from a height, but with a distinctive hollow echo to it. The sound could only be heard by one person and no one else, unless someone grabbed hold of them and then they too could hear it. Yet another highly unwelcome noise in the deep of night was the sound of something heavy being laid outside the entrance door. Such was the noise made by the delivery of a coffin. Similarly, the sound of muffled murmurs made by an assortment of human voices around the house was taken as forewarning of a funeral party to be held there.

Unexpected occurrences could cause great anxiety, particularly if a mirror or a portrait fell of a wall. And if it was your portrait – the mortal terror of all mortal terrors - your death was said to be imminent. Lights might be seen around the house.

One of these was the 'dead candle' – a pale bluish light that slowly moved around when a death was about to take place, and could also be seen along the route to the graveyard where the coffin was to be carried. Something similar to the 'dead candle' turns up in *Dracula*. Jonathan Harker is in a horse-drawn coach travelling to Count Dracula's castle when he sees blue flickering flames out of the window: 'Once the flame appeared so near the road, that even in the darkness around us I could watch the driver's motions. He went rapidly to where the blue flame arose, it must have been very faint, for it did not seem to illumine the place around it at all, and gathering a few stones, formed them into some device.' Count Dracula explains the phenomenon in a later chapter: 'that on a certain night of the year, last night, in fact, when all evil spirits are supposed to have unchecked sway, a blue flame is seen over any place where treasure has been concealed.'[152]

All sorts of strange omens could be taken as a portent of death. The manner by which a tallow candle burns could give rise to concern. A 'coffin-spehl' might form whereby wax dripping down the side of the candle, having solidified, was left standing proud while the rest of the candle burned to a stub. It was the sign of a coming death in the family. Three drops of blood from a bleeding nose indicated that a close relative of that person was about to die. If a sick person never sneezed, this was not a good sign. Sneezing was thought to mark the turning point towards recovery.

When someone in the family fell seriously ill, it was possible by a somewhat grim procedure to divine whether they were going to die or not. Two pits were dug in the earth to resemble graves; one would be nominally assigned the living grave, the other the dead grave. The ailing patient would be laid between them and watched carefully. If they turned to face the living grave, they would recover. If they turned the other way they were deemed not long for this world.

A dying person was said to be having a 'sair fecht' (sore fight). A similar phrase is sometimes heard in Scotland today, 'it's a sair fecht to make yer daily breid' (It's a sore fight to make your daily bread) - often used as a gently sarcastic retort to someone who has just informed you of their trivial woes. At the actual moment of death, the doors and windows of the house were flung open to allow the spirit to escape. It should be on its way as quickly as possible lest an evil influence capture it. Precautions were taken to ensure that the spirit didn't linger in the house. A sharp iron object such as a nail or a knitting needle was stuck into any material that might feasibly harbour the spirit, such as cheese, butter, meat, oatmeal, butter or whisky. Whisky had been known to turn as white as milk if the precaution wasn't taken. In some Aberdeenshire fishing villages, butter and onions were thrown out. Any milk in the house was poured down the drain.

Further precautions were necessary. The furniture was sprinkled with water as were the clothes of the dead. All the cats and dogs were shut up safe for the duration that the body lay unburied, because if a cat or a hen jumped over the body, the first person to meet the creature could expect to go blind at some time during their life. In one fishing village no earth could be moved until the body was buried.

The clocks in the house were stopped; it was a symbol that time had now ceased to have any significance for the deceased. Mirrors were covered up with a white cloth as were any pictures hanging on the walls. You wouldn't want the spirit of the dead lingering here. It's curious to note that stopping clocks and covering up mirrors after a death is a widespread superstition throughout Europe and one that persists today. Even more curious is the widespread belief, common to many cultures, that the spirits of the dead can come back to cause problems amongst the living. There doesn't seem to be such a thing as a happy ghost.

Once these precautions were out of the way, a carpenter was asked to provide a wooden 'striking' board on which the body could be placed. The corpse was wrapped tight with a winding sheet (shroud), and according to Walter Gregor, 'Many a bride laid up in store her bridal dress, to be made into her winding sheet, and her bridal linen and bridal stockings, as well as her husband's, to be put on when life's journey was ended.'[153] If the eyes of the deceased remained open or would not shut completely, coins were placed on them. This is a similar tradition to the Ancient Greek custom of placing a coin in the mouth of a corpse; the coin was intended to pay the ferryman Charon for rowing the souls of the dead across the rivers Styx and Acheron. A bowl containing a small amount of salt was also placed on the breast of the body to keep away the evil spirits. This tradition derives from a Christian source; salt is a sacred substance in the Bible. One or two candles were kept burning next to the body. On occasion a calamity arose when the candles fell over and set light to both the shroud and the body within it. This struck horror into the hearts of the mourners. It was a sign that the deceased had been up to no good while alive; perhaps having gained specialist skills from the Devil.

Once the body was laid out, it was watched very carefully day and night. The night watch was called the 'lyke wake' and it was the scene of an extraordinary tradition; one that raised the wrath of the Church ministers. Of the two main books about Aberdeenshire folk traditions, Reverend Walter Gregor writing in 1881 is by far and away the more circumspect about what happened on the night of a death:

> The time was ordinarily spent in reading the Scriptures, sometimes by one, and sometimes by another of the watchers. Some of the passages usually read were the ninety-first Psalm, the fifteenth chapter of St John's Gospel, and the fifteenth chapter of Corinthians. Other passages were read besides these. All conversation was carried on in suppressed voice.[154]

He did, however, drop hints that the occasion wasn't always so solemn. Reverend James McPherson's account, written in 1929, shows how far this could go:

> The Christian idea of a night vigil, during which the Scriptures were read, prayers offered and hymns sung, was observed among some portions of the community, but that is not the lykewake that appears in the Church records: and it was no Christian motive that called it into being.[155]

Let's hear more... He quotes the following excerpt from John Ramsay's 1888 book *Scotland and Scotsmen in the 18th Century*, and wryly comments that judging by church records it was only too true:

> Nothing went on in the house of mourning but dancing and other amusements. Even the ties of nature and affinity seem to have been suspended, for a widow who had just lost her husband, her and her infant's only support, was constrained by the fashion to suppress her sorrow, and to join in the expressions of joy and merriment. The nearest relation of the deceased, together with the stranger of most distinction, commonly began the dance . . . there are strong traces of this custom not only among Eastern Highlanders but even among the bordering Lowlanders not long ago.[156]

Abundant supplies of tobacco, whisky, bread and cheese were provided; and from all accounts the whisky wasn't spared. 'We read about profaneness, unseemly carriage, exercises, sports, the singing of bawdy songs, fiddling, dancing and gaming'.

Reverend McPherson explains why these extraordinary events took place:

> This pagan celebration never took its rise in a Christian rite. It sprang from a heathen past, when the noise and revelry were invoked to ward off evil spirits and thus maintain the morale of the living... It was altogether a survival of "heathenism," as the Church Courts described it. With a veneer of Christianity, the natives in the great crises of life and death reverted to the practices of their heathen ancestors.[157]

Returning to the somewhat reticent Reverend Walter Gregor, he does actually mention one example of unusual behaviour at a wake - practical jokes. A mourner would pretend to be the body lying under the covering blanket, and once the guests had arrived would start to move, 'at first gently, then more freely, and at last he spoke imitating as far as possible, the voice of the dead, to the utter terror of such that were not in the secret.'[158]

On the day of the funeral the body would be laid out with the coffin resting on two chairs. All would pay their last respects before returning to inspect the body for the last time. Whisky was drunk as a toast to the departed; sometimes several toasts were made. The funeral rites could last from ten o'clock in the morning to mid afternoon. On occasions, too much whisky was drunk and

100

it had been known for the funeral party to set off for the churchyard without the body.

A parting gesture was made to the corpse. The men removed their caps and laid their hand on the breast or brow of the dead, uttering gestures to the deceased such as 'he will be sorely missed' or 'she is such a bonny corpse'. There may have been more than just the expected trepidation involved in doing so. If the corpse was felt to be soft and flabby it indicated that another body would soon be carried out of the household. The body was then covered up, the coffin lid closed, and a mort-cloth draped over the coffin. A mort-cloth was a black embroidered cloth that was hired out by the parish church for funerals. It provided a source of income for the church funds.

The chairs on which the coffin had been resting on were overturned. They would not be turned upright until after sunset or the funeral was over and everyone had returned to the house. The coffin was then carried by the bearers to the graveyard. A keen interest would have been shown in the weather that day; a shower of rain landing on the earth of the open grave was a good sign, the departed soul was in a happy place. But should a hurricane blow up, the living would look at each other askance. Some wickedness must have been committed which had never been revealed, perhaps the deceased had even made dealings with the Devil himself.

The funeral procession always took the path that the deceased took to church, no shortcuts were permissible. According to the local custom, either a bellman would toll the funeral march, or the church bells would be rung as the procession neared the churchyard. Should the route to the church be a long one, a rest was taken along the way. A special flat stone existed for this purpose. The coffin was laid on top of it, and while everybody was getting their breath back more whisky would be drunk. In the more remote parts of Aberdeenshire, the coffin could be carried by hand as much as ten miles to the church. The funeral procession eventually arrived at the graveyard and the coffin was then lowered into the grave. All the men removed their caps as a mark of respect. Family and close friends then returned to the house where dinner would be served.

Exceptions were made to the normal funeral procedure. The funeral of still-born children or children who had died before they could be baptised took place before sunrise. Only in this way could their spirits be permitted to enter heaven, otherwise they were consigned to linger on in limbo floating endlessly through the regions of space.

If a poor unfortunate soul committed suicide this caused great problems as to where they could be buried. The Christian Church considered suicide to be the sin of self-murder, and it was common practice not to allow the victims of suicide to be buried in a churchyard. One attempt to do so in Banffshire resulted in a major fracas:

> By an early hour all the strong men of the parish who were opposed to such an act so sacrilegious were astir and hastening to the churchyard with their weapons of defence – strong sticks. The churchyard was taken possession of, and the walls were manned. The gate and the more accessible parts of the wall were assigned to picked men. In due time the suicide's coffin appeared, surrounded by an excited crowd, for the most armed with sticks. Some, however, carried spades sharpened on the edge. Fierce and long was the fight at the gate, and not a few rolled in the dust. The assailing party was beaten off. A grave was dug outside the churchyard, close beneath the wall, and the coffin laid in it. The lid was lifted, and a bottle of vitriol poured over the body. Before the lid could be again closed, the fumes of the dissolving body were rising thickly over the heads of actors and spectators. This was done to prevent the body from being lifted during the coming night from its resting-place, conveyed back to its abode when in life, and placed against the door, to fall at the feet of the member of the family that was first to open the door.[159]

A sense of the ancient stigma against suicides is recorded in *Dracula*. Lucy is upset to be told by a local fisherman that her seat at a churchyard in Whitby is resting on the grave of a suicide victim. She remonstrates with him, 'Oh, why did you tell us of this? It is my favourite seat, and I cannot leave it; and now I find I

102

must go on sitting over the grave of a suicide.'[160] It was not altogether an advisable place to sit either; the novel hints that this is where Count Dracula was hiding during his stay in Whitby.

Another curious echo from *Dracula* sounds in Reverend Gregor's book: 'The mould of the churchyard... was used in acts of sorcery.' He gives two examples. Churchyard mould thrown into a mill stream will stop a mill wheel from turning. An Aberdeenshire witch is recorded as having built a mound of graveyard mould at her enemy's gate with evil intent (although what effect this would have had on her enemy was not mentioned).[161] Count Dracula arrives at Whitby onboard a schooner with its cargo, 'a number of great wooden boxes filled with mould.' This was consecrated earth from his native homeland - bedding for vampires it transpires.

Certain superstitions hung around graveyards. When a new graveyard opened up and was made available, it proved very difficult to persuade families to use it for their departed relatives. In one Aberdeenshire coastal town the old graveyard had been closed and a new one opened. Although there was no real choice, the population showed great reluctance to use it. The problem was solved by the local shoemaker who announced to his customers that a 'yird swine' had been seen in the old graveyard, and he produced the body of one to show them (it was actually a water vole which has a passing resemblance to a rat). From there, the rumours circulated rapidly through the village, and the former graveyard was shunned for ever more.

The dreaded yird swine was popularly believed to be a beast that burrowed in amongst dead bodies and ate them. It was a topic that saw a lively correspondence in the letters page of the *Aberdeen Free Press*. One correspondent was told by a mole-catcher that the creature was half rat, half mole. Another reckoned it to be the grey rat, only to be reminded in reply that the yird swine had been known about long before the grey rat displaced the black rat locally. One person wrote that he had it on good authority that the animal could be heard gnawing through a coffin on the way to its feast.[162]

Graveyards were reckoned to be haunted. A curious superstition is mentioned by Reverend McPherson. It was believed that the ghost of the last person buried in the churchyard haunted the entrance gates with the intent of guarding against the burial of a suicide or unbaptised child in the consecrated ground. They would continue in the role until relieved of their duties by the spirit of the next body to turn up. An unfortunate consequence of this belief came about when two funeral processions approached the churchyard at the same time; there would then ensue a mad rush to be the first to enter. Unseemly fist fights were known to have happened on these occasions; nobody wanted the spirit of their recently departed hanging around.[163]

Death meant much more to Aberdeenshire residents than a full stop at the end of life; it had supernatural significance. The spirit world gave signs that death was coming, and once it arrived, the soul was believed to leave the body and to fly away to another place. Sometimes the soul lingered close to the mortal realm; they could haunt churchyards for instance.

Did these superstitions influence Bram Stoker while he was in residence in Aberdeenshire? Perhaps, but what's more likely is that they were in keeping with his mystical views about life and death, and provided confirmation of them. He wrote in *The Jewel of Seven Stars*: 'Did men know that the portals of the House of Death were not in very truth eternally fixed; and that the Dead could come forth again!'[164] The boundary between life and death was a subject that fascinated Bram, providing a recurring theme in his novels. And he wrote large parts of these books in a village where supernatural beliefs about death were widespread.

9
THE OCTAGONAL ROOM

It's the summer of 1895 and the Stokers have returned to Port Erroll for another holiday. They arrive at the Kilmarnock Arms Hotel where they sign the guest book. Bram's signature is bold and confident, Florence signs underneath in delicate and flamboyant letters. Noel's turn is next. His signature is small and neat, and he adds at the end of his name - London & Winchester College. He's 15 years old.

Sometime in 1894 Bram Stoker started writing *Dracula*. It's not known exactly when or where. He was interviewed in June 1897 following the publication of the novel and told the journalist 'he had spent about three years in writing it.'[165]

The serious effort may have come later. According to his biographer Harry Ludlam the book came to life in August 1895 on the author's third visit to Port Erroll: 'And here one day, to the sound of the sea on the Scottish shore, Count Dracula made his entry.' Ludlam also writes: 'Jonathan Harker's alarming experiences in the Castle Dracula, comprising the first chapters of the book, were written at Cruden Bay.' His source of information was Noel Stoker.[166]

As we know it now in its published form, *Dracula* starts with a train journey. The opening sentence of the book is an extract from Jonathan Harker's journal: '*3 May. Bistritz.*-Left Munich at 8:35 P.M., on 1st May, arriving at Vienna early next morning; should have arrived at 6:46, but train was an hour late.'[167] It's not the most memorable first line for a novel. Nevertheless, the journey works beautifully as a narrative device. As Jonathan Harker penetrates deeper into the heart of rural Eastern Europe, the brooding atmosphere builds up as he gets closer to Count Dracula's castle.

Jonathan Harker's itinerary at the start of *Dracula* mirrors the trip that Bram Stoker would have taken to get to Port Erroll in 1895. Jonathan Harker sets off from London on a long train journey across Europe to Bistritz in Transylvania. From there he travels by horse and coach on the road to Dracula's Castle. Bram took the train from London to Ellon in Aberdeenshire; and from there by horse and trap to Port Erroll. Slains Castle would have loomed large on the skyline as he approached the village. Altogether the journey would have taken him at least fourteen hours. One can easily imagine Bram Stoker writing out this section of *Dracula* during or just after the train journey north in 1895.

The train journey wasn't the original start to the novel. The first chapter was removed at the recommendation of Otto Kyllmann, the chief editor of Bram's publisher Constable Ltd. There has been much debate amongst academics and *Dracula* fans as to what might have happened to the original first chapter. Yet, the answer has been out there since 1997 when Peter Haining and Peter Tremayne published their book *The Un-Dead - The Legend of Bram Stoker and Dracula*. The title appears to have been overlooked by enthusiasts, possibly because it was written as a mass-market book for the British public. Yet the eagle-eyed amongst them could have noticed that it had been issued by Constable, the original publishers of *Dracula*. Investigation of its contents reveals that the book's authors clearly had access to the publisher's archives.

Otto Kyllmann asked for the first chapter to be removed because it had too many echoes of a previous vampire novel. This was *Carmilla* written by Joseph Sheridan Le Fanu. The editor, while recognising that Bram had intended it as a tribute to *Carmilla*, anticipated that the critics would react unkindly to its inclusion.[168] Bram agreed to the removal of the intended first chapter. It was subsequently discovered by Florence Stoker after her husband's death. Part of it was used as the basis for a short story published in 1914.

The short story, *Dracula's Guest*, is set in the Munich area on Walpurgis Night (April 30th). 'Walpurgis Night was when, according to the belief of millions of people, the devil was abroad – when the graves were opened and the dead came forth and walked.' An unnamed Englishmen, presumably Jonathan Harker, goes on an excursion to visit an abandoned, 'unholy' village. He encounters an un-dead beautiful countess and is pounced upon by a gigantic wolf, but not with evil intent. A hailstorm has chilled the air, and the wolf lies on top of him to keep him warm. A platoon of horsemen arrives to rescue him. They had been asked by Count Dracula to take care of his guest: 'He is English and therefore adventurous. There are often dangers from snow and wolves and night.' And the grateful Count finishes his telegram by informing the horsemen: 'I answer your zeal with my fortune.'[169]

The novel benefits enormously by starting with the train journey because it leads directly to the main action. The intended first chapter didn't add anything that mattered. The author's purpose may have been to portray Jonathan Harker as an innocent abroad. What was he doing visiting an unholy village on Walpurgis night? Nevertheless, a clear sense of his vulnerability is established during the journey to Dracula's Castle without the earlier section. Jonathan Harker hurtles into the depths of Middle Europe with an increasing sense of foreboding. He is a stranger in a strange land and Castle Dracula beckons.

Slains Castle dominated the skyline of Port Erroll just as Castle Dracula dominates the first four chapters of *Dracula*. It has a huge presence in the novels of Bram Stoker; the Aberdeenshire castle made a big impression on him.

Slains Castle is about a mile from the village in a spectacular setting perched on the edge of a granite cliff. From there it looks out onto the grey waters of the North Sea. The castle stands out to dramatic effect in a situation emphasised by its surroundings: a bleak, treeless landscape with no building nearby to distract the eye. The jagged, red rocks of the cliffs add to the grandeur of the scene.

The castle was built on a promontory called Bowness, named after a distinctive double rock arch at its far end. The arches form two eye-shaped holes of similar size with the 'eyes' stacked one above the other. To the modern view, they are eyes and have been named as such in the Doric dialect, 'the Twa Een' or the Two Eyes; centuries before, the rock arch was seen to resemble a bow.

Bowness is a natural spot for a castle because it is located on a narrow sea-bound rocky headland surrounded on three sides by 75-foot-high cliffs. Slains Castle can only be approached by land from a southerly direction through a strip 200 yards wide, and this made for a defendable position in times of war. The castle is built on the cliff top on the south-east side. It was said that a stone dropped from the windows of the library would fall directly into the sea.

Slains Castle is represented explicitly or in disguised form in several of Bram Stoker's novels. It is specifically mentioned in the two books set in the Cruden Bay area, *The Watter's Mou'* and *The Mystery of the Sea*. It appears in *The Jewel of the Seven Stars* as Kyllion: 'A great grey stone mansion of the Jacobean period; vast and spacious, standing high over the sea on the very verge of a high cliff.' And like Slains Castle, one could hear, 'the crash and murmur of waves breaking against rock far below...' In *The Man* it becomes Lannoy Castle, within sight of the sea and to the north of a curving bay backed by sandhills. Whereas Cruden Bay has the Skares, Lannoy has a dangerous reef of low-lying rocks named the Skyres. In *The Lady of the Shroud* the Castle of Vissarion in the Land of the Blue Mountains also stands on steep cliffs close to the sea. As we will see later, *Dracula* can be shown to contain elements of Slains Castle.

Slains Castle was inhabited by an aristocrat with the title of the Earl of Erroll. During Bram Stoker's time in Port Erroll this was the 20th Earl, Charles Gore Hay. The Hay family name was part of an aristocratic lineage extending back, some say, to the tenth century when a battle was fought between the Scots and the Vikings at Luncarty near Perth.

It had not been looking good for the Scots Army at Luncarty. A rout appeared likely - the Scots were faltering as they faced a slashing storm of swords and axes, the Vikings demonstrating that mad fighting spirit which gave them the nickname - 'Beserkers'. Here and there some of the Scots soldiers yielded and ran, raging Vikings harrying them in close pursuit. The fleeing soldiers cascaded down a narrow pass leading from the battlefield only to come face to face with farmer Hay and his sons.

These doughty fellows stood their ground, striking at anyone who tried to pass them with the yokes of their ploughs, be they fleeing Scots or pursuing Vikings. The rout was stemmed and the

108

Scots held firm to win the battle. Farmer Hay was subsequently rewarded with a country estate in the area, and this was said to have been the origin of the Errolls' aristocratic line.[170] The incident went into the history books where it caught the attention of William Shakespeare. He used it for his play *Cymbeline*, albeit he moved the action to Roman times.

Down the years since then, the various earls and family members stepped in and out of major historical events as they affected Scotland. Gilbert Hay of Erroll supported Robert the Bruce and fought at the Battle of Bannockburn in 1314. Francis the 9th Earl of Erroll was caught up in a conspiracy theory in the years following the Spanish Armada in 1588; Queen Elizabeth's court produced evidence purporting to suggest that he had invited a Spanish invasion of Scotland. The 11th earl was fined £2000 sterling by Oliver Cromwell for his involvement with the Scottish coronation of King Charles II in 1651.

The father of the 14th earl, Lord Kilmarnock, took part in the Jacobite rebellion of 1745 and was the commander of Bonnie Prince Charlie's horse grenadier guards at the Battle of Culloden. The Jacobites lost that one. Lord Kilmarnock was captured and subsequently beheaded at the Tower of London.[171] To a limited degree he was fortunate. He avoided the far ghastlier fate of being hung, drawn and quartered as had happened to several of his fellow Jacobites. A swift chop to the neck with a sharp blade was a preferable final exit compared to that slow lingering death whereby a traitor was dragged by horse to the gallows, hung almost to the point of death, emasculated, disembowelled, beheaded and the body then chopped up into four separate pieces.

The Slains Castle perched on its dramatic cliff-top setting wasn't the first castle of that name. The original Slains Castle is located six miles along the coast to the south, although there is not much of it left; only one corner survives. The castle was blown up in November 1594 on the orders of King James VI. The 9th Earl Francis Hay having taken part in a failed Catholic insurrection in the north of Scotland then fled to the continent. The earl returned to Scotland in 1596. He was allowed to remain after pledging allegiance to the king, and much more reluctantly, to the Protestant faith.[172] In 1597 he moved into a tower on the cliffs north of Cruden Bay. Construction work took place over the years, and the extended building was later renamed Slains Castle after the original family home.[173]

Dr Samuel Johnson and James Boswell visited Slains Castle in 1773 on their way to the west coast of Scotland and the Hebridean Isles. They took a somewhat indirect route, travelling up the east coast for part of the way. Samuel Johnson had been invited to Aberdeen where he was awarded the freedom of the town at the town hall. This is a symbolic honour granted by the city to notable individuals in a practice which started in the twelfth century and continues today. While dining at Ellon to the north of Aberdeen, Johnson and Boswell received and accepted an invitation to visit the Errolls. 'We came in the afternoon to Slanes Castle,' wrote Dr. Johnson, noting that it is, 'built upon the margin of the sea, so that the walls of one of the towers seem only a continuation of a perpendicular rock, the foot of which is beaten by the waves.'[174] He was impressed by the view: 'From the windows the eye wanders over the sea that separates Scotland from Norway, and when the winds beat with violence must enjoy all the terrifick grandeur of the tempestuous ocean.'

They spent the night in the castle, although James Boswell did not sleep well: 'I had a most elegant room; but there was a fire in it which blazed; and the sea, to which my windows looked, roared; and the pillows were made of the feathers of some sea-fowl, which had to me a disagreeable smell: so that, by all these causes, I was kept awake a good while.' Not only that: 'I saw, in imagination, Lord Errol's father, Lord Kilmarnock (who was beheaded on Tower Hill in 1746), and I was somewhat dreary. But the thought did not last long, and I fell asleep.'[175] When the two travellers left the next day on their northwards journey they discussed their visit to Slains Castle. Samuel Johnson had been impressed with its grandeur and elegance.

The castle was rebuilt in 1836 and 1837 following the marriage in 1820 of the 18th Earl William George Hay to Elizabeth Fitz-Clarence, one of the illegitimate daughters of William IV. The king had been a busy man, siring no less than ten illegitimate children by the actress Dorothea Bland, better-known in her day by the stage name of Mrs Jordan. Elizabeth was one of five daughters by this union.[176]

The earl, having married into royalty, now felt the need to build a royal palace to house his Lady Elizabeth, the new Countess of Erroll. Much of the original castle was modified to create what was essentially a Victorian mansion in neo-Tudor architectural style with a touch of Scottish baronial influence. The entrance on the south face of the castle was at first floor level through a huge wooden door at the top of a flight of fourteen granite steps flanked by octagonal buttresses. The castle was so much exposed to the elements, it was said that if a wind blew up along the coast it was almost impossible to make it to the top of the stairs. Two round towers with conical roofs were set in the south face of the castle, and these added to its Tudor-like appearance. A large bay window looked out onto the sea from the library.

In Bram Stoker's time Slains Castle was the size of a palace, including seven reception rooms, 14 main bedrooms and two bathrooms. Not much is known about what it looked like inside from those years; only a handful of photographs of the interior survive that I know about. Reverend Pratt gives a partial description in his book *Buchan*. He mentions, 'the magnificence of a storm as seen from the windows of Slains Castle', and how you could hear on a dark November night, 'the booming waves as they beat against the rocks, or rush up the broken gullies, almost impelling the belief, in spite of the stability of one's footing, of having slipped cable and being fairly out at sea.'

He continues:

Nor is the view from the windows less impressive when the full-orbed moon, slowly traversing the heavens, touches with her silver beams a line of rippling waves, crossed by some chance vessel in its tranquil passage over the glittering expanse of water. It is at such a time that the singular charm of this seaboard residence is delightfully realised.

Reverend Pratt describes one of the rooms in detail: 'The library, in the north-east angle of the castle, is a fine room, fitted up with oak book-cases. It contains upwards of 4000 volumes.'

He was impressed with the collection, holding as it does 'splendid editions of the Fathers of the Church, and numerous works of note on divinity and ecclesiology...' However, with heavy heart he reports that: 'In the end of the last century this library was remarkably rich in manuscripts, many on vellum; but, sad to relate, these were recklessly destroyed in the menial services of the household.'[177]

It's part of local myth that the sight of Slains Castle inspired Bram Stoker to write *Dracula*. This is incorrect because Bram had been researching the background to *Dracula* long before he visited the area. His early notes from 1890 mention that Count Dracula lived in a castle. This was a castle in the abstract sense - the author probably didn't have any specific castle in mind. Not long after he found line drawings of Transylvanian castles in the books he used for researching his novel. These show castles on top of dramatic rocky mounts and that was good enough to get going with.

When Bram started writing the early chapters of *Dracula* in Port Erroll, he sought to fill out the skeleton plot with descriptive detail. It's plausible that the location of Slains Castle on its cliff-top setting would have helped him during the imaginative process of writing. Slains Castle may have stood in as a proxy for Castle Dracula in Transylvania while the words spilled out onto the page.

Slains Castle contains a distinctive room with a lookalike in the novel.[178] Jonathan Harker has just arrived at Dracula's castle and is shown to his bedroom: 'The Count halted, putting down my bags, closed the door, and crossing the room, opened another door which led into a small octagonal room lit by a single lamp, and seemingly without a window of any sort.' Compare this with the description of Slains Castle from a 1922 sales document: 'On the Principle Floor: Entrance Hall (heated with stove) leading to Central Octagonal Interior Hall (heated with stove and lighted from above)...'[179] The southern entrance to Slains Castle led via a stairway to a vestibule and a connecting corridor to the octagonal hall. It acted as the focal point connecting to various parts of the castle.

Although the castle is now a ruin, the octagonal hall has survived intact. Three arches leading from it at first floor level. One arch faced onto to the north wing of the building where bedrooms were situated, while the east arch opens to a corridor which connected to the drawing room and the library. The octagonal hall (or the salon as it was referred to by the occupants) was used as a reception room for visitors to the castle, and Bram may have known it well. The lamp that hung there survives, and is now in a house in London owned by a member of the Hay family.[180]

It's possible that the description of the other parts of Dracula's castle were inspired by Slains Castle, the library for instance, although perhaps the comparison shouldn't be pushed too far. The main entrance to Slains Castle led up a flight of granite steps, whereas the door to Dracula's Castle is at ground level. Another difference: Castle Dracula had a central courtyard whereas the rebuilt Slains Castle did not. If Bram Stoker had made Slains Castle too obvious a model for Castle Dracula it would have implied that the occupant, the 20th Earl of Erroll, was a blood-sucking monster in league with the Devil. A libel action might come his way and no author wants that.

Although there is no record that Bram Stoker actually set foot inside Slains Castle, it's likely that he did. The earl would not have passed up the opportunity to meet someone so well-connected with London society. It's plausible that Bram Stoker visited the earl in Slains Castle in 1894 or 1895. I'm told that the long-standing memories of the Hay family are that he was invited for an evening soiree at the castle during at least one of his early visits.[181]

Let's imagine what might have happened. An invitation arrives from the earl, and one evening Bram makes his way from the village to the castle. On the way he hears dogs barking behind him. He finally arrives at Slains Castle, walks up the steps, and knocks on the huge front door. 'I heard a heavy step approaching behind the great door, and saw through the chinks the gleam of a coming light. Then there was the sound of rattling chains and the clanking of massive bolts drawn back.'

113

The butler appears; he's framed in the opening and backlit from behind by gas light. That makes an impression. He beckons Bram inside, leads him through a long corridor, 'and crossing the room, opened another door, which led into a small octagonal room lit by a single lamp, and seemingly without a window of any sort,' telling him to wait there while he goes to inform the earl that his guest has arrived. The earl greets him and leads him into the library. Bram notices 'the extraordinary evidences of wealth which are round me. The table service is of gold, and so beautifully wrought that it must be of immense value. The curtains and upholstery of the chairs and sofas... are of the costliest and most beautiful fabrics, and must have been of fabulous value when they were made...'[182]

Although Slains Castle looks to play a minor role in the description of Castle Dracula, it's difficult to avoid the impression that it infuses the novel and provides inspiration for the text. There is an ambience about the situation of Slains Castle that would have been picked up by Bram Stoker. The castle is located about a mile from the village of Port Erroll and is quite separate from it. This sense of isolation from the rest of the community is also a characteristic of Castle Dracula; it adds to the psychological landscape in the early chapters. Count Dracula living in his castle is a lonely soul. He tells Jonathan Harker: 'I long to go through the crowded streets of your mighty London, to be in the midst of the whirl and rush of humanity, to share its life, its change, its death, and all that makes it what it is.' Perhaps we even believe him.

10

'I THINK STRANGE THINGS, WHICH I DARE NOT CONFESS TO MY OWN SOUL'

Once Bram Stoker started writing *Dracula* he became preoccupied with it to an alarming degree, Florence telling a reporter in 1927:

> When he was at work on *Dracula*, we were all frightened of him. It was up on a lonely part of the east coast of Scotland, and he seemed to get obsessed by the spirit of the thing. There he would sit for hours, like a great bat, perched on the rocks of the shore, or wander alone up and down the sandhills thinking it out.[183]

The creative intensity made Bram very tetchy and intolerant of any interruption. He demanded absolute isolation while working on the novel, and became emotionally distant from his family at other times.[184] It hadn't helped that they were cooped up together in hotel rooms. Perhaps the 15 year-old Noel Stoker was finding his teenage years difficult to cope with, and had been in a sulk at spending another month in a remote Scottish fishing village with nothing to do. Bram escaped to the 'rocks of the shore' and thought about the evil doings of Count Dracula. These were almost certainly those of the Sand Craig at the far end of Cruden Bay beach. It was the last year the family spent in the Kilmarnock Arms Hotel; in subsequent years Bram rented cottages with more rooms to escape to.

Once Bram fixed the next part of the plot of *Dracula* in his head he would write it down, perhaps on notebooks balanced on his knee while sitting on the Sand Craig. On other occasions he may have worked on the novel back at his hotel room. He told someone he met at a dinner party that *Dracula* had been written sitting up in bed on summer mornings with the birds singing outside in a garden scented with geraniums and carnations.[185] This was plausibly his room at the Kilmarnock Arms Hotel overlooking the garden. In one of his Port Erroll novels he describes the location of the hotel next to 'the western bank of the

Water of Cruden with a fringe of willows protecting its sunk garden which was always full of fruits and flowers.'

Why was Bram acting so strangely? Here's an explanation: he was aiming for authenticity of tone in his prose. Many authors live their novels through one or several characters. It's akin to method acting, whereby an actor who is learning a specific role will try and become that person, to behave like them and to think like them. By doing this, they believe that they can appear more authentic when they portray the character on stage.

Henry Irving practiced an early version of this technique in the Lyceum Theatre. Bram referred to it as 'dual consciousness'. In his book *Personal Reminiscences of Henry Irving* he quotes the actor:

"It is necessary to this art that the mind should have, as it were, a double consciousness, in which all the emotions proper to the occasion may have full swing, while the actor is all the time on the alert for every detail of his method... The actor who combines the electric force of a strong personality with a mastery of the resources of his art, must have a greater power over his audiences than the passionless actor who gives a most artistic simulation of the emotions he never experiences."

And again quoting Henry Irving: "With the true artist the internal force is the first requisite - the external appearance being merely the medium through which this is made known to others."[186]

Could Bram Stoker have used the literary equivalent of method acting while writing *Dracula*? His biographer Daniel Farson thinks so, although this was based on hearsay. Farson had been told this from someone who knew an elderly woman who knew Florence... Still, it's worth recounting what he passed on – Florence was terrified when her husband wrote his horror novels, 'because he 'became' the personality he was writing about and behaved very strangely at home.'[187]

Other authors have used similar methods to get authenticity into their prose. Here's how the French writer Georges Simenon, best known for his Maigret detective novels, wrote his literary (i.e. non-detective) novels. It was a writing procedure that was so hard on the nervous system, Simenon would get a check-up from his doctor before he even started. The main issue of concern was his blood pressure. Only once he had the doctor's approval would he get going.

His basic requirement was total isolation from the world so he could live like a monk. He would not see anybody for the duration, nor would he take any phone calls. Only now could the writing process start. He imagined the beginning of the story, and taking the part of the main character created a situation whereby they are taken to their psychological limit. Their lives totally change in consequence and they are subjected to tremendous stress. He became that character, feeling what he or she felt and enduring what he or she went through. This happened with such great intensity, he was living inside their skin. He kept going like this for eleven days in a row. 'And it's always unbearable after five or six days,' he said. It is especially 'awful' when the character has been driven to the absolute extreme. After eleven days the novel is complete and written in full; it had to be or its author would have gone crazy.[188]

Let's be somewhat fanciful and speculate that Bram Stoker sat on the Sand Craig or walked along Cruden Bay beach imagining that he was inside the waxen skin of Dracula. Here he acted out the Count's ghastly deeds in his mind's eye and thought his evil thoughts. Perhaps his inspiration had come from watching Henry Irving playing the archdemon Mephistopheles in the play *Faust*. Young Noel Stoker had certainly been impressed. As a seven year old he had been taken by his father into Henry Irving's dressing room during a run of the play *Faust*. '...a quaint fancy struck the actor. Telling the boy to stand still for a moment he took his dark pencil and with a few rapid touches made him up after the manner of Mephistopheles; the same high-arched eyebrows; the same sneer at the corners of the mouth; the same pointed moustache. I think it was the strangest and prettiest transformation I ever saw.'

Every now and again Bram would look up and see Slains Castle on the cliff top; it would have stood in as a proxy for Castle Dracula in Transylvania. He could envisage Count Dracula scaling its walls: 'my very feelings changed to repulsion and

117

terror when I saw the whole man slowly emerge from the window and begin to crawl down the castle wall over the dreadful abyss, face down with his cloak spreading out around him like great wings.'

Could it have been that Bram Stoker was unhappy with the tone of an early draft of the novel, and then rewrote it in its current form? It's possible because a version of *Dracula* differing from the published book as we know it was used for a Swedish and Icelandic translation.[189] Was this an earlier draft written in 1894? On rewriting the book, this time round he would strive to get an authentic tone to his gothic horror novel: he was Count Dracula: Cruden Bay was Transylvania: Slains Castle was Castle Dracula...

So what was it about Port Erroll and Cruden Bay that put Bram on track to write *Dracula*? Let's list the possibilities. He had found a beautiful secluded spot with the peace to write his books. It also gave him an important facility; a coastline to trudge along in isolation while thinking about how to put a book together. He had rediscovered nature and this invigorated him giving him renewed energy for his writing efforts. Perhaps the simplest explanation why *Dracula* was written is this: His return visits to Port Erroll every August provided a regular slot of time to be dedicated to writing. However, it's one thing to allocate the time and yet another to find a suitable project to work on. Perhaps Bram had run out of ideas for his books with the next monthly time slot for writing looming large and empty before him. What to do? Needs must; so the notes for the vampire story were dusted off; 'My scruples about this one can go hang,' he might have thought, 'a man has to keep himself busy.'

And there was something else that may have got *Dracula* under way. Bram was receiving cues everywhere he went in Port Erroll; cues which resounded with the supernatural subject matter of the book. He had discovered that pagan superstition and traditions survived in this remote part of Aberdeenshire, all tangled up with the terror of death, omens of death and what happened to the soul at the moment of death.

Bram may have come across yet another feature of local village life that resonated with the subject matter of his book. The evening tales that the rural inhabitants of Aberdeenshire told each other at the fireside have been described by Reverend Walter Gregor:

> The story was for the most of the supernatural – of fairies and their doings, of waterkelpie, of ghosts, of witches and their deeds, of compacts with the Devil, and what befell those who made such compacts, of men skilled in *black art*, and the strange things they were able to do. Sometimes riddles formed the subject of amusement. As tale succeeded tale, and the big peat fire began to fade, the younger members of the family crept nearer and nearer the older ones, and, after a little, seated themselves on their knees, or between them and the fire, with the eyes now fearfully turned to the doors, and now to the chimney, and now to this corner, whence issued the smallest noise, and now to the next, in dread of seeing some of the uncanny brood.[190]

These were stories that aroused fears which lay deep within the human frame – the fear that unseen and malevolent agencies are out to get you. Out of all the possible tales which humans tell each other, these are the ones that grab the undivided attention of the listener. They raise a frisson of horror at the unimaginable proximity to death. A good story is crafted as an emotional rollercoaster as it unfolds, and a tale of terror will be the one to yield the highest peaks and the deepest troughs.

Bram added an extra dimension of hideousness to the mix. There's something special about the vampires in *Dracula* which puts them in a class of their own. They tap into our deepest fear, the fear of being attacked and killed by a predator with sharp teeth. This undoubtedly arose from our origins on the African plains millions of years ago. Our ancestors were apes ejected from the tropical forest when the trees died out during a prolonged drought. Forced out into the open plains, they became naked apes in an environment patrolled by big cats and starving dogs. Our terrified ancestors depended only on their wits and weapons. Yet, they survived on that dusty plain of terror: the human species now became much more than just another creature struggling for existence in the natural environment, vulnerable to teeth and claw. Nature didn't master us, we mastered nature.

In our civilised state today, humans don't normally get eaten, save for the occasional shark attack in tropical waters or the unwary soul venturing too close to a crocodile-infested river. Yet that age-old terror lingers deep within us, and what could be more horrific than an un-dead ogre gorging on human blood; your blood, your precious fluid of life.

By the end of the summer holiday in 1895 Bram still wasn't close to finishing the novel. It would take longer than he usually took with a book. On his return from Port Erroll, Bram Stoker departed with the Lyceum Theatre Company on their fifth American tour; it lasted nine months. He was writing notes for *Dracula* while in the States. One of the pages, on hotel notepaper from Philadelphia, is in three columns, each with separate dates from November 1895, December 1895 and March 1896.[191] It appears that half the novel had been written by this stage. The notes concern the events in London and the end of the book.

It's curious that when Bram Stoker returned to Scotland in the summer of 1896 he went on a tour, exploring the north coast of Aberdeenshire and Banffshire. He certainly appreciated the trip, writing later in *The Mystery of the Sea* that 'a lovely coast' is found between Banff and Gardenstown. There was no rest from the attentions of Henry Irving even though his manager was on holiday. He was sent a letter concerning legal issues of Lyceum Theatre business to the Garden Arms Hotel in Gardenstown which was received by Bram Stoker on the 25th July. On July 30th the author had been tracked by letter to the 'Marine Hotel, Banff'. The same legal issues were raised and Irving mentions in passing that he hopes Bram is enjoying himself.[192]

What was going on here? Why was he on holiday? Didn't he have a book to finish? What had happened to the intense creative drive that had been there the year before? I don't know the answers, but here's some speculation. Perhaps there was a problem finding accommodation in Port Erroll at the end of July. Or maybe he just needed to get in a relaxed mood before setting out on the big push that would see the last chapters of *Dracula* written. Florence might have insisted on it after all the tensions of the previous 'holiday'.

Although Bram Stoker visited Aberdeenshire in the summer of 1896, I don't have any direct evidence that he was in Port Erroll that year. The last signature in the Kilmarnock Arms guest book is from 1895, there is nothing for 1896, although the pages for most of that year are missing. Nevertheless, I reckon he was probably in the village, and had only spent a week or so on tour.

It may have been that 1896 was the year that Bram moved to what became his main base for his visits to Port Erroll. This was Hilton Cottage, located 200 yards up Bridge Street from the Kilmarnock Arms Hotel. Hilton Cottage would now become their preferred holiday home in Port Erroll in the years to come. It's also known that they also spent one year in Roselea Cottage, a house next door to the hotel, when everywhere else in the village was full. It's not known which year that was, although this was probably after 1899 when accommodation in Port Erroll was in particularly high demand.[193]

Hilton Cottage occupied one half of a new villa which had been built by James Cruickshank in 1895 on a south-facing ridge overlooking the hotel.[194] The western half of the villa provided accommodation for the staff, and was called Lilybank Cottage; the eastern half is Hilton Cottage, and was in use as an annexe to the hotel. An advert from a 1908 tourist guide lists the cottage as having two sitting rooms and three bedrooms. When not in use as an annexe during the summer, it was the family home for James Cruickshank and his wife June. Two daughters were born later; Ethel in 1899 and Mary Jane in 1901.

Today the two semi-detached cottages have been combined into a single private residence which retains the name Hilton Cottage. I talked to the present owner who has lived there since the 1970s. There have been some changes since Bram Stoker's time. The outside aspect hasn't changed too much, although a new porch has been added onto the front. An old photograph shows that the porch has replaced the front doors for the original cottages.

A long garden at the front slopes down to the hotel. Back in the day a series of grass terraces gave way to a vegetable garden which provided produce for the hotel menu. The front garden is much as it was, although the vegetable garden on the lower slope has been replaced by a grass lawn and shrubs. Two narrow terraces are laid out in grass next to the house with flower beds to one side. I was shown the spot on the lower terrace opposite the drawing room of Hilton Cottage where Bram had been seen at a small round table writing his books on a warm summer's day. The owner had been told by a neighbour that she had often seen the author at work there. The neighbour was James Cruickshank's daughter Mary Jane who was then living in Sunnybank Cottage next door. Others have mentioned that they saw Bram sitting at a table in the front garden of Hilton Cottage on fine days.[195] One woman told the reporter Gordon Casely that as a little girl she had seen Bram Stoker writing there when a sudden gust of wind blew his papers away. She helped him to pick them up.

It's certainly a great spot to write books. I stood there and looked around. There is a clear view south over the sand dunes. Beyond the dunes can be seen the headland with the houses of Whinnyfold visible on the horizon. One can also see towards the harbour and the sea that lies beyond. The upper floors of Slains Castle were once visible from the garden. Trees now obscure this line of sight, although the faint outline can still be made out in winter when the trees lose their leaves.

Hilton Cottage suited Bram more than the Kilmarnock Arms Hotel as a writing den. He could find seclusion to write in the garden while looking out onto an impressive vista. Even if the weather turned nasty, there were still plenty of rooms in the cottage to escape to where he could be on his own. But most important of all, it was a place where the Stoker family could live together in peace and harmony.

11
'OH, THANK GOD FOR GOOD BRAVE MEN!'

It was the summer of 1896 and Bram Stoker had a novel to finish; yet to come was the effort to write the dramatic ending for *Dracula*. The heroes of the tale are about to set out to put an end to Count Dracula's evil doings with no thought for their own safety. They promise each other that they will act, 'to find out the author of all this our sorrow and to stamp him out'. 'Oh, thank God for good brave men!' says Mina Harker.[196]

Bram's trips north to Aberdeenshire provided him with one final cue for the book, one to inspire him to complete *Dracula*. He admired the bravery that was shown whenever a shipwreck happened in the area and men's lives needed to be saved. Everyone along the coast made every effort to rescue the sailors no matter what risks were involved. These were fearless people carrying out daring deeds. 'Cowardice is pretty well unknown in Buchan,' Bram had written in *The Watter's Mou'*.

The fishermen of Port Erroll confronted the reality of death on a daily basis. They risked disaster every time they set out in their boats on daily fishing expeditions. It may have been a calm day with blue skies when the fishing boat left the harbour, but once out to sea and far from shore, a gale could blow up very quickly. The reality that Bram found in the village was a long way from London and his job in the Lyceum Theatre. Bram encountered real drama in Port Erroll. And most dramatic of all was the regular occurrence of shipwrecks around the coast.

The rocky Aberdeenshire coastline between the villages of Collieston to the south and Boddam to the north has been the site of many a shipwreck down the centuries. It lies close to the most easterly point of the Scottish mainland, and for ships sailing north and around the top of Scotland the distance could be shortened by skirting the shore here. It's a dangerous course to take, although it's one that will save time and money for the owner of the vessel. Many of the ships wrecked on the coast sailed from England or the European countries. The local fishermen were much more wary of their own shoreline.

The occasion of a ship in distress brought out the best in the local people. Great efforts would be made to save any sailor caught up in a shipwreck; their heroic deeds verged on the extraordinary. The first indication of a ship in trouble in an Aberdeenshire village was when two rockets were fired from the lifeboat house and exploded above the houses. 'A fisherman can never mistake the sound that the call-rocket for the crew of the life-boat makes when it goes whizzing up into the air,' wrote John McGibbon in *The Fisher-folk of Buchan*. The reaction shown by everyone is instantaneous, 'down goes nets, food, or anything they may be working at, and then pell-mell towards the shore. If you were walking homewards through the streets of a night, and there was not a person to be seen except the lonely policeman on his nightly rounds, and the bang, bang of the life-boat rocket were to sound out of the still night air, in a second of time the streets would be filled with flying crowds of people hurrying in the direction of the sea front.' Everybody seems to know instinctively where to go, 'you never need to ask where the wreck is; all you have to do is to follow the crowd. There will be fishermen who are pulling on their jerseys as they run, others will be pulling on their jackets and buttoning them up. Women will be wrapping their shawls around them as they run...'[197]

In the village of Newburgh, 11 miles south of Cruden Bay, the artist James McBey tells of how everyone reacted immediately to the rockets, be they the postman or the school teacher. They dropped everything in their hurry to help launch the lifeboat.[198] Newburgh is located on an estuary cutting through a long stretch of sandy beach. Ships were often stranded on the shoaling bank of the beach hundreds of yards offshore. It often proved impossible to launch the Newburgh lifeboat into the estuary during an easterly gale or when a strong tide was running. In this situation, the boat would have to be hauled onto a long-wheeled carriage and dragged by ropes along the beach, men, women and children helping. All the while, the villagers would pull determinedly ahead buffeted by slashing rain, sleet or snow. On one occasion the lifeboat was dragged seven miles before it was in a position to be launched; their mission to save the crew members of the *Imperial Palace* held fast on the stormy foreshore of the beach. Four trips were made to the trawler to recover the crew.

If the conditions were too bad to launch the lifeboat from the beach, a rescue of last resort was carried out. This involved a feat of the utmost bravery by the villagers. They formed a human chain of men and women, which extended out from the beach into the tumultuous breakers until they reached the storm-battered ship. One slip or a loosened hold meant certain death. The sailors were then passed along the chain to dry land. James Leatham mentions that this happened several times.[199]

Where the local lifeboat couldn't get in about the wreck, particularly on rocky shores, the rocket brigade was sent for. These were the volunteers responsible for the 'Board of Trade Rocket Apparatus' which they transported to the shore opposite the shipwreck on a horse and cart. On arriving opposite the stricken ship, a powerful rocket was fired with a line attached. Once the line was secured by the men on the stranded vessel, a steel hawser was attached at the shore end, and the men on the ship hauled it onboard. A 'breech buoy' was then pulled over on the hawser, a cradle and harness device that could be used to transport the sailors to safety one by one.

John McGibbon describes a rescue on the Peterhead coast which involved a superlative act of bravery.[200] A steamer making her way north had become lost in fog. Before long it collided with the rocks on the shore. The heavy sea was pounding the stranded ship incessantly against the rocks, and it wasn't going to remain in one piece long. Once it broke up the men would be flung to the raging sea and a certain death.

The strong winds from the south-east made it very difficult for the lifeboat to approach the vessel. The only realistic hope now lay with the rocket brigade. After many attempts, they eventually managed to get a rocket to carry a rope across the deck of the stranded vessel. Unfortunately there was no sign of life onboard the ship which meant that there was nobody on deck to secure the rope and pull aboard the hawser and the breeches buoy. This looked grim. 'It was then that one of our brave skippers volunteered to try and swim aboard the ship with a line, and so establish communication with the shore. From different points he made two or three attempts without success, until he gave up in despair...'

The skipper was determined to try again and 'suggested that he should go out in the lifeboat and attempt to reach the wreck from the sea.' As he got close to the ship he put on a cork jacket, 'and tying about his waist a thin strong line he plunged himself into as strong a sea as you could get about this coast. He floated on the top of a great wave that carried him high over the ship's side, and left him clinging to the shrouds.' From there he made his way down below to check on the condition of the crew:

'When he appeared again he waved his hand and shouted something that was swallowed up in the roar of the storm. In the intervals between the great waves he managed to seize the rocket line, and to work his way into the shrouds again. Clinging there with his feet, and his teeth - as he afterwards told us - he was able to untie the rope that was about his waist, and to tie himself with it to the mast. Then slowly we saw the rocket line move, until we felt the hawser that was attached to it begin to move towards the wreck.'

The men were inside the ship and barely alive. All were rescued by breeches buoy; the heroic skipper also made it back onshore to a resounding cheer from his fellows.

Numerous ships were wrecked around the coast during the years that Bram Stoker visited Port Erroll, some with significant loss of life. The highest frequency of shipwrecks in the area occurred on the Skares, the low-lying reef of rocks which extend offshore from near Whinnyfold for almost half a mile. They have been the site of many a shipwreck down the centuries; some of the ships are still down there around the rocks. Houses along the coast around Whinnyfold were once graced with sheds, coal cellars and hen houses made with wood salvaged from wrecks over the years, some of them with recognisable name boards from the ships. Plates, cutlery, bed and table linen, all bearing the names of the ships they came from, ended up inside the houses.

The following were the more dramatic wrecks that occurred in the area during Bram Stoker's time.

126

On the 10th October 1894, the steamer *Chicago* was on route from Sunderland to Baltimore with 130 tons of cargo. The ship, heading north, skirted around the Skares at the southern end of Cruden Bay in bad visibility and a stiff following wind. A short time after, the second officer on watch noticed they were heading directly towards a light which couldn't at first be identified. What was that light? As they got closer, they realised to their horror that it was beaming from the windows of Slains Castle, and they were heading straight for the cliff underneath it. The engines were put full astern although this was not enough to prevent the steamer hitting the cliff. The impact was so violent, a large block of granite broke off, the ship's three forward compartments were breached and the ship jammed fast on an underwater ledge. A coachman at the castle, having heard the collision, warned the coastguard. The steamer could not be refloated, so rocket lines were fired, secured to the ship and the 22 crew were taken onshore. A servant's ball was being held at the castle that evening which explains the light the second officer had seen. The party came to a halt as everyone rushed outside to watch the unfolding drama below.[201]

On the 16th September 1898, the *SS Milwaukee* hit the Skares with no loss of life. The captain had run aground due to a navigation error. A photograph of the shipwreck hangs on the wall of the Port Erroll Congregational Church. It shows the Liverpool steamer lying next to the reef. It had been cut into two parts with the intention of refloating the sections separately. Both parts are upright with only a small gap between them; it's as if they had been pulled apart by a giant hand. One of the funnels is belching smoke. The two parts of the *Milwaukee* were later welded together and it steamed the seas once more. That is until 1918 when the unfortunate ship was torpedoed in the last year of World War One.

When Bram Stoker visited Port Erroll for his summer holiday in 1903, he would have known about the dramatic events that had taken place earlier that year. This was the shipwreck of the Danish steamer *Xenia*, and one of the most renowned rescue feats on the Buchan coast.[202] He probably knew all the fishermen involved in the rescue.

On the morning of Saturday the 31st January 1903, the *SS Xenia* left Newcastle on route to Boston in the United States with a cargo of coal. The next morning, when they were an estimated twenty miles offshore from Aberdeen, the wind changed, the sea became rough and heavy showers of sleet started to fall. Before long the storm intensified and they were blinded by thick snow to the extent that they had lost track of their whereabouts. The ship was proceeding at half speed, when at 7 a.m. they hit the rocks of the Skares. The sides were holed and the *Xenia* sank within ten minutes. Before it sank they lowered the three lifeboats. The first boat was swamped with water, and a fireman, John Johansson, who had jumped into it, was drowned in front of the crew. A second crew member, Ernest Raff the third engineer, was lowering himself by rope into one of the other lifeboats, when he lost his grip and was also drowned.

A woman in the village spotted the steamer on the rocks and alerted everyone immediately. The Port Erroll lifeboat crew were also informed. The lifeboat put to sea while the rocket brigade rushed around the coast to Whinnyfold. Unfortunately the lifeboat couldn't get in about due to a strong flood tide flowing across the northern side of the Skares. The *Xenia* was too far out for the rockets to reach her either. The men were doomed or so it appeared.

On hearing the alert, nine Whinnyfold fishermen immediately put out to sea in the small fishing boat, the *Vine*. The fishermen were Joseph Cay, Thomas Gray, William Morgan, Alexander Cay, James Freeland, James Phillips, John Hay, William Hay and James Hay. It was an astonishing act of bravery given the extreme storm conditions. The superb seamanship showed as the small boat rode the high waves out to the Skares under severe risk of being swamped or smashed against the rocks. With a heroic effort and much battling with the waves, they managed to get alongside the Xenia's lifeboats. Thomas Gray boarded one and William Cay the other and both lifeboats were landed ashore with 20 of the Xenia's crew onboard.

Five of the Xenia's crew including the captain were still left on the stricken vessel. Without hesitation the Whinnyfold fishermen went back out again to pick them up, this time in one of the lifeboats. After much effort, they eventually got close enough to the shipwrecked *Xenia* to throw a line onboard. One by one the remaining crew members were pulled through the raging surf onto the lifeboat. Great difficulties were experienced in getting the captain on board, a big fat man from all accounts, although this was eventually achieved.

Once ashore, the crew members were cared for by the villagers, Captain Kruse being lodged at the Crookit Lum cottage in Whinnyfold where he was looked after by Isy Cay. She would later become Bram Stoker's landlady when he stayed in the village.

'During my thirty-five years' experience at sea this is my first serious mishap,' Captain Kruse told the *Aberdeen Daily Journal*, 'but I could not have fallen into the hands of a more hospitable people and I will never forget their kindness although I live to be a hundred years old.' The captain returned his thanks by inviting Isy Cay to Copenhagen to meet his family, and she took him up on the offer. The fishermen were awarded with medals from both the British and Danish governments. A ceremony was held at the Port Erroll Public Hall where the rescuers were each presented by the Countess of Erroll with a bronze Board of Trade medal for gallantry in saving life at sea. They also received £2 cash. Lord Erroll said, '...within the last twenty years upwards of 90 lives had been saved by the Whinnyfold fishermen.' Referring to the *Xenia* rescue, he added that 'a braver or more gallant act was never done.'[203]

The greatest loss of life in the Cruden Bay area took place in January 1912 when two ships were wrecked within successive days. On the 17th January, the Aberdeen Collier *Frederick Snowdon* was spotted about 12.30 p.m. by the coastguard at Port Erroll listing heavily to port and being over-run by waves. The ship turned over at 1 p.m., and sank at a distance of one and a half miles from shore. Thirteen crew members were drowned. A court of enquiry concluded that the cargo had probably shifted during the storm, causing the ship to list and become unmanageable. The coxswain of the Port Erroll lifeboat reported that he had never seen the sea quite so rough before, adding that it had been impossible for the lifeboat and crew to put to sea. A board bearing the ship's name was later found floating off Peterhead Harbour.[204]

The next day proved even more calamitous when the 3,000 ton steamer *Wistow Hall* ran aground at the Temptin' Rock, a large tooth-shaped rock that rises out of the sea three miles north of Cruden Bay.[205] Fifty three members of the crew were drowned and only four survived including the captain.

One rescue on the Buchan coast is so spectacular it ought to be much better known. The story would be difficult to believe was it not for the fact that an entire village witnessed what happened. 'Cowardice is pretty well unknown in Buchan,' writes Bram Stoker, a tribute that applies not only to humans but also to their dogs.

In October 1904 the German ketch *Maria* was making its way from London to Wick. Five men were on board. In the hold was a cargo of metal hoops to be used in the manufacture of barrels for storing fish.[206] The ship was close to Wick when a violent storm blew up. The northerly gale blew it all the way across the Moray Firth, driving it onto the rocks of the northern Aberdeenshire coast near the village of Rosehearty.

The coastguard arrived on the scene, and watched by a large crowd of onlookers from the village, fired rockets out to the ship from the shore to try and get a line onto it. Unfortunately, the rockets had to be fired into the face of a howling gale and not a single one reached its target. More rockets were brought in from Fraserburgh but these also failed to get anywhere close. It was looking dire for the five seamen onboard the *Maria*.

At this point Mr Shirran, the local banker, arrived with his big black retriever, Don. Without any prompting and to the total astonishment of all watching, the dog ran to the rope the coastguards had been trying to fire offshore, took one end in his mouth and swam towards the shipwrecked vessel with it. His first two attempts were unsuccessful, and he was forced to return to the shore both times. Setting off a third time, he disappeared from sight several times as the waves engulfed him. An eye witness account mentions how the onlookers gasped every time the dog's head resurfaced, many thought the dog to be drowned. The drama of the situation overwhelmed the onlookers; children and adults

130

were openly weeping, others fervently prayed.

Slowly and relentlessly the dog swam towards the ship. He was getting close, and the crew could be seen at the side of the boat frantically shouting and urging Don to get even closer; their lives depended on it. The brave dog approached the ketch such that the crew were able to grab hold of the rope with a grappling hook and then fasten it to the mast. The job done, Don returned safely back onshore, shook himself dry and wagged his tail happily as he was now the centre of attention in the middle of a wildly cheering crowd. The line having now been secured, the coastguards brought the five men onshore by breeches buoy.

A ceremony was held for Don in a packed village hall at Rosehearty. The sailor's friend was rewarded for his bravery with a solid silver collar. It was inscribed with the words:

> Presented to 'Don', the noble dog of A.M. Shirran Esq. of Rosehearty by Mrs Braybrook, Vice President of the Canine Defence League for his courage in swimming out to the wrecked schooner 'Maria' & bringing back a rope & thus saving the crew on Oct 4th 1904.

This was one truly remarkable dog.

12
'MR STOKER'S CLEVER
BUT CADAVEROUS ROMANCE'

The story line for *Dracula* is this: Jonathan Harker, an English solicitor, visits Count Dracula in his Transylvanian castle. The count wants to buy a London estate and Jonathan Harker is there to explain the purchase details. However, this is no ordinary aristocrat. It becomes increasingly obvious that this man is dangerous, has evil intent and will be a formidable opponent to stop. Jonathan ends up trapped inside the castle, all the doors have been locked and bolted. 'The castle is a veritable prison, and I am a prisoner!'

Not only that, Count Dracula has some very strange habits such as climbing up and down the castle walls like a lizard. Jonathan asks himself: 'What manner of man is this, or what manner of creature, is it in the semblance of man?' We will find out that he's a vampire: 'for centuries to come he might, amongst its teeming millions, satiate his lust for blood, and create a new and ever-widening circle of semi-demons to batten on the helpless.'

Jonathan eventually escapes from Castle Dracula after a failed attempt to kill the count by striking his face with a shovel. Meanwhile, Dracula embarks by ship making landfall in England at Whitby. Jonathan Harker's fiancée Mina Murray happens to be there at the time with her friend Lucy Westenra. Lucy is a sleep-walker, and one disastrous night she leaves her bed, walks along the cliffs and is attacked by the Count. The consequences are dire: she wastes away fast, 'all the time the roses in her cheeks are fading, and she gets weaker and more languid day by day. At night I hear her gasping as if for air.'

Professor van Helsing, an expert in obscure diseases, is called in to assess Lucy's condition. He eventually works out what has happened - vampires are involved. He tries to save her but to no avail; she becomes Dracula's first victim in the novel. Count Dracula then moves from Whitby to London where he is spotted by Jonathan Harker in the street. And what's our villain up to? He now starts preying on Mina. Count Dracula tells her she is to become, 'my bountiful wine-press for a while, and shall be later on my companion and my helper.'

The Count can only sleep on consecrated earth from his homeland and has brought 50 boxes to England for the purpose. Van Helsing and his helpers track down 49 of the boxes, rendering them unusable by adding in fragments of a holy wafer. It's looking tricky for the count, so he escapes with his last remaining box of untainted earth back to Transylvania. He is followed there by Van Helsing and his helpers. They track him to his castle. Count Dracula is found there resting in his coffin, 'deathly pale, just like a waxen image, and the red eyes glared...' There is no time to wait, the sun is sinking, and once the shadows of night darken his powers will return. 'On the instant, came the sweep and flash of Jonathan's great knife. I shrieked as I saw it shear through the throat. Whilst at the same moment Mr Morris's bowie knife plunged into the heart.' The result, 'before our very eyes, and almost in the drawing of a breath, the whole body crumbled into dust and passed from our sight.' Quincey P. Morris then dies from a wound sustained during the final attack. Mina survives, and we are told that seven years later she is the mother of a boy named Quincey. 'It is an added joy to Mina and to me that our boy's birthday is the same day as that on which Quincey Morris died.'[207]

The plot followed by *Dracula* is a fairly standard one; the bad guy arrives; mayhem erupts; the bad guy is dispatched. It's the basis for many a cowboy tale and science fiction story. This type of plot has momentum and leads to a satisfactory ending; another advantage is that it's easy to keep the action going throughout. When the novel was first published reviewers remarked that it was impossible to put the book down. The plot is helped along by Bram Stoker's skill at drawing the reader forward to see what happens next.

Having established the plot, Bram then sought out background material for his novel. He had never visited Transylvania, so research was required to make his descriptions appear real. He took to reading books and articles about the region. Anything suitably exotic was thrown into *Dracula* to create a sense of place. Here's an example of how some of these details ended up in the novel:

'The strangest figures we saw were the Slovaks, who were more barbarian than the rest, with their big cowboy hats, great baggy dirty-white trousers, white linen shirts, and enormous heavy leather belts, nearly a foot wide, all studded over with brass nails. They wore high boots, with their trousers tucked into them, and had long black hair and heavy black moustaches.'

At least there was something to show for the years of planning that went into *Dracula*. Bram is at his best in creating a sense of brooding atmosphere and the details in his notebook had helped him do this.

A book can suffer from structural problems - *Dracula* is not free of them. A novel, if it is to work, should follow a logical path such that the reader can follow the flow. This can be difficult to achieve. Dramas thrive on conflict between the characters: yet if they can't stand the sight of each other, how can you get them to come together? Writing a book often involves solving such difficult issues. The author James M. Cain has mentioned this in the *Paris Review Interviews*.[208] A brilliant plotter, he wrote *Double Indemnity* and *The Postman Always Rings Twice*, both novels made into classic films. Cain compared good writing to algebra. A book should be logical all the way from the individual sentence, to the structure of the paragraph, which in turn should add to the overall shape of the book.

The logical structure of the plot is a problem in *Dracula;* one which Bram probably agonised over and few readers have ever noticed. Count Dracula, having imprisoned Jonathan Harker in his Transylvanian castle, takes off to England and lands at Whitby. Jonathan Harker's fiancée Mina and her friend Lucy are on holiday in Whitby when Count Dracula lands. It's a remarkable coincidence of course. And once Dracula is let loose on the village, of the hundreds of people living there at the time, he picks on Lucy to attack vampire-style, yet another coincidence. And then he relocates to London, where amongst its teeming millions, he is noticed by Jonathan Harker, who by then

134

has returned home after fleeing from Transylvania.

Your typical author, full of self doubt that he can carry the story, will fret endlessly about situations that are contrived like this. The awkward thought surfaces that if a novel appears illogical to its author, it will be considered as such by its readers. Can the contrivances be avoided? Is there a better way of getting the plot to work? All so often there isn't anything that can be done if the story is to move from A to Z. Bram Stoker gets away with it because successful authors know the trick of how to make a dodgy plot appear reasonable. Your typical reader will not get too bothered by the logical disconnects providing there is a cracking good story. It also helps if they are distracted by all sorts of evil goings on and a suitably gothic atmosphere.

So Count Dracula is undead, not quite alive and not quite dead, but on the boundary somewhere in between. And as Arthur Holmwood asks Professor Van Helsing: "UnDead! Not alive! What do you mean? Is this all a nightmare, or what is it?" Van Helsing replies: "There are mysteries which men can only guess at, which age by age they may solve only in part." OK, so the author who wrote this doesn't know either. The reader will let you get away with it because they know that a work of fiction is in essence one big lie – they have bought into it for the purpose of being entertained.

Dracula is rooted in the supernatural realm, and a creepy castle is almost obligatory for a novel of this type. Ancient objects commonly form part of the story, such as instruments of torture or Egyptian mummies. An atmosphere of death looms large in the tale; tombs, crypts and catacombs are used as scenic backdrops; ghosts, spirits and all things sinister abound. A reviewer wrote when *Dracula* came out: 'Mr. Bram Stoker gives us the impression - we may be doing him an injustice – of having deliberately laid himself out in *Dracula* to eclipse all previous efforts in the domain of the horrible,--to "go one better" than Wilkie Collins (whose method of narration he has closely followed), Sheridan Le Fanu, and all the other professors of the flesh-creeping school.'[209]

As if this was bad! The ratcheting up of the fear and horror content in books and films is eagerly anticipated in modern times.

If anything, Bram underplays it. Professor van Helsing and his gang manage to quickly contain Count Dracula's activities in London before chasing him back to Transylvania. The public has hardly noticed he was there. Some events take place around Hampstead Heath, as reported in *The Westminster Gazette*, and a wolf escaped from London Zoo. That's about it. A modern writer would most certainly not have done this. They would have allowed the London element of the story to escalate to an apocalyptic scale with Count Dracula creating total mayhem as hordes of newly-created vampires storm the streets seeking fresh victims. The task of saving the world then becomes epic. The author will romp through the story with glee as the streets resound with battle on a grand scale. It will be a near run thing, and the tension reaches unbearable levels. The finale arrives, a violent clash between the vampires and the human survivors. The reader gasps with relief when the evil is dispatched and it's safe to walk the streets again.

A novel which did exactly this was published in 1898, the year after *Dracula* came out. *The War of the Worlds* by H.G. Wells is the tale of a Martian invasion of South East England. The alien foe was formidable, wielding the superior technology of a devastating death ray that incinerated all in its path. Humanity is saved only when the Martians are invaded in turn by the deadly microbes which kill them.

Bram Stoker missed another trick. As the tale unfolds, we learn that the correct way to put Count Dracula to eternal rest is to cut off his head and either burn his heart or drive a stake through it. Alternatively, a vampire can be dispatched by firing a sacred bullet into its coffin. What happens at the end of the story isn't quite this; Jonathan Harker and Quincey P. Morris both attack him with knives and Count Dracula crumbles to dust. This raises the question as to whether Count Dracula has truly been destroyed or not. It's intriguing to note that Bram made a last minute revision to the ending. In the typewritten manuscript sent to the publishers in 1897 Dracula's Castle and the hill it stood on are pulverised to fragments by a volcanic eruption. This section was then scored out and it never appeared in the final version of the book. The result was an ambiguous ending; perhaps deliberately leaving the story open to a nice money-earning sequel should the book do well.

No modern author would have shunned the opportunity – he or she at the merest hint of success would have shamelessly trotted out a sequel. Bram Stoker reportedly told an American fan that he planned a sequel to *Dracula* based in the United States, although there is no record of him ever having written out a plot summary for it.[210] One curiosity, discovered along with Bram's notes for *Dracula*, was a press cutting he kept from the New York World dated Sunday 2d February 1896. This is an article headlined *Vampires in New England. Dead Bodies Dug Up and Their Hearts Burned to Prevent Disease.* It's reported that age-old superstitions about vampires were still current in parts of New England and Rhode Island.[211] If Bram had wanted to base a vampire tale in the United States the evidence was there to do so.

Dracula is written as a plot-driven novel where the action comes first and the characters come second, that is, with the exception of Count Dracula himself. Nevertheless, it has to be said that a novel lives through its characters. The reader opens a book and quickly immerses themselves in the story. By doing so, they escape into a new world populated by its characters and are provided with interesting companions for a few blissful hours of relaxation. These are people you need to feel involved with; whooping with delight as the hero or the romantic lead wins out, hissing with outrage as the dastardly villain thwarts their plans.

An essential element of an author's technique is to make the characters seem real. They should have specific aims, good points and their little eccentricities; all in all they will be like you and me. But not quite like you and me; it helps if the protagonist has a unique characteristic that makes them remarkable, that special something that makes the story crackle and pop. Perhaps it's a special attribute, the hyper-logical mind of Sherlock Holmes or the cynical wisecracks made by Phillip Marlowe, Raymond Chandler's private eye. Alternatively, it's a character flaw – the hero suffers from vertigo, paranoid delusions or claustrophobia. Whatever the author decides, it will make the novel different from the thousands of others out there – a selling point that will get the novel published, talked about and emptied from the bookshop shelves.

The author will need to get their characters right because they will dread getting a letter from their publisher which rejects their book with the words: 'I couldn't empathise with the main character'. So an author will need to understand their characters better than anyone in their family: all their quirks, their back history, what gets them up in the morning. Some will write pages upon pages of notes on their characters including everything about their life history. One writing technique involves compiling a list of a hundred or more questions about a character and then answering each one. 'Does X have an allergy?' 'How much do they drink every week?' 'What is their biggest secret?'[212]

Bram Stoker isn't very good at making his characters stand out from the page. With exceptions such as Count Dracula, they are often one dimensional and come across more like wooden puppets than real people. The heroes are fearless men protective of their frail women. The women simper in awe at their men folk; Lucy is a bit flirty and that's about it. As a novel *Dracula* gets away with this because the reader is overwhelmed by the horror of it all; the garlic drowns out any subtle flavours that might have been in the recipe. Bram is oh so good at creating a sense of atmosphere with well-chosen words. Some of the phrases in the book are deservedly famous such as 'the children of the night' and 'a stranger in a strange land.'

The world found out something later that wouldn't have been appreciated by the author - the atmospheric set pieces in *Dracula* could have been written with view to a lucrative movie tie-in. It's a book that reads as if you are watching a film. Aptly enough, the motion picture camera had just been invented a few years before *Dracula* was published, and the first public showings of movie pictures overlapped with the writing of the book. One short film was shown in France in 1896, *The House of the Devil* - it could be described as the first-ever horror movie. Years ahead of its time, the three-minute film starts with a bat flying into a castle which then transforms into a demon. As the demon lands on the floor, he stretches out his arms and flexes his dark cape in a style that would become familiar from the vampire movies made over 30 years later.

Bram took much effort to get the character of Count Dracula right. It's one thing to have an evil monster carrying the tale, but if the book is to be any good only a monster that's interesting will keep the readers reading. So lots of little details were brought together to make him register on the page. The count is a tall and thin man dressed entirely in black. He's old with waxen skin in the first few chapters, although he can rejuvenate his appearance by drinking human blood. He is not much to look at; thick eyebrows almost meeting over blue eyes. Yes, blue eyes - they glow red when he is at his most fiendish and are usually described that way. He has a thin aquiline nose with peculiarly arched nostrils. The mouth is hard-looking with those sharp white teeth protruding over the very red lips. You wouldn't want him getting too close - his breath is described as rank. And you will notice that the palms of his hands are rather hairy.

Count Dracula is not your normal neighbourhood fiend, and we find out more about him as the novel progresses. The first ominous sign is when Jonathan Harker notices that he cannot see the Count's reflection in his shaving mirror. Later we find out that he doesn't cast a shadow; no vampire will, they are un-dead and not of bodily form. It gets worse. He can transform into a wolf or a bat or even elemental dust. He has absolute power over animals, 'the meaner things' such as wolfs and rats. But most horrific of all, by biting a human being he can transform them into undead vampires beholden to his will.

Yet, it's not easy being Count Dracula. He can only operate with his full evil powers at night; they don't work during the day. What to do? - Best to sleep in his coffin during daylight but only on consecrated soil from Transylvania. He can be driven off by garlic, a crucifix and a holy wafer. A branch of a wild rose left on his coffin lid will trap him inside.

There are occasions when Dracula surprises the reader. Early on we find him inside his Transylvanian castle, outside are howling wolves and terrified peasantry. So what is he doing to while away the hours? He's sitting on the sofa in his library leafing through books such as Whitaker's Almanac and the Bradshaw's Guide, a Victorian railway timetable and a travel guide for Great Britain. The count is an anglophile. And later in the novel Count Dracula escapes by ship out of London; his destination the Black Sea. The dock workers had noticed the evil one before he set off, because according to Professor Van Helsing: 'That he be all in black, except that he have a hat of straw which suit not him or the time.'

An author, having worked out the plot and characters, is now faced with the question: what point of view should be used to write the novel? They might want to pick one of the characters and write a first person narrative. One person tells the entire story as they see it. It creates a mood of intimacy such that the reader feels a growing familiarity with the narrator as the book proceeds. A good writer will reveal how the key character thinks and how they feel about the action as it takes place. Their inner life comes alive. As a reader you can get inside their head; some of their viewpoints you can empathise with; others will be unfamiliar and perhaps even surprising. Nevertheless, the experience should prove fascinating. For a few hours you are not alone as you become totally absorbed while reading the book.

Alternatively, the author can write in the third person as if they are an all-seeing being standing above the action and watching it all happen. The majority of novels are written like this. It's a colder, less intimate way of telling a story, but it's also easier to write. It provides a more complete way of understanding the plot, as you will be made aware of everything that happens through many points of view, and not just through the outlook of one person only. It's also a way of creating suspense because the reader will be told about things that the main characters do not know yet, especially if evil or retribution is about to come their way. Most thriller novels are written in the third person for this reason.

Bram picked a third method, writing *Dracula* as a series of letters and journal entries from different people - the so-called epistolary style. It's a way of combining intimacy with several points of view. Indeed the only major character we don't have the privilege of hearing from in *Dracula* is the villain himself. Each letter or journal entry serves to move the plot along while maintaining a broad overview of the action. Along the way, we get the reaction of more than one character to the horrific events in the book. Bram probably copied this style from *The Woman in White* by Wilkie Collins.

One tricky little detail required attention, the title for the book. Bram's original title had been *The Un-Dead* and this is what appeared on the original manuscript as submitted to the publishers. The publisher asked for the title to be changed. I'm not surprised. Make a submission to a modern publisher, and if he or she likes the idea of the book the next thing they will discuss with you is its title. A good title sells a book. I can imagine the publisher's reaction when Bram announced the title of his new book, *The Un-Dead*: "Ho, hum, it will do I suppose," while privately thinking that it comes perilously close to what is truly a horror story for any publisher: *The Un-Read...*

Dracula was the title that Bram Stoker came up with next, and the publisher probably jumped up and down with glee at this point.[213] It's a title that smokes of the other world, that peculiar k-sound at the end of the first syllable Drac which forces you to pronounce the last two syllables as Queue-la. It juxtaposes a K with a Q, something which sounds exotic to an English speaker and vaguely unsettling. Dracula - a name you would never give to a child and probably not a pet. No doubt about it, *Dracula* is a cracking good title for a horror tale.

The book was published by Archibald Constable and Company on the 26th May 1897. The first edition was bound in yellow cloth with the *Dracula* embossed in bold red letters and the authors name immediately below. Bram received congratulations for *Dracula*: Winston Churchill enjoyed reading it as did Arthur Conan Doyle. The author's biggest fan was his mother who wrote to her son, 'it is splendid, a thousand miles beyond anything you have written before, and I feel certain will place you very high in the writers of the day the story and style being deeply sensational, exciting and interesting.' And after reading a review of the book she wrote again a few days later: 'In its terrible excitement it should make a widespread reputation and much money for you.'[214]

The reviewers were more judgmental. *The Athenaeum* praised the novel for: 'An immense amount of energy, a certain degree of imaginative facility, and many ingenious and gruesome details.' The final note of the review was somewhat snotty: 'Mr Stoker has got together a number of horrid details and his object, assuming it to be ghastliness, is fairly well fulfilled. Isolated scenes and touches are probably quite uncanny enough to please those for whom they are designed.'

The Bookman was more positive, 'we must own that, though here and there in the course of the tale we hurried over things with repulsion, we read nearly the whole with rapt attention.' Further adding that, 'a grown reader, unless he be of unserviceably delicate stuff, will both shudder and enjoy...' The *Spectator* described the novel as 'Mr Stoker's clever but cadaverous romance.'

The first print run was for 3,000 copies only. The author was given no advance payment and received royalties of one shilling and six pence out of the cover price of six shillings only after 1,000 books had been sold. This was 'a safe investment from the publisher's viewpoint,' wrote Haining and Tremayne in a book about *Dracula* which was also published by Constable.[215] It was a poor deal from the author's point of view.

Dracula was a moderate success initially, with eight editions issued during Bram's lifetime. Since then it has never gone out of print. The book only became the run-away publishing sensation of later years after the first Hollywood film was released in 1931, long after Bram's death. *Dracula* had a limited international run early on; an American edition came out in 1899, and the book was translated into Icelandic and an unauthorised Hungarian edition. A paperback appeared in 1901.

Bram Stoker came away from *Dracula* with his reputation enhanced and his credentials as a novelist now firmly established. It never made him that much money and his cash problems were as before. He had no idea during his lifetime that he would become a household name in the years to come.

Dracula the novel would eventually rise from the dead after a long slumber, and unlike its villain it took over the world.

13
'THE BRIGHTON OF ABERDEENSHIRE'

On the 22d June 1897 and less than a month after the publication of *Dracula*, Great Britain and the Empire celebrated Queen Victoria's Diamond Jubilee. It marked the 60th anniversary of the monarch's accession to the throne. Bram Stoker was in London preparing for a special event; this is how he described it:

> Indian and Colonial troops were gathered in London for the "Diamond" Jubilee of Queen Victoria, Irving gave a special performance for them. It was a matinee on June 25.... Some two thousand troops of all kinds and classes and costumes were massed at Chelsea Barracks. The streets were cleared by the police for their passing as they marched to the Lyceum to the quickstep of the Guards' Fife and Drum Band, the public cheering them all the way. They represented every colour and ethnological variety of the human race, from coal black through yellow and brown up to the light type of the Anglo-Saxon reared afresh in new realms beyond the seas. Their drill seemed to be perfect, and we had made complete arrangements for their seating. Section by section they marched into the theatre, all coming by the great entrance, without once stopping or even marking time in the street. In the boxes and stalls sat the Indian Princes and the Colonial Premiers, and some few of the foreign guests. The house was crammed from wall to wall; from floor to ceiling; the bill was Waterloo and The Bells. No such audience could have been had for this military piece. It sounded the note of the unity of the Empire which was then in celebration; all were already tuned to it. The scene at the end was indescribable. It was a veritable ecstasy of loyal passion.

Up and down the land beacons were lit on prominent hillsides to mark the occasion. In Port Erroll the celebrations for the Jubilee bore a distinctly pagan tinge. They were organised by a local social club with an unusual name, The Caledonian Order of Oddfellows. The events during the day were conventional enough. A gala was held in the recreation park with a picnic and free refreshments provided. Sports were held for the children including a tug of war competition for teams from local schools. A band played in the afternoon and boards were set out for the villagers to dance to the music. This was followed by a bicycle race along the beach, won by James Cruickshank, proprietor of the Kilmarnock Arms Hotel and village over-achiever.

At seven p.m. the children were put to bed and the main event started. Horse-drawn carts and wagons covered in decorations brought in people from the surrounding countryside. As night time fell torches were lit, and a fiery procession led by the Oddfellows set off from the village hall and marched up Aulton Road. The dense mass of waving torches produced an admirable effect according to the *Buchan Observer*.[216] They passed by the schoolhouse and then turned left, making their way up to the top of the Hawklaw, the prominent hillock overlooking the beach. When they reached the summit, they found an old wooden herring boat laid out surrounded by wood shavings. Acting as one, the assembled marchers threw their burning torches into the boat and it erupted into a mass of flames. The celebrations finished at midnight leaving the bonfire blazing furiously. It was still alight at dawn.

The old was about to give way to the new; proposals were afoot to transform Port Erroll into an upmarket holiday resort. One of the moving forces behind the project had been James Cruickshank. The concept envisaged the construction of a luxury hotel and a golf course near the beach. Visitors would arrive there by a new railway; a branch line connecting to a junction on the existing main line twelve miles inland.[217] The Great North Railway Company found the proposal attractive, and now started to work out the commercial feasibility of the project. They liked what they saw. The company's hotels in Aberdeen were profitable; a success that could potentially be repeated at Port Erroll.

Plans were drawn up for the new hotel, and the company prepared to build the railway line. It would link Ellon with the

144

coastal village of Boddam and pass through Port Erroll. A ceremony was held to mark the start of work on the line in September 1895. Two train-loads of dignitaries, 550 in number, were brought from Aberdeen to Ellon. They met up with Lord and Lady Erroll who had arrived from Slains Castle with a small party. The weather was dismal, blowing a north-westerly gale with frequent heavy rain showers.[218]

Lady Erroll was dressed for the occasion in a green satin mantle with jet trimmings, a black satin dress and a hat kitted out with black feathers. Buffeted by wind and rain, she started proceedings by lifting four square turfs with a silver spade, dropping them deftly onto a ceremonial oak wheelbarrow. She then wheeled the barrow a short distance along a gangway and upended the turf onto the track of the proposed railway. Everyone clapped and cheered. Her labouring duties over, lunch was then held in a marquee tent within the grounds of Ellon Castle. Speeches followed. When the Chairman of the railway company finally stood up to speak, he announced: 'The salubrious climate of Port Erroll has grown rapidly in popularity as a summer resort, and the inhabitants may feel themselves justified in claiming for the village the name of the Brighton of Aberdeenshire, and there seems little doubt that when, in the near future, the railway system is completed, the claim will be undisputed.'[219]

He then presented Lady Erroll with a 'magnificent silver model of a railway wagon.' Her husband now stood up to give his speech. Once the line was opened, the earl said, Port Erroll and London 'would be placed within twelve hours' reach of each other, and that it would be perfectly possible to breakfast at the one and dine at the other.' All present at Ellon Castle expressed great hopes for the venture to come.[220]

Not everyone shared their boundless enthusiasm. Reverend Ross, minister of the Cruden Parish Church, gave a gloomy prediction as to the likely consequence of the proposed development: 'One thing is certain, that the quiet retirement of Cruden, which to many was one of its chief recommendations of old, has already taken flight and will not return.'[221]

It was a bold venture to build a tourist resort on this scale in the north of Scotland. The 'Brighton of Aberdeenshire', which, at

145

over 500 miles from London, is somewhat less accessible by comparison to the original at 50 miles from the capital. The climate on the south coast of England is also noticeably warmer in the summer.

Cruden Bay Railway Station was opened on 2d August 1897. It was located about half a mile south of the village, and was intended to serve the nearby hotel; the service provided to the local population was of secondary consideration. If the villagers had to walk that bit further to get there then they should consider themselves grateful for the amenity provided. The station was named 'Cruden Bay' rather than Port Erroll because Cruden Bay sounded more like a desirable destination for a seaside resort than a 'port'. It caused confusion in the years to follow whereby the village of Port Erroll was served by Cruden Bay Railway Station - some of the passengers may have missed their stop in consequence or would not have known where to go in the first place. It's probably for this reason that the village's name was change to Cruden Bay in 1924.

There were five trains a day from Aberdeen to Cruden Bay station with an extra train on Saturdays. A day return during the May to October season was issued at five shillings first class and two shillings and sixpence third class. A four-day return ticket to London was available as a specially-reduced fare at 38 shillings and six pence.[222]

The new hotel was still under construction when the railway station opened in 1897; the work had fallen behind schedule. It was being built out of pink granite in the baronial architectural style then popular in Victorian Scotland; the design showed a 98 feet high tower rising above the main entrance and flanked at each corner by turrets. The hotel was to have all the modern facilities of its time including lifts, together with an electricity generating plant and a laundry. When it opened in 1899 it would have 94 bedrooms. The cost of construction had been anticipated as £22,000.

The Aberdeen Journal reported on October 22d 1897 that directors and officials of the Great North of Scotland Railway Company had visited Port Erroll.[223] They were there to inspect progress on the work to date. Their first stop was the Bullers of

146

Buchan, a coastal beauty spot two miles north of Port Erroll, and a local fishing boat transported them from there to the village. Some of the visitors then moved to the golf course which had already been completed and was now playable. They enjoyed a game there while the rest of the party investigated the construction site for the hotel. The work was at an advanced stage and it was already possible to see how it was going to shape out.

The visitors then walked to the village, noting that a building boom had already started in anticipation of the new railway opening up the area. Houses were being built in all directions and the prediction was made, that 'in five years there will be a populous town at the place.' It was also reported that 'the Earl of Erroll has had a feuing plan prepared...' That last comment needs explanation. A feuing plan is roughly equivalent to a development plan as might be prepared today by the planning officials in a municipal council; the big difference is that back then local planning was under the control of the aristocracy. The Laird decided what should be built where.

One of the oddities of Scottish legal system up until recently was the survival of a law from the era of medieval feudalism. House owners in Scotland could buy and sell properties but were obliged to pay an annual feu duty to the local aristocrat who nominally controlled the land. The law changed and feudal duties were abolished in the year 2004. I remember as a teenager watching as my father wrote out a cheque for feu duties. It wasn't a large sum, nevertheless everyone was obliged to pay, and it was collectively a significant source of income for the local Laird.

The feuing plan for Port Erroll was published by the local press, and it showed a patchwork of building plots which if realized would result in a significant expansion of the area covered by the village. As we continue to read the report in *The Aberdeen Journal* from 1897, a surprise awaits us: 'Mr Bram Stoker, the litterateur and Lyceum manager, who has resided at Cruden Bay, and has written a charming story of *The Watter's Mou'*, is amongst those who have secured a feu, and the most distinguished and popular actress on the British stage is expected to erect a marine residence at this charming spot.'

Now that's interesting. It chimes with a comment in Bram's

1902 novel *The Mystery of the Sea*. The hero of the book, Archibald Hunter, reports that, 'I arranged to take a feu at Whinnyfold and to build a house overlooking the Skares for myself. The details of this kept me constantly going to Whinnyfold, and my house to be was always in my thoughts.' If Bram Stoker had bought land in Port Erroll or Whinnyfold, he never built a house there. Likewise the distinguished actress, who is almost certainly Ellen Terry, never built a house in the area either.

The Scottish Land Registry, the organisation that looks after the Scottish land and property registration, has thoroughly checked the records. Bram Stoker's name does not appear in them.[224] The Earl of Erroll's feus are listed under 'The Lands and Estate of Cruden and Ardendraught'. There are many feus and sales which were checked from 1876 to 1900 but none of these correspond to the name Stoker.

That's strange. I suspect that the idea of Bram Stoker securing property in Port Erroll was a fantasy of both the railway company and the man himself. It's entirely plausible that Bram Stoker wished to build a house at Whinnyfold, perhaps even a retirement home. He may even have made enquiries about securing a feu. The timing of the newspaper report is of interest, because it was written six months after *Dracula* was published. Could it be that Bram had anticipated the novel bringing in enough money to build his dream house in Whinnyfold? Well that didn't happen. *Dracula* was moderately successful when it came out but did not make its author a fortune.

The Cruden Bay Hotel officially opened for business in Easter 1899. Everything had now come together, the hotel, the railway and the golf course; Port Erroll was now a holiday resort. To mark the official opening of the latter a professional golf tournament was held with a prize fund of £120; £30 was the first prize.

The station was a bit out of the way from the hotel, and to ease the passage of their high society clientele a tramway was built between them, a distance of about a third of a mile. Two electric trams were put in operation and the hotel guests travelled in great luxury. The trams, which could seat 16 passengers, were made of highly-polished teak, 'polished so highly you could see your reflection in them. The glass too was sparkling clean' and the trams 'glided along as smooth as anything.' They displayed the purple and cream colour of the railway company's coach livery with the letters 'CRUDEN BAY HOTEL' along both sides. If the sun was too bright, the gold-coloured velvet curtains could be drawn shut. The trams were said to be as fine a sight as the hotel itself.[225]

Cruden Bay Hotel was marketed for its health benefits. The guests could play golf, tennis, bowling or croquet. Inside the hotel was a huge cycling hall.[226] They could also bathe on the beach with wooden bathing huts provided. Old photographs show a long line of white bathing huts along the length of the beach. One cannot imagine the guests spending too long in the North Sea, the average water temperature even in August is a chilly 14 degrees Celsius (57° Fahrenheit).

The interior of the hotel was sumptuous. For instance, the drawing room was kitted out with furniture of Chippendale mahogany in Louis XV style. No luxury was spared; the kitchens were staffed with French and Italian chefs. The local village historian, Margaret Aitken, was told by a woman in Cruden Bay how she once walked down the red-carpeted staircase to take part in her first ball at the hotel, meanwhile 'admiring her silver-trimmed, blue silk dress in the full-length mirrors of the entrance hall.'[227]

The guests were prominent businessmen of the time, including Sir Jeremiah Colman, whose business made Colman's Mustard, and Sir William Burrell from Glasgow, best known today for bequeathing his art collection to the city of Glasgow. Many returned year after year.

Port Erroll had now become a busy place during the summer and this lasted for about ten years after 1899. The newly bustling village was described by Alex Inkson McConnochie in 1901:

> The Bay was alive. Red-coated golfers were in evidence, and solitary ladies read books in the open or trifled at tennis; here and there we could note a couple of visitors looking more at each other than at the glorious sea in front of them, and picnic companies were numerous.

Some had come by rail, and had even indulged in a "special" for the occasion; others had driven in farmers' carts from neighbouring parishes... It was a busy scene ashore; nor was the sea idle. Little boats were" bobbing" in the Bay, many of them with fishers, amateur or otherwise, on board... The sea had retired far from the bathing coaches, and children gambolled and lovers walked on the firm sand, the barefooted urchins steering clear of the jelly-fish then so plentiful.[228]

Large villas were built on the Aulton Road between the Kilmarnock Arms Hotel and the approach road to the Cruden Bay Hotel. Many of these were rented out for the summer to those who couldn't get into the hotels. Residents in the older houses were also advertising rooms for rent. Port Erroll could now boast a bank, a public hall, three general merchants, a baker, butcher, fish shop, two shoe makers, a chemist, two tailors, a carpenter, a blacksmith and a builder. The locals were advertising their expertise at organising boating and fishing expeditions. The boys in the village made good money by caddying for nine pence at the golf course; some made huge tips from the millionaire visitors. Not everyone was happy. Complaints were made about the golf course being used on Sundays and thereby desecrating the Sabbath day. The local paper defended the practice, arguing somewhat unconvincingly that the Cruden Bay Golf Course was attracting idle fellows out of Aberdeen; otherwise they would have annoyed worshippers there by loafing about church doors, a common complaint it was said.[229]

Bram Stoker's feelings about the changes around Port Erroll from 1897 onwards are not recorded; although it's likely that he wasn't happy about them. He was not alone with nature any more during his August outings. He walked along a beach set out with long rows of bathing huts and crowded with visitors. 'In those days it was rare to see anyone on the beach,' he wrote in *The Mystery of the Sea* about his early visits to the area. Not just the beach, the trippers were walking over his beloved path to Whinnyfold where the enterprising locals were selling cream teas and scones.

Port Erroll benefitted from the money tourism brought into

the area. It was a lifeline to the village economy because its other main industry, fishing, was in decline at the end of the nineteenth century. Much of the blame was apportioned to the trawlers, which had started to come into prominence from around 1830. The trawl net had evolved from the drift net of old, a curtain-like net hung from floats with the intention of catching any fish that swam into them, particularly herring. The trawl net was dragged by the boat rather than left passively hanging in the water. The development of steam-driven trawlers had provided the power to drag the heavy nets.

Aberdeen became the main trawler port from about 1880. The numbers grew from there, 38 trawlers were registered in Aberdeen in 1892, 148 in 1900 and 230 in 1912. Fish catches had been declining and the trawlers were blamed for this. This is mentioned by Bram Stoker in his 1902 novel '*The Mystery of the Sea.*' The hero, Archibald Hunter makes conversation with a fisherman on a quay at Peterhead Harbour:

> I had been thinking of the decline of the herring from the action of the trawlers in certain waters, and fancied this would be a good opportunity to get a local opinion. Before long I strolled over and joined this son of the Vikings. He gave it, and it was a decided one, uncompromisingly against the trawlers and the laws which allowed them to do their nefarious work... certain fishing grounds, formerly most prolific of result to the fishers, were now absolutely worthless...[230]

The downward trend continued. Reverend Adam Mackay wrote in 1912 that the fishing was not prosperous. Line-fishing was now almost non-existent, and Port Erroll Harbour was seldom used by ships of any size except for carrying coal and grain. The concentration of large-scale fishing in the bigger ports had taken away many local fishermen.[231] He notes that the population in the parish had decreased by 200 since 1901, and fishing was dying as an industry in Port Erroll. By the 1930s, the landings were poor with the returns barely justifying the expenses of running a boat. Haddock and whiting had become very scarce. Commercial fishing eventually came to an end in 1965. Salmon fishing lasted longer and kept a small number of men at work up until ten years ago, although it has ceased as an occupation today. The salmon bothy is a private house and the wooden storage sheds have recently been pulled down, a modern house has taken its place.

The grand plan to turn Port Erroll into 'the Brighton of Aberdeenshire' came to nothing in the end. After an initial success, the profitability of the hotel slumped and losses were recorded for the years 1909 and 1910. The hotel slipped between profit and loss for the years thereafter. It was unfortunate for Bram that having discovered somewhere where he could be alone with nature, it had become a popular resort during the later years he visited Port Erroll. And after his last visit in 1910, that popularity waned considerably.

Port Erroll faced two major problems as a tourist resort, the season was short, it effectively ran from June to September, and the hotel was far too distant from the major centres of population. A guide book to the Cruden Bay area, written in 1908, records that the rail journey from London took 13½ hours. Bram was happy to make the effort given that this was his special place. For others in the capital city there were also the competing charms of Paris and the continent, much easier to reach than the North of Scotland.

Once the numbers of tourists dropped off from about 1910 onwards, the railway line became more dependent on farm and fishing freight, but given the decline of the latter this never brought in much revenue. Things came to a head when there was a major fire at the station in April 1931. This took place during the economic depression that followed the Wall Street Crash of 1929. The railway company could not justify the expense of rebuilding the station, and the branch line through Cruden Bay to Boddam was subsequently closed to passenger traffic in October 1932. A Rolls Royce car was purchased to transport hotel guests from Aberdeen station instead. Freight continued to be carried by railway up until 1945, when the Boddam branch line closed for the last time on the 7th November. The tracks were removed in 1950.

The Cruden Bay Hotel stayed open to the public up until the start of the Second World War. As the hotel shut, the Italian chef

152

was seized and made a prisoner of war. In 1940 it was put into use as an army barracks for the Gordon Highlanders. They sent their recruits to Cruden Bay for a month's field training. At the end of the war the railways were nationalised, and both the hotel and the golf course were surplus to requirements during a time of national austerity. The hotel had been trashed by the soldiers – they hadn't been too careful where they stubbed out their cigarettes - and then it was partly destroyed by a fire. Cruden Bay Hotel was eventually demolished in 1953. The last bit to go was the granite tower which was blown up with explosives. The granite building stone was reused; part went into the construction of a big house south of Aberdeen; the rest was used to build a block of flats in Kirk Street, Peterhead. Some of the bedroom doors were reused to build a shed for a house in Whinnyfold.

The intent had also been to return the golf course to agricultural land. It was saved from this fate when a group of local businessmen bought it from the government. The consortium included the then owner of the Kilmarnock Arms Hotel, Angus Carmichael, who was keen to see the golf course continue as otherwise the hotel would not be profitable without it. Today, it is considered one of the best golf courses in the world, consistently within a list of the top 100 all-time favourites.

Perhaps the busy atmosphere around Cruden Bay explains why Bram took a short break during the summer of 1897. He explored Deeside, spending part of the time at the Banchory estate of his London neighbour Henry Rivière.[232] A cycling trip down the Dee Valley from Braemar to Aberdeen provides an episode in *The Mystery of the Sea*, and is probably based on an actual trip. There are hints in the novel that the developments in Port Erroll had caused him problems in writing it. Although *The Mystery of the Sea* was written after both the hotel and golf course opened in March 1899, the action takes place over the two previous summers of 1897 and 1898. One of the scenes in the book involves a ghostly procession through the sand dunes. It would not have had the same impact if the ghosts had crossed a golf course. Even so, the ghosts of the drowned sailors making their way to St Olaf's Well on the evening of July 31st 1897 would have had to skirt their way around a golf course already under construction. The author neglects to mention this.

Bram also writes in the same novel: 'I followed the devious sheep track amongst the dunes covered with wet bent-grass, every now and again stumbling amongst the rabbit burrows which in those days honeycombed the sandhills of Cruden Bay.'[233] There are no rabbits in the dunes anymore, or none that I have ever seen. Yet, in the short story *Crooken Sands* based in Port Erroll, Bram Stoker wrote in 1894 about the same sand dunes, 'where the rabbits are to be found in thousands.'[234] Rabbits and golf courses are mutually exclusive it would appear. The construction of the golf course must have displaced much of their natural habitat. The loss of the rabbits would have upset Bram with his sensitivity to nature.

One feels sorry for Bram Stoker. Not only was his beloved Port Erroll getting a bit less peaceful after 1897, the next two summers of 1898 and 1899 were calamitous and probably a wipe-out as far as serious writing was concerned. The year 1898 had not started well for Bram and the Lyceum Theatre Company. The off-site building, which stored all the scenery and props, burned down in February 1898 with all the contents destroyed. The total value was over £30,000. Shortly before this happened, Henry Irving had told Bram to reduce the insurance cover from £10,000 to £6,000.[235] Apart from the financial loss, there was also the cost and time involved in getting new scenery and props made.

In early August 1898 Florence's elder sister Philippa was knocked down in Dublin, and this probably cut short the Port Erroll holiday. It was a bad year and the misfortune continued. Henry Irving was performing in Glasgow that October when, just as he was about to appear on stage for the second act, he called for Bram, who found him collapsed in a chair. He complained that every breath was like a sword stab although it didn't stop Irving from going on to complete the play. A doctor examined him once the final curtain closed and he was diagnosed with both pneumonia and pleurisy. He was laid up in bed in Glasgow for seven weeks. At the age of sixty he had suffered the first major illness of his life.

The summer holiday for 1899 was no better. Bram caught a chill while out cycling, and was confined to his bed. He had been due to attend a ceremony at Glasgow University on the 20th July - Henry Irving was to be awarded an honorary degree. However, as he wrote later: 'That was, I think, the only honourable occasion of Irving's life since 1878 at which I was not present. But it was quite impossible; I was then in bed with a bad attack of pneumonia.'[236]

Dr. James Harvey Stewart was called from the medical practice located in the nearby village of Hatton to treat Bram for the pneumonia bout.[237] He had just recently graduated from Edinburgh School of Medicine in 1899, and was probably working as an intern at the time. He practised as a full doctor in the Cruden Bay area from 1902 until his death in 1917.

A letter from Henry Irving arrived at the village on the 8th August. He mentions that he is glad of good news and hopes that Bram will gain strength every hour. Bram eventually returned to London on the 2d September.[238] No experience is ignored in his novels and the fever bout made it into his next book. He wrote in *The Mystery of the Sea*:

> I walked home by Cruden sands in a sort of dream. The chill and strain of the night before seemed to affect me more and more with each hour. Feeling fatigued and drowsy I lay down on my bed and sank into a heavy, lethargic sleep. The last thing I remember is the sounding of the dinner-gong, and a dim resolution not to answer its call....
>
> It was weeks after, when the fever had passed away, that I left my bed in the Kilmarnock Arms.[239]

According to the doctor's daughter-in-law, Anne Stewart, Bram later presented Dr. James Harvey Stewart with an engraved silver cigar case and matchstick holder. The date on the cigar case is 18th July 1906.[240] Mrs Stewart also recalls a story her mother had told her about the occasion when Dr Stewart invited Bram and Florence for Sunday dinner at their house in Hatton. They accepted but had made an unfortunate oversight in doing so. No trains ran on Sunday from Port Erroll to Hatton, so they had to walk two and a half miles along the railway line instead.[241] One guesses it wasn't one of their happier walks together.

1898 and 1899 look to be the lost years in Bram Stoker's

writing career. No novels appear to have been worked on at this time, although he did write some short stories. This demonstrates the importance of his Aberdeenshire holidays for his writing output. In 1897, the year when *Dracula* was published, he had been rewriting *Miss Betty*. The original version had been written years earlier. It was a romantic novel without the bite of his recent success and had been rejected by his publisher. He now rewrote the ending, and it came out to indifferent reviews in 1898.

He picked up the pieces again in 1900 when he returned to Port Erroll. His normal routine continued and the summer of 1900 was mercifully incident free. The only activity making it into the local newspapers was when Bram Stoker took part in a concert at the village hall (although one misspelled his name as Brain Stoker). He is reported to have given a recital, although what he read out was not recorded. The concert was held every summer on the day of the sale of work at St James's Church for the poor of the parish. Only the visitors to Port Erroll were allowed to perform at the concert. It was a grand occasion in the local social calendar, and was followed by 'a dance in which all participated, the villagers, the visitors and the maids from the hotel.'[242] Bram's writing task that year was to revise *Dracula* for a paperback edition, cutting its length by 26,000 words.[243]

The increased popularity of Port Erroll had failed to deter him from coming every year, yet it's to be wondered how Bram reacted on the occasion when he was asked to open the Peterhead Flower Show. The Lord Provost (mayor) of the town introduced him with the remark that he done much to publicise the attractions of the area, particularly as having come to Port Erroll before the Great North of Scotland Railway. The author would have politely beamed a smile to the Provost while stifling a pained grimace. One has to keep up appearances in public.

14
THE LATER YEARS

As time went by, a trip to Port Erroll became increasingly a welcome escape for Bram Stoker. His job at the Lyceum Theatre in London had become highly stressful. The theatre company was running into serious financial difficulties and was eventually sold to a consortium, although the financial problems continued. They eventually moved out of the Lyceum Theatre, giving the last performance there in July 1902.

Even this was not enough to save the company and it was liquidated the following year. Irving now intended to retire but not before he completed a two-year farewell tour. It was at this stage that Bram now realised that his income from Henry Irving was about to come to an end. He would have to depend on his writing before long. Five novels followed. These were *The Jewel of Seven Stars* (1903), *The Man* (1905), *Lady Athlyne* (1908), *The Lady of the Shroud* (1909) and *The Lair of the White Worm* (1911).

Of particular mention is *The Jewel of Seven Stars,* a spooky thriller involving an experiment to revive an ancient Egyptian spirit. It's possible that Bram got the idea for the book from long-remembered conversations with Oscar Wilde's father over thirty years previously. As a young man, William Wilde had toured the Middle East and had written a book on his travels. He investigated the ancient tombs of Egypt, returning to Dublin with some of the mummified remains he found there.

Another source of inspiration for the novel may have been Arthur Conan Doyle's short story *Lot No. 249* published in 1892. Its plot also involves the revival of an Egyptian mummy: 'This fellow Bellingham, in his Eastern studies, has got hold of some infernal secret by which a mummy — or possibly only this particular mummy — can be temporarily brought to life.'[244]

I reckon *The Jewel of Seven Stars* would qualify as Bram's best-written novel had it not been for the feeble ending. It's written in a pacy style, builds up to a climax and then comes to a premature stop. When the ancient spirit manifests itself in the modern world, everybody except for the narrator dies, and that's it. You feel on finishing the book that it deserves a final chapter to wrap everything up - something to explain the significance of everything that had just happened and how the surviving character felt about it. This would provide emotional closure for the main character and the reader. *The Jewel of Seven Stars* does nothing of the sort, finishing on these sentences:

> I did what I could for my companions; but there was nothing that could avail. There, in that lonely house, far away from aid of man, naught could avail.
>
> It was merciful that I was spared the pain of hoping.[245]

Bram must have assumed that the proof of concept, whereby an ancient spirit had been revived, was good enough to impress, and had left it at that. A version of the book with a revised ending was issued in 1912. This time the experiment failed and everybody lived. That one was even less satisfactory.

A curious episode happened at the start of his visit to Port Erroll in 1903. Bram arrived in the village with a dog. He was then told that the Kilmarnock Arms Hotel enforced a strict no-pets policy in its rooms, and this included the Hilton Cottage annexe. He was obliged to ask around the village to see if anyone would look after the dog for a month. He didn't have to go far. He knocked on the door of Clifton Cottage, two doors along from Hilton Cottage. The servants of the house were more than happy to look after the dog. I was told by their daughter, Marna Cruickshank, that Bram was very grateful and sent her parents a big box of chocolates when he returned to London. 'I remember the chocolate box well', Marna told me. 'It had beautiful silk violets on the front of it.' The box has since been lost. Marna couldn't remember anything else about Bram Stoker. 'My parents mentioned him but I didn't take any notice at the time.' I was curious to know who owned the dog and what its name was. Marna didn't know.

The year 1903 also saw the publication of a novel by the son of the Earl of Erroll, and he probably took *Dracula* as his inspiration for writing it. The novel is *Ferelith* and its author is

Victor Hay, named after his godmother Queen Victoria. He will eventually become the 21st earl. Ferelith, a girl's name, is an anglicised version of the Gaelic word *forbhlaith* meaning 'true sovereignty', and is still occasionally used today. Princess Anne of Denmark, and a cousin of Queen Elizabeth II, was christened Anne Ferelith Fenella Bowes-Lyon.

It is not known if Bram helped Victor Hay to write the book. Nevertheless, *Ferelith* contains a line of narrative which appears to pay tribute to *Dracula*: 'I become intoxicated with the magic touch of his filmy arms, I drink red nectar from his gossamer lips.'

The action of *Ferelith* opens by introducing an Englishman called Bill Bramble. Having made his fortune and wishing to be accepted by high society, he marries Lady Ferelith Sidlaw. Next up he buys 'Gowrie Castle' in Scotland, which is obviously modelled on Slains Castle: it lies next to the cliffs 'on the very edge of the rock.' Bill Bramble then moves in with his wife, and his sister Anne joins them. Anne narrates the tale as the book proceeds. It centres on Lord Gowrie, who had died over a hundred years previously. His portrait hangs on the wall, 'it was dark and handsome, but if ever black sin showed in a countenance it was there,' and his ghost walks the stone floors of the castle at nights.

Bill Bramble gets nowhere with his attempts to be accepted by high society, so he takes off to America, remaining there for over a year. He leaves his wife and sister to be looked after by the servants in the castle. In his absence, the ghost of Lord Gowrie appears to his wife and tells her, 'I bode you no ill. I am but an unhappy spectre, and I long for a moment's sympathy'. The lonely Ferelith falls in love with him - and as she records in her diary - a night comes when the ghost gets frisky. She implores the ghost to, 'stop!' But there's no stopping the spectre:
"Nay, nay. You are mine – mine after a hundred years," his lurid voice hissed at me, and he threw the last shreds of restraint to the winds... for ghostly arms were about me, arms that strained me to a ghostly breast...

Before long she writes in her diary: 'I am going to be a mother. The idea seems too fantastic.' It's a sentiment shared by the reader. A daughter is born and Lady Ferelith dies in childbirth.

The book was reviewed in the February 1903 edition of *The Academy and Literature*, 'the plot of the story is on familiar lines, but it is treated with some distinction.' This was damning with faint praise, and the novel also failed to inspire the public. The main interest of the book is historical. It gives a flavour of what it was like to live in Slains Castle at the beginning of the twentieth century. The future earl didn't appear to enjoy the experience that much, '...my first impressions remain the most vivid – a dim, shadowy mass, grey and impalpable in the mist, lonely, uncanny, weird. This is what it will always be to me... its real self is as I first saw it, mournful and hopeless in the drizzling mist.'

The description of the nearby village and its fisherfolk are also handled in an unsympathetic manner:

Few people were to be seen, most of the fishers being away for the herring season. There was an unpleasant smell of stale fish about. A few haddocks were drying on a tumbledown railing.

We met one man, weather-beaten and grizzled, and with a very dour face. He did not even look at us. William addressed him. "Is there going to be a storm?"

"A dinna ken [I don't know]," was the answer, and the old fisherman went on his way.

William was annoyed. We walked on further till we came across a little knot of fisherfolk, men, women and children, some twelve in all. They regarded us suspiciously and ceased their talk.

William was embarrassed, and could find no appropriate remark to break the ice. He stammered out:

"What sort of fishing have you had?"

None answered him. [246]

The relations between the fisherfolk and the family of aristocrats living in Slains Castle must have soured by this time. Victor Hay also wrote a couple of plays which quickly fell into obscurity. He made the headlines in August 1910 when he was accidently shot and badly wounded by King George V during a hunt in the grounds of Balmoral Castle. The King was 40 yards away when the gun went off, either unintentionally or Victor Hay happened to get in the way of the intended target. He was peppered with shot around the head and body. Victor survived the incident although he was badly hurt.[247]

The Errolls left Slains Castle shortly after 1900. The earl had duties elsewhere, and money was running short for its upkeep. The Hay family fortune had dwindled; a combination of taxes, the extravagance of building the castle extension in the 1820s, the cost of the 19th earl's good works in Port Erroll and an extravagant life style split between Slains Castle and drawing rooms in London. The family still have in their possession a model of the castle which was built by one of the butlers and given to the earl as a present. Measuring several feet long, it was made out of champagne corks picked up by the butler in the castle.[248]

For the next few years after 1900 the castle was advertised as a high-class holiday let; the Prime Minister Herbert Asquith rented it three times. The Errolls eventually sold off the castle and estate to a shipping magnate in 1916. The contents of the castle library, 3,000 books in total, were sold separately to the Mitchell Library in Glasgow. Some of the more exotic contents of the castle came up for sale at an Aberdeen auction room that year. These included the pocket handkerchief of Frederick Duke of York, and some memorabilia connected to William IV; a pair of gloves worn on opening his first Parliament; a stone thrown at him by a mad sailor at the Ascot races, and a two-foot-long section from the last horse to have been ridden by the king.[249]

Slains Castle was sold again in 1923. An advert in Country Life magazine stipulated a minimum price of £10,000 for the castle, together with 332 acres of land. Up to 7,200 acres of additional land, including Cruden Bay Golf Course, could be had if desired. The remaining contents and fittings came up for sale at a public auction within the castle in April 1925. The building was bought by a contractor intent on dismantling it for profit. The roof was removed; this proved to be doubly profitable because the owner now avoided paying an annual tax ('rates') to the local council and the lead lining on the roof was stripped and sold. The lead was said to have brought in more money than the contractor

161

paid for the castle.

In 1926 an advert was placed in the *Buchan Observer* advising that joists, windows, doors, flooring, bathroom fittings, 1,000 tons of dressed granite and other splendid building material were now available for immediate delivery from Slains Castle.[250] There couldn't have been many takers. The Aberdeen architect Tom Scott Sutherland mentions how he was allowed to take away stonework for free which he then used to build a new wing for a country mansion.[251] The castle has since been left as a ruin and is gradually disintegrating.

Two reports from 1904 suggest that Bram had become deeply immersed within his mystical views of the universe as bound up with nature. He was invited to open the Peterhead Flower Show that year and give a speech. The show was advertised in a local newspaper beforehand, mentioning that Bram Stoker 'writes exceedingly well and should be interesting.' There was some hedging of bets here as if to say, don't blame us if we are wrong! The newspapers found the speech worthy of reporting when it came. In it the author professed his great love for this part of Scotland which he had visited for many years. He hoped to come there as long as he lived, mentioning to laughter and applause that he intended to live on herrings all the time. Bram went on to say:

> "A flower show was a most excellent help to social and educational progress. In a thousand different ways it helps... flowers were things of beauty, common to all, and which should be had by all... In every branch of life whatever was beautiful helped to elevate and refine, and those of them who had been about the world, and seen the rough places as well as the smooth, could easily understand what it was so difficult for young people to understand. Vice itself lost half its evil while losing all its grossness. There was in the economy of nature a wise provision in all the beauty they saw. The colours which attracted their eyes were part of the great scheme of creation, and the insects, who carried the fructifying pollen from flower to flower served a very useful purpose. The flowers, the animal, the vegetable and the

mineral world acted and reacted upon one another, so that in time they began to understand, with their hearts if not their heads, some of the great schemes of the all-wise creator, the 'only' God."

He then told the tale of two drunken workmen staggering around outside Covent Garden Market in London; one is a believer and the other is an 'infidel'. They argue about the meaning of the universe, and this reaches the point when the believer picks up some petals from the flower of a white lilac lying on the street. He holds them up and asks the other workman if he sees the petals - because yes, it was possible to see them but a workman couldn't ever make such a thing. Bram concluded with the moral of the story as recounted by the drunk believer: others who called themselves Christians, "did not give enough thought to the cause of the beautiful, and to the beautiful things they saw around them, for he could tell them that not the best, or the wisest, or the most learned, or the most clever could even begin to understand the purpose, or the lesson, or the mystery of the meanest flower that grows."[252]

It was a subtle lecture praising a pantheistic view of nature, and hinting that something mystical extended beyond the realms of Christian belief.

That same year Henry Irving and his theatre company were on stage at Her Majesty's Theatre in Dundee. A reception was held in a private house after one of the performances and Bram came along. Also present was Norval Scrymgeour who 33 years later gave an account of an after-dinner conversation. They were at a table in the dining room next to a blazing fire, Bram smoking a huge cigar. 'Sitting there beside me, sometimes laying his great hand on mine, the author of *Dracula* spoke as if he were in a dream, his eyes misted as with sleep.'

Norval concluded that, 'Bram Stoker was a mystic. The red-haired Irish giant was a child, sensitive of the elemental experience which the materialist ridicules or ignores.' [253] Bram told him a series of stories about the supernatural, mostly focussing on the subject of second sight. Many were from the Western Highlands of Scotland and were clearly inspired by his reading of J.G. Campbell's books on the folklore of the region.

The year 1905 brought the death of Henry Irving on the 13th October. The actor had been in Bradford on tour. Bram was at supper at his lodgings close to midnight, when one of his assistants arrived by carriage to tell him, 'Sir Henry is ill. He fainted in the hall of the hotel, just as he did at Wolverhampton.' They rushed to the Midland Hotel and found Henry Irving laid out on the floor surrounded by three doctors. One of the doctors spoke to Bram, 'he is dead. He died just two minutes ago.' Bram was stunned. This was the man he had dedicated his working life to, and now he was dead. Once he had collected himself together, he knelt down and felt Henry Irving's heart. There was no movement. He then closed the actor's eyelids.

Money was now a concern. His friend Horace Wyndham explains:

> Irving's untimely death must have been in many ways a great blow to Bram Stoker. Apart from the sudden severance of a close friendship between them that had existed for some forty years, it meant the abrupt and entire cessation of his sole source of income. He had drawn a large (but well-earned) salary from the Lyceum treasury, and had lived up to every penny of it. Accordingly, on Irving's death, the problems of ways and means began to press rather hardly. Still, despite the fact that he was getting on in years, Stoker had plenty of grit, and thrust himself into the rough-and-tumble anew, and with characteristic vigour. But he met with many rebuffs, for the Lyceum tradition was not wanted in the quarters where he offered his services. He even went after a five-pound-a-week job at Manchester Exhibition, and when the committee turned him down, he did his best to get it for me instead.
>
> In addition, however to theatrical management, which he knew from A to Z, Stoker had a second string to his bow. This was writing "shockers" of the "Dracula" type, with which he had years earlier made a considerable success. To keep the domestic pot boiling, he also did a bit of journalism when the opportunity offered...[254]

164

Two of these shockers are worthy of mention. The *Lady of the Shroud* is a bizarre tale that centres on a shroud-clad beautiful woman who appears at night in a castle in the Balkans. She appears to be a ghost but is in fact a living person employing a disguise.

Even odder is Bram Stoker's last book, *The Lair of the White Worm*. Lady Arabella March, an aristocrat resident in the ancient kingdom of Mercia, holds a dark secret. An ancient snake-like creature, the white worm of the title, lives in a pit under her house. Lady Arabella is evil and resorts to murder – it is suggested that she is the snake-like creature in human form. The book ends with an explosion that destroys the creature and its lair.

In the last few years of his life Bram fell seriously ill. His health started to decline from 1905. He had been laid low with kidney disease. There is even a suggestion that he suffered from syphilis; something which is argued over at length by his biographers with no agreement ever having emerged. Bram had a paralytic stroke at the beginning of 1906 and was unconscious for 24 hours. He would require the use of a magnifying glass to read and write from now on, returning to work a few months later.

Bram visited Port Erroll in 1906. He spent the summer correcting the proofs of a book he had been writing about Henry Irving, and which was intended as a memorial to his late friend. *Personal Reminiscences of Henry Irving* was published the following year.

I have no documentary evidence that Bram came north for the summers of 1907, 1908 and 1909. He may have been in the village; it's just that there is no definite proof of it. Illness may have had something to do with this.

If he had been in Port Erroll in 1908, and I suspect that he was, he would have been aware of the dramatic events that took place at Slains Castle that summer. They involved Winston Churchill and his near-disastrous attempts to sort out the conflicts of his love life only weeks before his wedding that September. The bare bones of the events were given in newspapers at the time, although it wasn't until Michael Shelden published *Young Titan - The Making of Winston Churchill* in 2013 that the full story was made public.[255]

Only the year before Bram Stoker had interviewed Winston Churchill for a newspaper article: 'When I met him in his library he explained more fully in words: "I hate being interviewed, and I have refused altogether to allow it. But I have to break the rule for you, for you were a friend of my father." Another reason was given: "And because you are the author of *Dracula*." Bram added in explanation: 'This latter was a vampire novel I wrote some years ago, which had appealed to his young imagination.'[256]

They were not close friends on the basis of what is said here, yet Bram was invited to Churchill's wedding a year later. Had something happened in Port Erroll that summer to warrant the invitation? - Something that required the utmost discretion perhaps?

Let's tell the story from the beginning using the information from Michael Shelden's book, and I'll add in extra details from local sources. Winston Churchill's love life had been unimpressive in his youth. He had proposed to three women and all three had turned him down. Surprising you might think – this was a man with prospects. His taste was for beautiful women, no less would do. Yet, there was something about Winston which did not impress the ladies. Perhaps it was his height; at five foot seven inches he was not a tall man, or his slightly bulging eyes, or because he wasn't that wealthy despite his aristocratic background.

He now looked to be having some success with Violet Asquith, the daughter of the soon-to-be Prime Minister, Herbert Asquith. Violet was twelve years younger than Winston. When she met him she was immediately entranced; they now went on to meet socially at balls and dinner parties over the next few months, often hiving off to talk for hours in some private corner. Violet was eminently marriageable not the least because of her political connections. She used her influence over her father when he became Prime Minister in April 1908, urging him to make the most of Winston. The announcement of an engagement seemed nigh.

Alas for Violet, Winston had met someone else, fallen in love and had quickly proposed marriage. He was accepted. This was Clementine Hozier, the granddaughter of the Scottish aristocrat, the Earl of Airlie. Winston may have been unsure of where he stood with Clementine at first. She was 22 years old and had already been engaged twice, breaking off both engagements. Clementine was by no means a sure catch, and Winston was no sure catcher either. He had first met Clementine in 1904; however, it was when he met her again at a dinner party on March 15th 1908 that they both sensed a deep connection between them. Winston became convinced of Clementine's interest after she had expressed great concern following his escape from a house fire. That clinched it. The engagement was announced on August 15th and the wedding was set for less than a month later on September 12th.

The engagement was announced while Violet was on holiday with her family in Slains Castle. Not that she knew anything about Winston's furtive goings-on up until a day before the engagement was made public. A letter arrived at Slains Castle, and it was only now that Winston informed her he was marrying someone else. When Violet read the letter she is said to have fainted.

He needed to smooth things over with both Violet and her father, so Winston now made the long journey north to Slains Castle on the 24th August. Meanwhile Clementine, his bride to be, had been vastly unimpressed that with their wedding imminent, her new fiancé had taken off to a castle in Scotland to meet his former girlfriend. She was furious and threatened to call off the engagement. She was talked out of it by her brother Bill, who had argued that to do so would have been disastrous for the political reputation of both Winston and Prime Minister Asquith.

Winston and Violet spent much time together walking and clambering amongst the cliffs. They also explored Port Erroll, and I'm told were seen walking past my house in the village. The Prime Minister played a game of golf every day at the Cruden Bay Golf Course (the locals were not impressed with his standard of play). Winston also visited the course and played golf with the Asquith family and their guests on two separate occasions.[257] One evening Winston informed Violet that he had made the right decision to marry Clementine, although nothing would stop them from continuing as friends. Winston then left for London and

Violet stayed on in Slains Castle with her parents.

Violet's emotional distress surfaced again on September 19th, a week after the wedding. In the late afternoon she left the castle, taking her dog and a book with her, and walked north along the cliffs. Night fell with no sign of Violet. Family, guests and servants set out to search for her. An hour later, she still hadn't been found, and her father now contacted the coastguard and the local policeman. They roused the villagers to help look for Violet, before setting off with rope ladders and lanterns to climb down the cliffs with the intention of investigating the shore below.[258]

Family memories survive in Cruden Bay of the night this happened; servants from the castle walked along the shore carrying lanterns, fishermen searched caves burning anything to hand to light up the interior. One story doing the rounds of the village afterwards was that even fur coats were burnt in the desperate efforts to find Violet.[259] She was eventually found at a distance of over two miles along the coastal path, the barking of her dog alerting the search party. She was unconscious. Her mother was of the opinion that Violet had staged the episode as a cry for attention after experiencing an emotional breakdown. Violet Asquith eventually married the politician Maurice Bonham Carter in 1915; the actress Helena Bonham Carter is her granddaughter.[260]

In 1910, Bram Stoker experienced a breakdown which he attributed to overwork. He was in a bad way, although this didn't stop him from taking the train trip north for one last time. He had cause to celebrate following his son Noel's wedding in England on the 30th July.

Bram and Florence on this occasion rented rooms in the village of Whinnyfold. The Crookit Lum Cottage where they stayed stands in the first line of houses in the small village of Whinnyfold. It has a clear view of the sea, in particular looking out to the Skares. The name 'Crookit Lum' is the Doric dialect for 'crooked chimney' and refers to the chimney stack which leans outwards on the northern gable end of the house.

The Stokers' landlady at the Crookit Lum was Isy (Isabella) Cay – both her surname and the 'I' in Isy rhymes with high.[261] Isy lived with her aging mother Jane, and when the summer season came round they both moved into the wash-house, the northern end of the house with the crooked chimney. The rooms in the main part of the cottage were rented out.[262] An enterprising woman, she ran a tearoom in her wash-house. Visitors would walk over the beach from the hotel and take afternoon tea there. Her scones were a speciality; boiled eggs were also on offer. Before they used the Crookit Lum Cottage as a holiday home, Bram and Florence had got to know they place when they stopped off at Isy Cay's tearoom following their walks across the beach.[263]

A family photograph shows Isy Cay sitting down looking at the camera.[264] She has an oval face framed by straight dark hair parted in the middle. Her eyebrows are prominent, untrimmed and arched; they accentuate a distracted, almost doleful expression in the eyes. Her nose is long and meets with a straight mouth over a strong chin. Isy appears to be in her thirties which would suggest that the photo was taken 15 years before the Stokers first met her.

Isy's relatives still live locally, and I talked to one of them, her grandniece Elsie Watt. She remembers Isy as an old lady living at the Crookit Lum in the 1940s. Elsie was between eight and ten years old at the time. 'Aunty Isy' - she calls her relative - although she was her mother's aunt.

Elsie's friends Flora and Margaret used to help look after Isy. While I was visiting her, Elsie picked up the phone and gave Flora a call; she provided extra information. Flora and Margaret used to cycle the three miles of road to Cruden Bay every Saturday to fetch her groceries from the shops. They received six pence for their trouble providing they also cleaned the front room.

Four years after Bram Stoker stayed in her cottage, Isy married John Main a marine engineer. Flora remembers that she moved to Aberdeen where she took up a post as a housekeeper to look after his three children. The children came from his first marriage after his wife had died. This is a less romantic story than the one previously told – that John Main was a sea captain whose ship had been wrecked on the Skares, and that he had met Isy Cay when he returned to the village to claim the salvage.[265] Isy died aged 82 in April 1946 and is buried in St James's churchyard near Cruden Bay.

Whinnyfold seems an unlikely place for a fishing village, located as it is on a cliff top facing a rocky coastline above the reefs of the Skares. There is no harbour here, only a pebbly beach to drag the boats up onto. The fishermen were there because earlier in the nineteenth century as the herring boom took hold, any location that could be feasibly used for a fishing village was settled in, even if that looks rather unlikely now.

They had noticed back then that in amongst the rocks were two deep channels leading up to the pebbly beach. Bram described these as 'natural channels with straight edges as though cut on purpose for the taking in of the cobbles belonging to the fisherfolk of Whinnyfold.' These trochs (troughs), as they were called in the local dialect, provide direct access to the sea. It wasn't an ideal location because getting in and out was dangerous during bad weather; many fishing days were lost as a result.

Another drawback was that fishing tackle and baskets had to be lugged up and down a zigzag path cut into the side of the cliff. It runs 'down to the stony beach far below where the fishers keep their boats and which is protected from almost the wildest seas by the great black rock—the Caudman,—which fills the middle of the little bay...' The women of the village trudged down to fetch the fish from the boats and then up again after loading them into creels on their backs.

Elsie remembers the fishermen and women baiting the lines outside their houses or in their sheds if the weather was not great. She collected limpets from the rocks on the shore, using a chisel to prise them off. 'All the children did that'. When the boats returned the fish was carried up the zigzag path and stored in 'farlins', boxes lined up in a row along the side of the road. Lorries regularly came to pick up the fish.

She was proud of the fishermen's skills, particularly in negotiating the reefs of the Skares on their way out to sea. 'They knew where all the rocks were and kept clear of them'. I asked her about the local superstitions. The fishermen would not mention salmon, and did not like to meet a minister or a black cat on the way to the boats. They were comfortable with meeting women on the way; indeed the practicalities involved with fishing off Whinnyfold meant that the womenfolk had to help out in lugging creels up and down the zigzag path.

It's possible that Bram visited the Crookit Lum Cottage more than once, although there is no clear evidence that he did. One of his biographers, Barbara Belford, states that he used the cottage from as early as 1902 - this is incorrect.[266] He was renting Hilton Cottage up until at least 1904.

The reason for the move to Whinnyfold was probably financial. Port Erroll was undergoing a short boom as a holiday resort with a high demand for quality accommodation. As such the summer rates had probably increased for the let of Hilton Cottage at a time when Bram Stoker could least afford it.

Less expensive accommodation was available in the area. The demand from summer visitors had prompted the let of several private houses in Port Erroll and Whinnyfold. My neighbour Ann Findlay had been told by her mother that this was common practice locally, and when 'the toffs came' the residents would move into the sheds they used for storing fishing equipment. Some were large sheds equipped with fire places so it wasn't necessarily a hardship.

A guide to Cruden Bay, written in 1908, gives a list of properties to let. Bram Stoker could easily have picked a cottage to rent in Port Erroll and one less expensive than Hilton Cottage. I suspect there were other reasons why he chose the Crookit Lum cottage in Whinnyfold. Cruden Bay was getting too busy, and may not have provided the peace and seclusion that Bram needed to write his books. I also reckon that Whinnyfold was his favourite spot in the Cruden Bay area.

Apart from visitors to Isy's teashop, Bram would have found plenty of peace and quiet in Whinnyfold during the summer months. Normally a busy place with a population of 119 recorded in the 1901 census, there would have been no fishermen around during August. Between mid May and the end of August the men left the village for the summer herring season and rented accommodation in Peterhead.

He needed that peace and quiet. He was recuperating after a winter of illness. Mrs Cruickshank from the Port Erroll Post

Office recalls visiting him in Whinnyfold. 'It was plain to see he was very ill.'[267] Local resident George Hay mentions how Bram Stoker would lie in a hammock for hours at a time staring at the Skares. On other occasions he would rise up and go for a walk along Cruden Bay beach, 'the tall, bearded Irishman, his cloak flying in the wind tamping about the heavy sand, prodding it with the heavy stick, waving his arm and shouting at the great rollers as they thundered up the beach, and altogether behaving in such an outlandish way that George's second cousin, Eliza, who worked at the Kilmarnock Arms, was afraid to walk home across the sands to Whinnyfold, and took the long way round.' These observations tie in with a comment by his biographer and relative of Bram Stoker, Daniel Farson, who was told by his mother that by this stage he was 'rather dotty.' When Farson queried this, she replied, 'Well, really very dotty.'[268]

Despite his illness Bram was able to write. According to Harry Ludlam his publishers had asked for a new thriller, and he started writing *The Lair of the White Worm* at Whinnyfold.[269] Two Victorian inkpots were discovered on the old Whinnyfold village rubbish dump in the 1970s raising speculation they had once belonged to him.

Bram was in a bad way in 1910 and it was his last visit north. He became increasingly bed-bound in his later years and died at the age of 64 on the 20th April 1912. His body was cremated and the ashes are kept in an urn at Golders Green Cemetery in London. The author of *Dracula* died unaware that he would become famous in the years ahead.

The obituaries in the newspapers were brief and focussed mainly on his work with Henry Irving at the Lyceum Theatre. The newspapers were short of space following a major disaster which had taken place five days earlier. The Titanic had sunk after hitting an iceberg in the Atlantic Ocean en route to New York. Over 1,500 passengers and crew died.

Later in 1912 the Cruden Parish Church issued a booklet *Cruden Recipes and Wrinkles* as a souvenir for a bazaar to be held in the church grounds.[270] The recipes had been contributed by the congregation and friends. In amongst them are the 'wrinkles' – pithy phrases of wisdom and advice. Two of the

172

recipes attract attention. First up is:

SAVOURY
(Mrs BRAM STOKER, 26 St George's Square, London, S.W.)
Stone some French plums. Roll each in a very thin slice of bacon (prepare them as for "angels on horseback")[2]. Fry and serve each on a fried crouton cut in an oval shape.

The second recipe is under the section 'Salads, Sauces, etc':

THE "DRACULA" SALAD
(Mrs BRAM STOKER, 26 St George's Square, London, S.W.)
Arrange alternate slices of ripe tomatoes, and ripe, purple egg-shaped plums in dish, and dress with oil and vinegar French dressing.

The recipes were included within the booklet to honour the long-standing association between Bram Stoker, Port Erroll and his novel *Dracula*. They were Florence's memorial for her late husband.

---

2 The dish "angels on horseback" is made by rolling oysters in bacon and then baking them in an oven.

Salads, Sauces, &c.

SALAD.

(Mrs PIRIE, Bank House, Lonmay).

Wash and pick two heads of lettuce. Shred them, and add the white of a hard-boiled egg cut in rings. Pound the yolk. Add a little salt, a large teaspoonful of made mustard, one breakfastcupful of cream, and a little vinegar. Mix well. Pour over the lettuce, and turn over the whole a few times wtih a spoon and fork. If liked a few slices of tomato may be added.

THE "DRACULA" SALAD.

(Mrs BRAM STOKER, 26 St George's Square, London, S.W.)

Arrange alternate slices of ripe tomatoes, and ripe, purple, egg-shaped plums in dish, and dress with oil and vinegar French dressing.

BREAD SAUCE.

(Mrs J. SMITH, Easterton, Peterhead).

½ pint milk.	2 cloves.
1 small onion.	2 oz. bread crumbs.
Pepper and salt.	1 oz. butter.

Stick the cloves in the onion. Put the milk in a saucepan. Add the onion, and set at the side of stove for half an hour. Warm it, but do not boil. Shake out the onion and add the crumbs, butter, salt, and a good pinch of pepper. Stir until the bread crumbs have absorbed the milk.

174

15
'FATHER AND BROTHER AND WIFE TO HIS SOUL'

Two questions were asked at the start of the book. How did Bram Stoker come to write *Dracula*? And what was in the mind of the man who wrote it? The previous chapters deal with the writing of *Dracula*. The following chapters address the second question: What was in his mind?

The straightforward answer is that we don't know for sure, Bram left no memoirs or diaries that might have revealed these. However, what was not in the uppermost thoughts of our author was an obvious tendency to dwell on the evil and the morbid. Bram was a jolly fellow full of jokes.

The huge influence on Bram Stoker's thoughts has always been in plain sight to anyone acquainted with his life story: namely the poems and writings of Walt Whitman. The enthusiastic reader with a lot of spare time can demonstrate this for themselves by first browsing through the poems of Walt Whitman and then reading Bram Stoker's books. Although Bram rarely cites Walt Whitman, his books contain many allusions to his poetry. These include echoes of lines in the poems, episodes used to provide incidents in the novels, passages influenced by Whitman's spiritual outlook and in one instance in *The Jewel of Seven Stars*, a long section of descriptive writing which copies the style of a Walt Whitman poem.

Dennis Perry's technical paper *Whitman's Influence on Stoker's Dracula* notes that Count Dracula sometimes speaks in a way that is characteristic of the rhythm and balance of Walt Whitman's verse.[271] The poet wrote in a manner influenced by the style of Biblical prose and Bram imitates this. For example, Count Dracula tells Jonathan Harker in Transylvania: 'Here I am noble. I am Boyar. The common people know me, and I am master. But a stranger in a strange land, he is no one. Men know him not – and to know not is to care not for.'[272]

One of Bram's books stands out for its intimate connection to Walt Whitman's poetry - *The Mystery of the Sea*. Published in

1902, it appears to capture much of what was in Bram's mind at the time. The main character is a barely-disguised version of himself, and reveals what appears to be Bram's mystical musings about nature and the supernatural. The novel is a celebration of Bram's passion for the Cruden Bay area together with his admiration for Walt Whitman. Although Whitman isn't mentioned in the novel, it's the Bram Stoker book above all that abounds with references to his poetry.

Before discussing *The Mystery of the Sea* in detail, I'll start by giving a summary as to how Walt Whitman saw the universe and his place in it. Bear in mind that Bram appears to have shared the same outlook.

Walt Whitman's poetry is difficult. At first glance the poems appear simple enough to understand - he uses plain words in plain sentences. Read on and you will find a long series of evocative images which appear to fuse into a world view, but what exactly is the poet getting at? Walt Whitman once said that only a few, very few, managed to get the meaning. It was deliberately concealed and sometimes left obscure on purpose. As he explained:

> There is something in my nature *furtive* like an old hen!
> You see a hen wandering up and down a hedgerow,
> looking apparently quite unconcerned, but presently she
> finds a concealed spot, and furtively lays an egg, and
> comes away as though nothing had happened! That is
> how I felt in writing *Leaves of Grass*.[273]

The poems express Walt Whitman's mystical views about human beings and their interaction with both the material and the largely-hidden spiritual world. Now I'm not an expert on the subject, so I've been helped by reading books about Walt Whitman's poetry and by friends who 'get the poetry' because it accords with how they see things.

His biographers note that the young Walt Whitman was in the prime of health. He took care to avoid what he considered to be unhealthy fare such as alcohol, tobacco and coffee. It was also important for him to keep his soul healthy; he deliberately avoided the trappings of wealth acquisition and ducked out of any fraught relations with his fellows.[274] This glowing sense of fitness prompted him to believe that the human body was god-like; he could feel it glow within him. From there, he took the logical leap that if his god-like being was part of the universe, then the entirety of the universe is equivalent to God and he was part of God.

To feel god-like is a supreme sensation. His great poem *Song of Myself* starts: 'I celebrate myself and sing myself.' It salutes total and uncritical self-acceptance:

Welcome is every organ and attribute of me, and of any man hearty and clean,

Not an inch nor a particle of an inch is vile, and none shall be less familiar than the rest.

I am satisfied — I see, dance, laugh, sing...

It's a triumphantly joyful outlook for the human spirit.

One more demon had to be slain before Whitman could rejoice in all that is gloriously human and godlike. He ignored the gloomy sermons of the Christian Church whose ministers preached that the body is the source of all sin. According to his biographer Gay Wilson Allen, Whitman had been much influenced by reading *A Few Days in Athens* by Frances Wright (who was born in Dundee). Frances had set out in her book to explain the ideas of the ancient Greek philosopher Epicurus. The core message is that humans should strive to enjoy life and be happy. In this view, good is that which yields pleasure, evil is what brings pain. Frances Wright saw religion as perverting what she saw as the ideal purpose of all human beings; she didn't hold back:

We have named the leading error of the human mind, - the bane of human happiness – the perverter of human virtue! It is Religion – that dark coinage of trembling ignorance! It is Religion – that blind guide of human reason! It is Religion – that dethroner of human virtue! which lies at the root of all the evil and all the misery that pervade the world![275]

Gloriously celebrating the rude spirits of a healthy body and banishing the concept of sin from tainting his mortal being, Walt Whitman aimed to go through life as the rarest of creatures, a perfectly natural human being. Prejudice and selfish urges would not thwart his path. It would be a life 'that shall be copious, vehement, spiritual.'

Whitman decided that his views on spirituality would be his own and not those handed down by the clerics. He believed that the universe and everything in it are equivalent to God such that the two share a common identity. It's the pantheism we encountered in chapter five. The word 'God' is a convenient label that is used to refer to a concept which lies beyond definition. It's something vast, elusive, yet it encompasses all. 'The one' or 'the totality' could be taken as alternative labels. This is not the concept of a Christian God who is separate and distinct from the products of his creation including humans on earth.

Yet, there is room in Whitman's universe for the Christian God and all other gods and spirits too. They are encompassed by the whole. He accepted all faiths, rejecting none. If someone somewhere on earth worshipped a god or spirit, it was meaningful and real to them. And if this was meaningful to them, it was meaningful to him. He wrote in his poem *Song of Myself*:

I do not despise you priests, all time, the world over,
My faith is the greatest of faiths and the least of faiths,
Enclosing worship ancient and modern and all between ancient and modern...' [276]

And having taken in the teachings of all faiths, he wrote in *Without Antecedents*:

'I adopt each theory, myth, god, and demi-god,
I see that the old accounts, bibles, genealogies, are true, without exception...

Keep this in mind, because it's a view that provided a big influence on Bram Stoker as we will see later.

In a universe that is identical to a totality or 'God' humans have a privileged place. They are self conscious and aware of all that surrounds them. In his poetry Whitman developed the theme that everyone has a god-like presence that manifests itself everywhere. He would imagine himself and the reader soaring through space and time as a means of connecting with a greater understanding of the totality. He wanted to feel his body becoming utterly immersed within the universe; to encounter the

178

intensity of his being streaming through existence.[277] His poetry aims to share that experience.

By way of these mystical musings, Walt Whitman was delving into the mysterious aspects of the spiritual. Yes, there is a material world in view, physical objects that can be seen and touched. Nevertheless, out there is also the spiritual essence; it's mostly hidden from our normal experience. But not quite, the soul or consciousness can find access to the spiritual essence.[278] He believed that the spiritual world interacts with the material world, and the signs of it are there if you know how to recognise them. It is important to become familiar with them. Only by comprehending the union of the body with the spiritual can one perceive the true nature of things. It's a common message in many eastern religions.

His outlook differs from eastern religious thought in that Whitman sought to connect with the spiritual realm, not through transcendental meditation or by received wisdom from gurus and saints, but through the perception of nature. To those of my friends who are in touch with this way of understanding, they tell me that it's not important how the spiritual world makes its presence known to the individual, it merely matters that it does.

Walt Whitman walked about in nature, tuned into its essence, and feeling a union with it. He wrote in his private notebook, 'The soul or spirit transmits itself into all matter - into rocks, and can live the life of a rock - into the sea, and can feel itself the sea ... into the earth - into the motions of the suns and stars.'[279] It's essentially the pagan view of nature.

Bram discovered an entire world-view in Walt Whitman's poems and connected with them. This was an outlook that led from his childhood connection with nature and progressed to an acceptance of pantheism. This encompassed and subsumed the Protestant faith of his boyhood.

Bram has given two accounts of how he discovered the poetry of Walt Whitman; the first in a letter written to Whitman, which is quoted in full below. The second is given in his book *Personal Reminiscences of Henry Irving*:

In 1868 when William Michael Rossetti brought out his Selected Poems of Walt Whitman it raised a regular

179

storm in British literary circles. The bitter-minded critics of the time absolutely flew at the Poet and his work as watch-dogs do at a ragged beggar. Unfortunately there were passages in the Leaves of Grass which allowed of attacks, and those who did not or could not understand the broad spirit of the group of poems took samples of detail which were at least deterrent. Doubtless they thought that it was a case for ferocious attack; as from these excerpts it would seem that the book was as offensive to morals as to taste.[280]

What had upset the critics of the time was the open celebration of the act of sex in the poetry. This was strong stuff for Victorian Britain, and when the Rossetti volume of poems was published here, the racier poems were left out, including the major poem *A Song of Myself*. Bram recounts the reaction in Dublin:

In my own University the book was received with cynical laughter, and more than a few of the students sent over to Trübner's for copies of the complete *Leaves of Grass* that being the only place where they could then be had. Needless to say that amongst young men the objectionable passages were searched for and more noxious ones expected. For days we all talked of Walt Whitman and the new poetry with scorn especially those of us who had not seen the book. One day I met a man in the Quad who had a copy, and I asked him to let me look at it. He acquiesced readily: "Take the damned thing," he said; "I've had enough of it!

I took the book with me into the Park and in the shade of an elm-tree began to read it. Very shortly my own opinion began to form; it was diametrically opposed to that which I had been hearing. From that hour I became a lover of Walt Whitman.[281]

Bram Stoker wrote two fan letters to Walt Whitman, the first unsent until he wrote a second letter four years later when it was then included. Both letters are quoted here in full as is the reply he received from the poet. They are extraordinary.

Dublin, Feb. 14, 1876.

My dear Mr. Whitman.

I hope you will not consider this letter from an utter
stranger a liberty. Indeed, I hardly feel a stranger to you,
nor is this the first letter that I have written to you. My
friend Edward Dowden has told me often that you like
new acquaintances or I should rather say friends. And as
an old friend I send you an enclosure which may interest
you. Four years ago I wrote the enclosed draft of a letter
which I intended to copy out and send to you—it has lain
in my desk since then—when I heard that you were
addressed as Mr. Whitman. It speaks for itself and needs
no comment. It is as truly what I wanted to say as that
light is light.

   The four years which have elapsed have made me
love your work fourfold, and I can truly say that I have
ever spoken as your friend. You know what hostile
criticism your work sometimes evokes here, and I wage
a perpetual war with many friends on your behalf. But I
am glad to say that I have been the means of making
your work known to many who were scoffers at first.
The years which have passed have not been uneventful
to me, and I have felt and thought and suffered much in
them, and I can truly say that from you I have had much
pleasure and much consolation—and I do believe that
your open earnest speech has not been thrown away on
me or that my life and thought fail to be marked with its
impress. I write this openly because I feel that with you
one must be open. We have just had tonight a hot debate
on your genius at the Fortnightly Club in which I had the
privilege of putting forward my views—I think with
success.

   Do not think me cheeky for writing this. I only hope
we may sometime meet and I shall be able perhaps to
say what I cannot write. Dowden promised to get me a
copy of your new edition and I hope that for any other
work which you may have you will let me always be an
early subscriber. I am sorry that you're not strong. Many

of us are hoping to see you in Ireland. We had arranged to have a meeting for you. I do not know if you like getting letters. If you do I shall only be too happy to send you news of how thought goes among the men I know. With truest wishes for your health and happiness believe me,

Your friend
Bram Stoker

The original letter is as follows:

Dublin, Ireland, Feb. 18, 1872.

If you are the man I take you to be you will like to get this letter. If you are not I don't care whether you like it or not and only ask you to put it into the fire without reading any farther. But I believe you will like it. I don't think there is a man living, even you who are above the prejudices of the class of small-minded men, who wouldn't like to get a letter from a younger man, a stranger, across the world—a man living in an atmosphere prejudiced to the truths you sing and your manner of singing them. The idea that arises in my mind is whether there is a man living who would have the pluck to burn a letter in which he felt the smallest atom of interest without reading it. I believe you would and that you believe you would yourself. You can burn this now and test yourself, and all I will ask for my trouble of writing this letter, which for all I can tell you may light your pipe with or apply to some more ignoble purpose— is that you will in some manner let me know that my words have tested your impatience. Put it in the fire if you like—but if you do you will miss the pleasure of this next sentence, which ought to be that you have conquered an unworthy impulse.

A man who is uncertain of his own strength might try to encourage himself by a piece of bravo, but a man

182

who can write, as you have written, the most candid words that ever fell from the lips of mortal man—a man to whose candour Rousseau's Confessions is reticence—can have no fear for his own strength. If you have gone this far you may read the letter and I feel in writing now that I am talking to you. If I were before your face I would like to shake hands with you, for I feel that I would like you. I would like to call you Comrade and to talk to you as men who are not poets do not often talk. I think that at first a man would be ashamed, for a man cannot in a moment break the habit of comparative reticence that has become a second nature to him; but I know I would not long be ashamed to be natural before you. You are a true man, and I would like to be one myself, and so I would be towards you as a brother and as a pupil to his master. In this age no man becomes worthy of the name without an effort. You have shaken off the shackles and your wings are free. I have the shackles on my shoulders still—but I have no wings. If you are going to read this letter any further I should tell you that I am not prepared to "give up all else" so far as words go. The only thing I am prepared to give up is prejudice, and before I knew you I had begun to throw overboard my cargo, but it is not all gone yet.

I do not know how you will take this letter. I have not addressed you in any form as I hear that you dislike to a certain degree the conventional forms in letters. I am writing to you because you are different from other men. If you were the same as the mass I would not write at all. As it is I must either call you Walt Whitman or not call you at all—and I have chosen the latter course. I don't know whether it is usual for you to get letters from utter strangers who have not even the claim of literary brotherhood to write you. If it is you must be frightfully tormented with letters and I am sorry to have written this. I have, however, the claim of liking you—for your words are your own soul and even if you do not read my letter it is no less a pleasure to me to write it. Shelley wrote to William Godwin and they became friends. I am not Shelley and you are not Godwin and so I will only hope that sometime I may meet you face to face and perhaps shake hands with you. If I ever do it will be one of the greatest pleasures of my life.

If you care to know who it is that writes this, my name is Abraham Stoker (Junior). My friends call me Bram. I live at 43 Harcourt St., Dublin. I am a clerk in the service of the Crown on a small salary. I am twenty-four years old. Have been champion at our athletic sports (Trinity College, Dublin) and have won about a dozen cups. I have also been President of the College Philosophical Society and an art and theatrical critic of a daily paper. I am six feet two inches high and twelve stone weight naked and used to be forty-one or forty-two inches round the chest. I am ugly but strong and determined and have a large bump over my eyebrows. I have a heavy jaw and a big mouth and thick lips— sensitive nostrils—a snubnose and straight hair. I am equal in temper and cool in disposition and have a large amount of self control and am naturally secretive to the world. I take a delight in letting people I don't like— people of mean or cruel or sneaking or cowardly disposition—see the worst side of me. I have a large number of acquaintances and some five or six friends— all of which latter body care much for me.

Now I have told you all I know about myself. I know you from your works and your photograph, and if I know anything about you I think you would like to know of the personal appearance of your correspondents. You are I know a keen physiognomist. I am a believer of the science myself and am in an humble way a practiser of it. I was not disappointed when I saw your photograph— your late one especially. The way I came to like you was this. A notice of your poems appeared some two years ago or more in the Temple Bar magazine. I glanced at it and took its dictum as final, and laughed at you among my friends. I say it to my own shame but not to my

184

regret for it has taught me a lesson to last my life out—without ever having seen your poems. More than a year after I heard two men in College talking of you. One of them had your book (Rossetti's edition) and was reading aloud some passages at which both laughed. They chose only those passages which are most foreign to British ears and made fun of them. Something struck me that I had judged you hastily. I took home the volume and read it far into the night. Since then I have to thank you for many happy hours, for I have read your poems with my door locked late at night, and I have read them on the seashore where I could look all round me and see no more sign of human life than the ships out at sea: and here I often found myself waking up from a reverie with the book lying open before me.

I love all poetry, and high generous thoughts make the tears rush to my eyes, but sometimes a word or a phrase of yours takes me away from the world around me and places me in an ideal land surrounded by realities more than any poem I ever read. Last year I was sitting on the beach on a summer's day reading your preface to the Leaves of Grass as printed in Rossetti's edition (for Rossetti is all I have got till I get the complete set of your works which I have ordered from America). One thought struck me and I pondered over it for several hours—"the weather-beaten vessels entering new ports," you who wrote the words know them better than I do: and to you who sing of your own land of progress the words have a meaning that I can only imagine. But be assured of this, Walt Whitman—that a man of less than half your own age, reared a conservative in a conservative country, and who has always heard your name cried down by the great mass of people who mention it, here felt his heart leap towards you across the Atlantic and his soul swelling at the words or rather the thoughts.

It is vain for me to try to quote any instances of what thoughts of yours I like best—for I like them all and you must feel that you are reading the true words of one who feels with you. You see, I have called you by your name. I have been more candid with you—have said more about myself to you than I have ever said to any one before. You will not be angry with me if you have read so far. You will not laugh at me for writing this to you. It was with no small effort that I began to write and I feel reluctant to stop, but I must not tire you any more. If you ever would care to have more you can imagine, for you have a great heart, how much pleasure it would be to me to write more to you. How sweet a thing it is for a strong healthy man with a woman's eyes and a child's wishes to feel that he can speak so to a man who can be if he wishes father, and brother and wife to his soul.

I don't think you will laugh, Walt Whitman, nor despise me, but at all events I thank you for all the love and sympathy you have given me in common with my kind.

Bram Stoker

He received a reply from the poet:

March 6, '76.
My dear young man,

Your letters have been most welcome to me—welcome to me as Person and as Author—I don't know which most—You did well to write me so unconventionally, so fresh, so manly, and so affectionately, too. I too hope (though it is not probable) that we shall one day meet each other. Meantime I send you my friendship and thanks.

Edward Dowden's letter containing among others your subscription for a copy of my new edition has just been received. I shall send the books very soon by express in a package to his address. I have just written E.

186

D.

My physique is entirely shattered—doubtless permanently, from paralysis and other ailments. But I am up and dressed, and get out every day a little. Live here quite lonesome, but hearty, and good spirits.

Write to me again.
Walt Whitman

Years later he would meet the poet in person on three separate occasions while on tour in the United States with the Lyceum Theatre Company. He described the first encounter:

When it came to my own turn to have a chat with Walt Whitman I found him all that I had ever dreamed of, or wished for in him: large-minded, broad-viewed, tolerant to the last degree; incarnate sympathy; understanding with an insight that seemed more than human. [282]

Bram Stoker had by this time been a Walt-Whitmanite for many a year; his poetry, a 'father, and brother and wife to his soul'.

16
THE MYSTERY OF THE SEA

Bram Stoker started writing *The Mystery of the Sea* in 1900. The novel is a mix of genres: part Gothic horror, part romance and part adventure novel. Within its pages are to be found ancient Spanish treasure, American secret agents, a villainous gang of kidnappers and a deadly shootout at sea. Much of the action takes place around Cruden Bay.

The main character, Archibald Hunter, is a barely-disguised version of the author. He shares much of Bram's autobiographical background and is an author too. The name Archibald Hunter's parallels Abraham Stoker, Bram Stoker's full name. Both have the same number of syllables in their first and second names; and the surnames end in 'er'. Could this have been the author's reaction to his experiences while writing *Dracula* when he became obsessed with the spirit of the novel and freaked out his family? If this time round he portrayed himself in the guise of the main character it would avoid the problem!

The Mystery of the Sea opens with a dramatic scene outside the Kilmarnock Arms Hotel in Port Erroll where Archibald Hunter is staying on holiday. Archibald is sitting on a wall next to the bridge when he sees a small group of people walking along the road; two women are being led by a man carrying a child's coffin. On the other side of the road stands an old woman who stares intently at him as he watches the grim procession. She crosses over and talks to him; her name is Gormala and she makes Archibald aware that he has a special gift. The small coffin carried along the road is bearing the body of a child drowned in the harbour; only this dreadful accident hasn't happened yet. He has anticipated the tragedy through the power of second sight, a mysterious ability to predict future events.

Sometime later on a visit to Peterhead, Archibald buys an old chest at an auction. Inside it are papers, some written in Spanish with dates between 1598 and 1610, the rest written in secret code. After some effort to decipher the text, he uncovers a document written in Spanish. It reveals the location of a Spanish treasure chest which was hidden in a cave on the Buchan coast during the Spanish Armada in 1588. He searches for the treasure with the help of an American heiress, Marjory Anita Drake. They had met when he rescued her from the rocks at the south end of Cruden Bay beach. She had been trapped there by the incoming tide. It was a memorable encounter for the two of them; during the course of the novel they fall in love and get married.

A subplot involves a gang of international criminals who attempt to seize Marjory Drake. They are thwarted by the actions of Archibald Hunter with the help of American government agents. In the meanwhile, he finds the treasure chest in a cave located directly under a house he has recently built for himself near the village of Whinnyfold. A hole dug in the floor of his house allows him direct access to the cave which is otherwise blocked by a rock fall at its entrance from the sea.

The plot involving Spanish treasure is partly based on historical fact. The source material for Bram's novel is James Dalgarno's book *From the Brig O' Balgownie to the Bullers O' Buchan,* a travel guide to the Buchan coast first published in 1890. Bram Stoker had probably read this book, not the least because the book contains an advert for the Kilmarnock Arms hotel and it's likely that the proprietor James Cruickshank owned a copy. The book describes an actual shipwreck in St Catherine's Dub near Collieston, believed to be a Spanish galleon from the sixteenth century.

The ship is still there amongst the rocks at the low tide mark, and several cannons and an anchor have been recovered from the wreck. No historical record has ever been discovered to explain where the ship came from and why it ended up on the Aberdeenshire coast. It has popularly been connected to the Spanish Armada in 1588, when several ships were wrecked around the coast of the British Isles during the severe storm which broke up an intended invasion of England. However, there is no record that any Spanish ships were wrecked on the Aberdeenshire coast during the Armada. The location of the wreck, St Catherine's Dub, suggests that *St Catherine* or the Spanish equivalent, *Santa Catalina,* is the name of the ship. Two ships of that name sailed with the Armada in 1588, the *Santa Catalina* and *La Santa Catalina.* Both returned home intact.

The alternative theory is that the Spanish galleon was sent with arms and money to support a Catholic rebellion in the north of Scotland during the reign of King James VI - the stirrings of which took place six years after the Armada. It's plausible because the site of the wreck is just over a mile from the castle of Old Slains, the residence of Francis Earl of Erroll. The earl was an ardent supporter of the Catholic cause.

One of the curiosities of Dalgarno's book is that it also mentions the discovery of a hoard of coins on farmland near Collieston, a short distance from the location of the shipwrecked Spanish galleon. The farmer found 297 old coins over an interval of 14 years, mostly old Scottish and English coins dating from the seventeenth and eighteenth centuries. According to Dalgarno these included 'an untarnished Spanish dollar of date 1555 and likely a relic of the Armada.'[283] A Spanish dollar and a relic of the Armada! But there is an alternative explanation as to why the coin was present in the hoard. Scotland in the eighteenth century was impoverished with only a small number of native coins in circulation. To keep commerce going numerous foreign coins were also used.[284] But let's not spoil the story too much. The elements for a mystery are present, a Spanish galleon and a hint of missing treasure.

The action in *The Mystery of the Sea* returns again and again to one particular landmark, the deadly reefs of the Skares near Whinnyfold. Bram was obsessed with them. The reporter Gordon Casely relates how Port Erroll residents told him that Bram Stoker would, 'stand on the cliffs above Whinnyfold staring at the breakers below.'[285] Likewise, James Drummond notes that when Bram rented a house at Whinnyfold, he would lie for hours at a time in a hammock looking over toward the Skares.[286]

Bram was intrigued by their geological origin. The Skares are formed from the layered rocks of the 600 million-year-old Collieston Formation – age-hardened muddy and sandy sediments originally deposited on an ancient seabed. Ancient crustal forces subsequently mangled the rock layers in the process of thrusting jagged mountains up over the primeval plains. The ancient mountains have long since gone, stripped away through millions of years of erosion by the incessant crash of sea waves and the action of fast-flowing rivers; a rock grain here and a rock grain there breaking loose, and on the continuance of this action over the aeons the mountains vanished, their inner core now exposed to view.

The Skares lie close to the edge of the Peterhead granite, the salmon-pink-coloured rock that forms the coastal scenery around Cruden Bay and along the cliffs further north. The boundary between the granite and the ancient layered rocks is seen in the cliffs 300 yards north of Whinnyfold. The granite was once red-hot molten magma which formed deep within the ancient mountain range 400 million years ago. Lighter than the surrounding rock layers, the incandescent liquid squeezed up forcibly through them, eventually cooling to form rock itself. You can still see where fragments of sedimentary rock have been caught up in the molten magma as it moved violently upwards. The rocky reefs of the Skares have formed just to the south of the edge of the granite mass.

These subterranean convulsions greatly impressed Bram Stoker: 'That union must have been originally a wild one; there are evidences of an upheaval which must have shaken the earth to its centre. Here and there are great masses of either species of rock hurled upwards in every conceivable variety of form...'

Past forces had exerted their impact on the present day by having formed the deadly reefs of the Skares. The evidence for crustal upheaval in the geological past makes for a theme that Bram repeats in his novels. For instance, in *The Lair of the White Worm* he writes: 'the geologic age—the great birth and growth of the world, when natural forces ran riot, when the struggle for existence was so savage...'[287] One is reminded of the description of Count Dracula's lair as 'full of strangeness of the geologic and chemical world'.[288] I suspect that Bram took evidence for geological convulsions as a tell-tale sign that a hot spot of mystic and savage forces was present in the surrounding area.

The Skares are the setting for a set piece of gothic horror in chapter five of *The Mystery of the Sea*. It's Lammas eve – July 31st – and the night before Lammas-tide, the traditional start of the harvest. The full moon is out and Archibald Hunter has taken a stroll over the dunes and along the cliff-top path to Whinnyfold. He comes into sight of the moon-lit rocky reefs of the Skares. Gormala has turned up and points to a fishing boat passing through. It is piloted by Lauchlane Macleod, a fisherman who Archibald Hunter had previously met on a quay in Peterhead Harbour.

The mast of the boat suddenly breaks, the fisherman is in the water and desperately swimming for his life amongst the deadly rocks. He cries as he strikes his arm against a sunken rock and injures it. 'Then he commenced a mad struggle for life, swimming without either arm in that deadly current which grew faster and faster every moment. He was breathless, and now and again his head dipped; but he kept on valiantly.' It was hopeless though, 'he struck his head against another of the sunken rocks. For an instant he raised it, and I could see it run red in the glare of the moonlight.'

This dramatic episode is not the product of Bram's imagination; it was inspired by the poem *Sleepers* in Walt Whitman's *The Leaves of Grass*. Here is the equivalent scene in the poem:

> I see a beautiful gigantic swimmer, swimming naked through the eddies of the sea,
> His brown hair lies close and even to his head--he strikes out with courageous arms--he urges himself with his legs,
> I see his white body--I see his undaunted eyes,
> I hate the swift-running eddies that would dash him head-foremost on the rocks.
>
> What are you doing, you ruffianly red-trickled waves?
> Will you kill the courageous giant? Will you kill him in the prime of his middle age?
>
> Steady and long he struggles,
> He is baffled, bang'd, bruis'd--he holds out while his strength holds out,
> The slapping eddies are spotted with his blood--they

bear him away--they roll him, swing him, turn him,
His beautiful body is borne in the circling eddies, it is continually bruis'd on rocks,
Swiftly and out of sight is borne the brave corpse. [289]

When Archibald Hunter retrieves the body of the dead fisherman something extraordinary then ensues: a procession of ghosts emerges from the sea, and from there they walk up the zigzag path to Whinnyfold:

Up the steep path came a silent procession of ghostly figures, so misty of outline that through the grey green of their phantom being the rocks and moonlit sea were apparent, and even the velvet blackness of the shadows of the rocks did not lose their gloom. And yet each figure was defined so accurately that every feature, every particle of dress or accoutrement could be discerned. Even the sparkle of their eyes in that grim waste of ghostly grey was like the lambent flashes of phosphoric light in the foam of moving water cleft by a swift prow. There was no need for me to judge by the historical sequence of their attire, or by any inference of hearing; I knew in my heart that these were the ghosts of the dead who had been drowned in the waters of the Cruden Skares.

The drowned ghosts 'were many for the line was of sickening length —became to me a lesson of the long flight of time.' It was 'the grim harvest of the sea' and they kept on coming:

At the first were skin-clad savages with long, wild hair matted; then others with rude, primitive clothing. And so on in historic order men, aye, and here and there a woman, too, of many lands, whose garments were of varied cut and substance. Red-haired Vikings and black-haired Celts and Phoenicians, fair-haired Saxons and swarthy Moors in flowing robes.[290]

The procession of ghosts passes along the path down to Cruden Bay beach and Archibald Hunter goes with them. They arrive at St Olaf's Well, inland amongst the sand dunes, where they disappear back into the bowels of the earth.

Some have said that the episode is based on local folklore,

it's not. When Robert Smith came to Whinnyfold in the 1990s to find stories for his travel book *One Foot in the Sea*, he talked to one of the residents. This was 80 year-old John Cay who had been born in Whinnyfold in 1911. John insisted that the ghost procession had nothing to do with any stories told in the village. This was a man whose working life involved sailing out by the Skares, day in day out. To John's mind the rocky reefs were fearful enough in their own right without having to worry about phosphoric lights and phantoms appearing out of the water.[291]

The inspiration for the ghostly procession was not from local folk lore; it too came from a scene in Walt Whitman's poem *Sleepers*:

> I am the ever-laughing - it is new moon and twilight,
>
> I see the hiding of douceurs - I see nimble ghosts whichever way I look,
>
> Cache, and cache again, deep in the ground and sea, and where it is neither ground or sea.
>
> Well do they do their jobs, those journeymen divine,
>
> Only from me can they hide nothing, and would not if they could,
>
> I reckon I am their boss, and they make me a pet besides,
>
> And surround me and lead me, and run ahead when I walk,
>
> To lift their cunning covers, to signify me with stretch'd arms, and resume the way;
>
> Onward we move! a gay gang of blackguards! with mirth-shouting music,
>
> and wild-flapping pennants of joy! [292]

The most memorable character in the book is the old woman Gormala. The name derives from a Gaelic name, Gormla or Gormlaith, meaning 'splendid princess'. J.G. Campbell, the Gaelic folklorist mentions that Gormshuil, a corruption of the first name Gormla, was a nickname given to witches in the Highlands and Islands of Scotland.[293] The hero of the novel Archibald Hunter has been granted with second sight and it's Gormala who makes him aware of this. She tells him about 'them that send forth the Voice and the seein'.' The second sight is a little bit of some great purpose, we are told.

J.G. Campbell defines second sight in his book *Witchcraft and Second Sight in the Highlands and Islands of Scotland*: 'The Gaelic name *da-shealladh* does not literally mean "the second sight," but "the two sights."' He goes on to explain: 'The vision of the world of sense is *one* sight, ordinarily possessed by all, but the world of spirits is visible only to certain persons, and the possession of this additional vision gives them "the two sights," or what comes to the same thing, "a second sight." Through this faculty they see the ghosts of the dead revisiting the earth, and the fetches, doubles, or apparitions of the living.'

Campbell explains the phrase 'apparitions of the living'. These turn up as a virtual copy of the original self and are visible to those with the second sight, yet their bodily counterparts, who may be sleeping or otherwise living their life, will be totally unaware of any of this. Nevertheless, the apparitions are connected to them somehow, either by a dramatic event that has occurred simultaneously with the vision or more often an event that is about to occur, a violent death for instance.[294]

The vision thus gives an insight into the impending fate of the person involved. If the apparition is observed in every-day clothes this is a good sign. But should they be dressed in a shroud it's clearly ominous. The higher the shroud on the body the sooner their death will occur. If the shroud covered the person's face their death was imminent. Bram was aware of this piece of lore. He used it for an anecdote he told at an after-theatre dinner party in Dundee. Bram had been invited on a shooting trip by a young Scottish earl, only to be informed by the gamekeeper that 'I see his sheet on him.' He returned the following year for another shooting party with the earl, who was still very much alive. He whispered to the gamekeeper that the earl looked perfectly healthy, only to get the reply, 'His sheet's higher up on his breast.' The earl dropped dead from an aneurism not long afterwards.[295]

He used this in *The Mystery of the Sea*, predicting the coming death of Lauchlane Macleod, the Peterhead fisherman. Archibald Hunter sees an apparition of the living man standing in front of him through the gift of second sight, 'he lay prone; limp and lifeless, with waxen cold cheeks, in the eloquent inaction of death. The white sheet—I could see now that it was a shroud—was around him up to his heart.'

The contrast is made in the novel between the old crone Gormala and Archibald Hunter's American fiancée Marjory Drake. When they meet for the first time Archibald gets the impression that, 'the New World was speaking to the Old.' Marjory is too good to be true. She is young, tall, and exceedingly beautiful with a superb figure and great dark eyes. She is sympathetic, generous of spirit, can read Archibald Hunter's moods and shows an eager intelligence. Yet, what impresses the narrator above all is her independence of mind, a readiness to be forthright and a willingness to assert her individuality with confidence. What's more she is a 'great heiress'. Her father 'left her a gigantic fortune; and her trustees have multiplied it over and over again.' She has money to spare – she has given a battleship to the American Government we are told.

The Mystery of the Sea was well-received when it came out in 1902. Arthur Conan Doyle, author of the Sherlock Holmes stories, was impressed. He wrote to Bram Stoker: 'My dear Bram - I found the story admirable. It has not the fearsomeness of "Dracula" but it is beautifully handled and the girl very admirable indeed.' He added below his signature: 'I've done a bit in cryptograms myself, but that knocks me out!' [296]

But what exactly is the mystery of the sea? The final chapters suggest several answers. The straight-forward solution to the mystery involved the cracking of the secret cipher and the discovery of the hidden Spanish treasure in a cave at Whinnyfold.

But nature also appears to be writing in a secret code. It was the topic of one of Walt Whitman's last poems before he died in 1892, and it was given the title: *Shakspere-Bacon's Cipher* (don't worry about Whitman's spelling of Shakespeare!). It contains the lines:

In every object, mountain, tree, and star--in every birth and life,
As part of each--evolv'd from each--meaning, behind the ostent,

196

A mystic cipher waits infolded.[297]

I suspect this is the true theme of the novel. *The Mystery of the Sea* is Bram Stoker's homage to both Walt Whitman and the natural environment in Cruden Bay. He drops a hint in the book about the Whitman influence; he mentions that the secret cipher which led to the discovery of the Spanish treasure in the novel was encrypted with a cipher invented by the sixteenth century English scientist Francis Bacon.

The various characters in the novel find their own solution to the mystery. Gormala solves her version of the mystery at her death, when she experiences her soul flying into the air, leaving her body behind. Archibald Hunter, by the means of second sight, grabs Gormala's body as she dies and experiences her spirit floating into the air. In this way he is able to see a panoramic view of the coastline of Cruden Bay from up on high, in much the same way as Walt Whitman's fancy takes to the air and flies around in his poetry. The meaning of what has happened to Gormala is clear - the soul survives death.

The mystery of the sea is also revealed to both Archibald Hunter and Marjory Drake. They have both made it to the end of the tale after having overcome near-death experiences. They conclude that the meaning of life is to love and be loved; death is nothing much to worry about.

Others are not so lucky.

The storm continued for a whole day, growing rougher and wilder with each hour. For another day it grew less and less, till finally the wind had died away and only the rough waves spoke of what had been. Then the sea began to give up its dead.[298]

This was also the underlying theme of Bram's previous Port Erroll novel *The Watter's Mou'*: 'The Angry Waters – which 'wishes ill to person & kills them then murmurs sorrowfully for ever.'[299] The pagan idea of the spirit of the sea comes to the fore again.

17

BRAM STOKER'S UNIVERSE

What was in the mind of the man who wrote *Dracula*? Or to put the question another way: how did Bram Stoker see the universe and his place in it? I've assumed that the author put his world view into his novels and expressed it through his characters. The views of the characters can then be used to paint a picture of Bram's metaphysical universe. Like any assumption it helps if the question is asked – why might it be wrong? An obvious answer is that the views of a fictional character are not necessarily those of the author: for example, writers of detective novels are not murderers. I would, nevertheless, back up my proposition by noting that the views expressed by Bram Stoker's characters are consistent across his novels and occasionally turn up in his non-fiction books. So let's see where this takes us.

In my opinion one book above all contains an abundance of clues to how Bram Stoker saw everything – it's *The Mystery of the Sea* again. The hero of the novel, Archibald Hunter, is awakened by his experiences in the Cruden Bay area. 'All the forces of life and nature became exposed to my view', he tells us.

Nature is the key to understanding Bram Stoker. Archibald Hunter continuously brings up variations on a single phrase again and again throughout the novel. The phrase is 'heaven and earth and sea and air', and it is sourced from the first line of a hymn written by the German psalmist Joachim Neander in 1680. Celebrating God and nature, its themes probably reflect how Bram felt during his daily walks along the shore. One can imagine him marching along Cruden Bay beach lustily singing the hymn:

Heaven and earth, and sea and air,
All their Maker's praise declare;
Wake, my soul, awake and sing:
Now thy grateful praises bring.

See the glorious orb of day

Breaking through the clouds his way;
Moon and stars with silvery light
Praise Him through the silent night.

See how He hath everywhere
Made this earth so rich and fair;
Hill and vale and fruitful land,
All things living, show His hand.

Lord, great wonders workest Thou!
To Thy sway all creatures bow;
Write Thou deeply in my heart
What I am, and what Thou art.

Archibald Hunter / Bram Stoker sense a spiritual significance to nature. The novel hints that the feelings are more pagan than Christian: the natural environment seems aware, alive perhaps. We are told of a mystical experience in *The Mystery of the Sea*:

The weather had changed to an almost inconceivable degree. The bright clear sky of the morning had become darkly mysterious, and the wind had died away to an ominous calm. Nature seemed altogether sentient, and willing to speak directly to a man in my own receptive mood... The sea before me took odd, indefinite shape. It seemed as though it was of crystal clearness, and that from where I gazed I could see all its mysteries. That is, I could see so as to know there were mysteries, though what they were individually I could not even dream. The past and the present and the future seemed to be mingled in one wild, chaotic, whirling dream, from the mass of which thoughts and ideas seemed now and again to fly out unexpectedly on all sides as do sparks from hot iron under the hammer. Within my heart grew vague indefinite yearnings, aspirations, possibilities. There came a sense of power so paramount that instinctively I drew myself up to my full height and became conscious of the physical vigour within me. As I did so I looked around and seemed to wake from a dream.

Naught around me but the drifting clouds, the silent

199

darkening land and the brooding sea.[300]

I can share a similar experience. Archibald Hunter saw all this from the road near Stirling Hill between Cruden Bay and Peterhead; I had been walking on Ward Hill above Port Erroll Harbour in the mid afternoon. Because I was high up I couldn't hear the sound of the waves, and there was no wind that day. It was eerily quiet except for the occasional bird clucking every now and again. Ward Hill provides a great vantage point to see a wide expanse of the sea for miles around. One also gets an impressive sense of the big sky that lies above. That day it was a dark grey sky full of voluminous black clouds. The grey-black sea was reflecting the colour of the sky. What made this experience so weird was that I could clearly see all the signs of a storm, yet there was no sound, no wind. The big black clouds were not moving at all.

My mind was boggling that afternoon, and I experienced similar perceptions to those of Archibald Hunter, a sky that was 'darkly mysterious' combined with an 'ominous calm'. I even felt a brooding presence, explaining it to myself as a psychological trick. The clouds were low in the sky and seemed to be enclosing me. My next thought was rational; it might be a good idea to go back home and take the washing in because it looked as if a storm was about to break. I was right about that.

Archibald Hunter went all mystical. 'Nature seemed altogether sentient, and willing to speak directly to a man in my own receptive mood.' The idea that nature is sentient and intent on communicating something to the author is a recurring theme of *The Mystery of the Sea*. It is also a vital part of Walt Whitman's poetry.

According to Gay Wilson Allen in his book *The Solitary Singer*, Walt Whitman walked the shore and looked at the stars genuinely believing that nature was speaking the answer to him in a literal sense; the sounds of moving water and the wind were part of the conversation. To understand this is to understand the imagery in much of his poetry.

What message is nature communicating? It's not in any language that humans can understand. Nature is acting to create a mood in much the same way that music creates a mood. The

200

message from nature is 'I am here'. By the act of communicating nature is signalling that it is sentient. Because it has made a statement, there is also the suggestion that nature has intent by doing so: that the recipient is considered worthy of contact within the grand scheme of things. It's all very pagan - this sense of a spirituality within nature.

Walt Whitman could only partly grasp the meaning of the message provided by the natural world. It was trying to draw him in to something - but to what? His hunch was that he had been granted with a purpose, and that this purpose involved growing into an increasing spiritual awareness of the universe. By this means he would achieve a degree of increasing purity over infinite time (and beyond physical death). His essence would then approach a state of god-like completeness. He sensed what this meant in practice. The greatest happiness of all is to love and to be loved. It is the totality of everything.

Archibald Hunter also appears to have believed that nature is sentient and was communicating to him with its various sounds. I'll quote three different passages from *The Mystery of the Sea* to make the point:

1) 'As one went through the country the murmur or rush of falling water was forever in the ears. I suppose it was in my own case partly because I was concerned in the mere existence of Lammas floods that the whole of nature seemed so insistent on the subject.'

2) 'The spirits of earth and sea and air seemed to take shape to me, and all the myriad sounds of the night to have a sentient cause of utterance.'

3) '...natural sounds such as the rustle of trees, the plash of falling water, or the roar of breaking waves wake into a new force that strikes on the ear with a sense of intention or conscious power.'[301]

I suspect that the coastal scenery around Cruden Bay strongly reminded Bram of the themes in the poetry of Walt Whitman. When you walk along Cruden Bay beach all alone with your thoughts, the constant sensation is the sound of the waves as they fall on the beach. The beach is shaped like an amphitheatre, and the sand dunes that border them form a wall that faintly echoes the sound. One of Whitman's poems in the *Leaves of Grass* comes to mind. The poem is *Out of the Cradle Endlessly Rocking*, and it tells the tale of what appears to have been a childhood experience when Whitman lived on Long Island in New York State. It is a poem that resonates in several of Bram Stoker's books and appears to have been of great importance to him.

Out of the Cradle Endlessly Rocking starts with a young boy walking along a beach. On the shore next to the beach he finds a nest in a brier bush occupied by a pair of mocking birds. He returns one morning and the female bird is absent; she is never seen again and is presumably lost at sea. Her mate cries out for her all summer long.

The boy, hearing the forlorn cries of the lonesome mocking bird, is saddened and profoundly affected by their sound. The cries prompt him to ponder the deeper meaning of the experience: he thinks of loneliness and love and song. Something stirs inside him. With great intensity he realises that: 'A thousand warbling echoes have started to life within me, never to die.' He is alert to the possibility that the experience will reveal something of great importance about the universe. He asks for a clue. But it's not the lonely bird that answers - the sound comes from the waves as they encroach on the sand: 'Are you whispering it, and have been all the time, you sea-waves?' And the sea answered: 'Death, death, death, death, death.' But the words in the poem are not used in any bleak sense; the word death is 'delicious' and it's 'the word of the sweetest song'. The sound creeps up to his ears, 'laving me softly all over.' The waves making this sound are unlike the cries of the lonely and lovelorn bird.

One senses that Walt Whitman's is attempting to explain how death transcends life's harshness, and is the means by which nature takes the soul into a sweeter place.

According to James Miller in *A Critical Guide to Leaves of Grass* the seashore is the symbol of the line that separates life from death in Whitman's poetry. It is also a symbol of death itself, in that it marks where the material life ends and the spiritual begins.[302] Did Bram walk along Cruden Bay beach thinking similar thoughts? On one side solid land and the physical universe; on the other side the sea, fluid and mysterious. And between the two, the shoreline that he tracked as he walked along, the waves sounding out a message to him.

I walk along the same beach every day trying to imagine what Bram Stoker was thinking when he walked there some 120 years ago. My suspicion is yes: Bram believed in a mystical universe, that land is the realm of the material world and the sea is the living embodiment of the spiritual world. It's essentially the age-old pagan belief of the Port Erroll fishermen; that a nameless spirit resides in the sea. That sea could become the angry sea. In *Dracula* we read: 'The waves rose in growing fury, each over-topping its fellow, till in a very few minutes the lately glassy sea was like a roaring and devouring monster.' Evocative writing perhaps – nevertheless, where a comparable sentiment appears in Bram's other novels it comes across as more than merely an expressive simile.

What sound do the waves make? Walt Whitman had the answer: the waves communicate a message from the spiritual world to the material world beyond the shore. But what did Bram think? The topic turned up in a conversation between Bram and his friend, the famous poet, Alfred, Lord Tennyson. Tennyson wrote plays as a sideline from his poetry. Henry Irving had secured the rights to stage one of the plays, *Becket* – a drama about the twelfth century archbishop who was murdered in Canterbury Cathedral.

In April 1892, Bram travelled to the Isle of Wight to meet the poet and to suggest some changes to the play. A crowd scene at Northampton Castle came up for discussion. Irving had asked for a rousing speech to be inserted at this point for dramatic effect. It would gain the support of the crowd kneeling before him. Tennyson asked Bram: 'But where am I to get such a speech?'

Bram describes what happened next:

As we sat we were sheltered by the Downs from the sea which thunders night and day under one of the highest cliffs in England. I pointed out towards the Downs and said: "There it is! In the roar of the sea!"

The idea was evidently already in his mind ; and when he sent up to Irving a few days later the new material the mighty sound of the surge and the blast were in his words.[303]

The 82 year old poet was frail and died seven months later. He clearly had not read Walt Whitman's poem or he would have understood the allusion.

The sound of the waves is found repeatedly as a theme in Bram Stoker's novels. In *The Mystery of the Sea* he describes the thoughts of the novel's hero Archibald Hunter as he walks along Cruden Bay beach with his beloved Marjory Drake:

> Unconsciously we walked close together and in step; and were silent, wrapt in the beauty around us. To me it was a gentle ecstasy. To be alone with her in such a way, in such a place, was the good of all heaven and all earth in one. And so for many minutes we went slowly on our way along the deserted sand, and in hearing of the music of the sounding sea and the echoing shore.[304]

Note that wonderful phrase, 'the music of the sounding sea and the echoing shore'. Back in 1885 Bram wrote a poem *The One Thing Needful*, and it's believed to be a tribute to Walt Whitman who was then still alive. Here's the last verse:

> One thing alone we lack. Our souls, indeed,
> Have fiercer hunger than the body's needs.
> Ah, happy they that look in loving eyes.
> The harsh world round them fades. The Master's Voice
> In sweetest music bids their souls rejoice
> And wakes an echo that never dies. [305]

The final two lines are a reference to *Out of the Cradle Endlessly Rocking*. In this poem, the waves sound 'the word of the sweetest song.' And the result of this: 'A thousand warbling echoes have started to life within me, never to die.' Bram's poem repeats the message of the Whitman poem, the ultimate meaning of the universe is love. It's a state of happiness where the 'harsh world' fades.

Near the end of *The Mystery of the Sea* Archibald and Marjory come close to death by drowning. They are trapped in a sea cave with the tide encroaching, their heads on the verge of being submerged by the water:

> "Dear one" I said "do as I wish, and I shall feel that even

death will be a happy thing, since it can help you." She said nothing but clung to me and our mouths met. I knew what she meant; if die we must, we should die together in a kiss.

In that lover's kiss our very souls seemed to meet. We felt that the Gates of the Unknown World were being unbarred to us, and all its glorious mysteries were about to be unveiled. In the impassive stillness of that rising tide, where never a wave or ripple broke the dreadful, silent, calm, there was no accidental fall or rise which might give added uneasiness or sudden hope. We had by this time become so far accustomed to its deadly perfection as to accept its conditions.

This recognition of inevitable force made for resignation; and I think that in those moments both Marjory and I realised the last limitations of humanity. When one has accepted the inevitable, the mere act of dying is easy of accomplishment.[306]

Walt Whitman could have written this. Death is not to be feared; it is when the spirit enters the Unknown World. Something glorious is involved in the process; it's the moment when the mysteries of the spiritual become known to the individual.

Bram had picked up from Whitman's poetry a sense that the soul is progressing into a state that is more complete, pure and god-like. And again it came from that poem *Out of the Cradle Endlessly Rocking*. Here are some extracts from Bram's novels that mimic the line in the poem: 'A thousand warbling echoes started to life within him'. It's the point when the little boy becomes aware of the spiritual aspect of nature and the significance it has for him. In Bram's novels this line is the call sign that his main character now understands the deeper significance of everything that has happened so far.

In *The Mystery of the Sea* Archibald Hunter muses: 'When I look back, it seems to me that all the forces of life and nature became exposed to my view. A thousand things which hitherto I had accepted in simple faith as facts, were pregnant with new meanings.'

In *The Jewel of the Seven Stars* Bram introduces the supernatural theme of the novel – the sentience of the ancient Egyptian spirit world – once the novel's main character Malcolm Ross has informed us:

> I began to realise more than I had yet done the strangeness of the case in which I was now so deeply concerned. When once this thought had begun there was no end to it. Indeed it grew, and blossomed, and reproduced itself in a thousand different ways.

And I have previously quoted a similar line from *The Shoulder of Shasta*, when the young girl Esse wakes up to find that, 'the full chorus of Nature proclaimed that the day had come.' The result, 'a thousand things impressed themselves on her mind.'

Professor van Helsing in *Dracula* isn't quite sure how to deal with the complex situation that confronts him: "I have been thinking, and have made up my mind as to what is best. If I did simply follow my inclining I would do now, at this moment, what is to be done. But there are other things to follow, and things that are thousand times more difficult in that them we do not know."

Bram Stoker even used this phrase in a speech. When he opened the Peterhead Flower Show in 1904, he introduced his musings on the mystical significance of flowers like this: 'A flower show was a most excellent help to social and educational progress. In a thousand different ways it helps...' [307]

So what else was in the mind of the man that wrote *Dracula?* And let's take into account his three other Victorian gothic novels, *The Jewel of Seven Stars*, *The Lady of the Shroud* and the *Lair of the White Worm*. How does his vision of the supernatural fit into his metaphysical universe?

Here's what I think. Bram Stoker's spiritual outlook appears to be more or less that of Walt Whitman: it encompassed all religions past and present and rejected none. If a religious belief was real to the person that held it, then their gods or spirits were real to Bram Stoker. That the fishermen of Port Erroll could simultaneously hold Christian and pagan beliefs would be seen as natural by Bram. He had every respect for the local fishermen, they were solid, competent and brave – these were serious people.

He thus envisaged a universe with many gods, all within the one enveloping spirit. Gormala says something like this in *The Mystery of the Sea*, that the 'Ministers o' the Doom be many an' various' and they gather as one from many ages and from the furthermost ends of the earth'. The phrase 'the Doom' in this context is defined in a later novel, *The Lair of the White Worm*: It is, 'the court from which there is no appeal.' In a universe where all gods coexist they gather together to form a committee. The 'Ministers o' the Doom' meet in the court of no appeal – and here the fate of the world and the individuals in it are decided by them. Once they have decreed what is to happen, nothing can change their minds. 'What is ordered of old will be done for true; no matter how we may try to work our own will. 'Tis little use to kick against the pricks', says Gormala.[308]

The concept of a grand committee where The 'Ministers o' the Doom' meet might explain the comment made by Bram Stoker in his non-fiction work *Personal Reminiscences of Henry Irving*:

Tennyson died on Thursday, October 6, eleven days after we had seen him... Before he died he spoke of May the spring seemed to be for him a time which the Lords of Life and Death would not allow him to pass.[309]

Every now and again Bram comes up with a phrase in his books that suggests he is fatalistic in attitude, that all in life is predestined. There is a sense of this in *Personal Reminiscences of Henry Irving*. 'More than five years elapsed before I saw Henry Irving again. We were both busy men, each in his own way, and the Fates did not allow our orbits to cross.' Note 'the Fates' here is written here with a capital F. In *The Mystery of the Sea* Gormala refers to the Fates (with a capital F) as equivalent to the 'Ministers o' the Doom'.

And what is the origin of this fatalistic attitude? Bram writes in *Dracula*: 'The fate amongst us has been sent down from the pagan world.' And yet again, a similar comment turns up in *Personal Reminiscences of Henry Irving*. Bram refers to Hamlet and his 'patient acquiescence in the ways of time - half pagan fatalism, half Christian belief - as shown in that pearl amongst

207

philosophical phrases:

> "If it be now, 'tis not to come; if it be not to come, it will be now; if it be not now, yet it will come; the readiness is all." '[310]

Whereas pagans yield to fatalism, Christians through the agency of prayer to God aim to influence the course of events.

Bram's pantheism encompassed all spiritual outlooks including both pagan and Christian. If some of the views expressed in his novels appear to be pagan, well they are. Nevertheless, it's a paganism that is wrapped up with all the other faiths in a pantheistic outlook.

A universe with many gods and spirits is the set-up for a theme of epic dimensions as outlined in *The Jewel of the Seven Stars*:

> Could we realize what it was for us modern mortals to be arrayed against the Gods of Old, with their mysterious powers gotten from natural forces, or begotten of them when the world was young... the reality of the existence of the Old Forces which seemed to be coming in contact with the New Civilization. That there were, and are, such cosmic forces we cannot doubt, and that the Intelligence, which is behind them, was and is. Were those primal and elemental forces controlled at any time by other than that Final Cause which Christendom holds as its very essence?[311]

This is Bram Stoker's big idea. The Victorian Gothic novel is set in the trappings of an ancient world with castles and instruments of torture, so why not bring in their gods and monsters too? We are told in the same novel: 'Their Gods had real existence, real power, real force.'

Make the spiritual essence of all gods real, and it adds an extra element to the story; it allows the author to contrast the new world with the old. Modern science and technology can be wielded to subdue a monster from the past. We can see science being used in the fight against Count Dracula, albeit it is Victorian science. Arrayed against the king vampire in the novel is an early version of psychiatric science, criminal profiling and research into hypnotism. But watch out! Count Dracula is smart enough to have adapted to the modern age. We read that he has studied politics, the law, finance, science and the social customs of England. He is a formidable enemy.

And in a universe where the ancient spirits can endure what does this mean for the world of mortals?

> We should be face to face with an inference so overwhelming that one hardly dared to follow it to its conclusion. This would be: that the struggle between Life and Death would no longer be a matter of the earth, earthy; that the war of supra-elemental forces would be moved from the tangible world of facts to the Mid-Region, wherever it may be, which is the home of the Gods. Did such a region exist? ...Was there room in the Universe for opposing Gods; or if such there were, would the stronger allow manifestations of power on the part of the opposing Force which would tend to the weakening of His own teaching and designs?[312]

What a grand concept! – A universe with opposing gods and a struggle for existence amongst the deities. Unfortunately there is one big flaw in the dramatic potential for a universe where gods battle for supremacy, and it was recognised close to the birth of literature in Ancient Greece. In Homer's *Iliad* the gods are immortal and they can't really do each other too much damage. And ever since then, the gods in literature have fought battles by proxy using mortal men as their foot soldiers. And so it is in Bram Stoker's gothic novels.

Today, Bram's universe frames the supernatural themes in our books and films. Because of his vision, vampires of old and the spirits of ancient Egypt walk the modern streets of popular culture.

So what was in the mind of Bram Stoker? – The words of Walt Whitman; some of the gentlest and most loving poetry ever written: sweet music to make the soul rejoice. And out of this came *Dracula*.

Bram Stoker. With permission from the Bram Stoker Estate.

Cruden Bay beach. Copyright Mike Shepherd.

The Sand Craig, Cruden Bay beach. Slains Castle is in the
background. Copyright Mike Shepherd.

Kilmarnock Arms Hotel. Copyright Mike Shepherd.

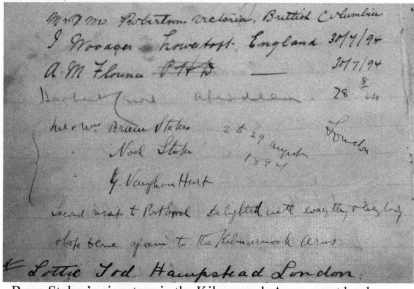

Bram Stoker's signature in the Kilmarnock Arms guest book,
1894. Photo copyright Mike Shepherd.

James Cruickshank. With permission from the Kilmarnock Arms Hotel.

Port Erroll. From Dalgarno, 1890.

The fishermen of Port Erroll. With permission of Dr Jean Kelman.

Harbour Street, 1902. With permission of Ann Findlay. Ann's mother Elizabeth is the young girl standing fourth from the left.

The estuary of the Cruden Water, Cruden Bay. Copyright Mike Shepherd.

The Watter's Mou'. 'The white cluster of rocks looked like a ghostly mouth opened to swallow whatever might come in touch.' Copyright Mike Shepherd.

Slains Castle from a 1913 picture postcard.

The Octagonal Hall in Slains Castle. With permission from Mrs George Dare.

Hilton Cottage. Bram Stoker's writing spot is on the lawn at the bottom right. Copyright Mike Shepherd.

Whinnyfold. The Crookit Lum Cottage is on the left. Copyright Mike Shepherd.

The Skares. 'Did the sea hold its dead where they fell, its floor around the Skares would be whitened with their bones, and new islands could build themselves with the piling wreckage.' Copyright Mike Shepherd.

Biography

Mike Shepherd is a geologist turned writer, so it was natural for his first foray into writing to be a geology textbook, followed by *Oil Strike North Sea*, a history of North Sea oil. The latter was nominated for the Saltire Society Scottish history book of 2016.

Dracula was written in his home village and this aroused Mike's curiosity. Nobody has ever ventured to Cruden Bay to investigate Dracula's origins in detail, tucked away, as it is, in a remote part of Scotland. That gave him all the inspiration he needed to find out more. From his investigations came a wealth of new information on an old and renowned subject. It is a fascinating story about how Bram Stoker, who otherwise mixed with the rich and famous, chose to write his books in an Aberdeenshire fishing village. Suffice to say that Mike found great joy in writing this book.

Thanks to:

Fiona-Jane Brown
Ewen Carmichael
Gordon Casely
Steve Cramphorn
Marna Cruickshank
Mrs George Dare
Steven Davie
Adelaide Duncan
Ann Findlay
Phyllis Gentle
Duncan Harley
Angus Hay
Dr Jean Kelman
Angelika and Kenny McKenzie
Jill McWilliam
Sylvia Munro
David Pybus
Michael Rochon
John and Gill Ross
Lisa and Iain Shearer
Eddie and Lindsey Savage
Adrian Smith
Sveta Shepherd
Dacre Stoker
Martin Taylor
Elsie Watt
Iulia Wright
Aberdeen Public Library
Aberdeen University Library
Aberdeenshire Libraries
Cruden Bay Public Library
National Library of Scotland
The Bram Stoker Estate
The Kilmarnock Arms Hotel

BRAM STOKER'S VISITS TO CRUDEN BAY

YEAR	EVIDENCE FOR VISIT	NOTES
1893	Ludlam	Kilmarnock Arms guest book 1894: 'Second visit to Port Erroll'.
1894	Signed Kilmarnock Arms guest book	
1895	Signed Kilmarnock Arms guest book	
1896	?	Visits Banffshire and north Aberdeenshire coast. Letters from Henry Irving.
1897	Letter from Henry Irving to Port Erroll	Visits Deeside. Letter from Henry Irving.
1898		No evidence for a visit.
1899	Letter from Henry Irving to Port Erroll	Bram Stoker in bed with pneumonia.
1900	Letter from Henry Irving to Port Erroll. Gave recital in Port Erroll Village Hall.	
1901		No evidence for a visit.
1902	Ludlam / Letter from Henry Irving to Ellen Terry, 'Stoker is in Cruden Bay'	Visits Mountblairy, Banffshire. Letter from Henry Irving.
1903	Ludlam	
1904	Opened Peterhead Flower Show / Letter from Henry Irving to Port Erroll	
1905	Letter from Henry Irving to	

	Port Erroll	
1906	Ludlam	
1907		No evidence for a visit.
1908		No evidence for a visit.
1909		No evidence for a visit.
1910	Ludlam	Stays at the Crookit Lum Cottage, Whinnyfold.

Twelve known visits to Cruden Bay.

---

1 Rev. John B. Pratt, 1901. *Buchan.* Fourth Edition, revised By Robert Anderson. Lewis Smith & Son. Aberdeen. Reverend Pratt mentions alternative derivations of the word Cruden, for instance after the old word for the Pictish kingdom, or from the Gaelic, circle on the hill, possibly referring to a circle of standing stones now removed.

2 *'She Remembers the Cheery Irishman Who Wrote Dracula.'* The People's Journal, January 5th 1963.

3 Bram Stoker obituary *Cleveland Plain Dealer* April 25, 1912 Reprinted in *The Forgotten Writings of Bram Stoker*, edited by John Edgar Browning, 2012, Palgrave MacMillan.

4 Bram Stoker, 1907. *Personal Reminiscences of Henry Irving.* William Heinemann, London.

5 Harry Ludlam, 1977. *A Biography of Bram Stoker Creator of Dracula.* New English Library.

6 Paul Murray, 2004. *From the Shadow of Dracula: A Life of Bram Stoker* Jonathan Cape.

7 Bram Stoker, 1907. *Personal Reminiscences of Henry Irving.* William Heinemann, London.

8 Bram Stoker, 1910. *Famous Imposters.* Sidgwick & Jackson.

9 Horace Wyndam, 1922. *The Nineteen Hundreds.* London: G. Allen & Unwin Ltd

10 Walt Whitman 1855, preface to *Leaves of Grass,* Brooklyn, New York.

11 Bram Stoker, 1907. *Personal Reminiscences of Henry Irving.* William Heinemann, London.

12 Bram Stoker, 1879. *The Duties of Clerks of Petty Sessions in Ireland.* John Falconer, Dublin.

13 Ken Sweeney, 2012. *Dracula Creator Bram Stoker Also had Painting in his Blood.* Independent.ie https://www.independent.ie/irish-news/dracula-creator-bram-stoker-also-had-painting-in-his-blood-26840498.html

14 Harry Ludlam, 1977. *A Biography of Bram Stoker Creator of Dracula.* New English Library.

15 *The Letters of Oscar Wilde.* Edited By Rupert Hart-Davis, 1962. Harcourt, Brace & World, Inc. New York.

16 Joseph Pearce, 2000. *The Unmasking of Oscar Wilde.* HarperCollins.

17 *'She Remembers the Cheery Irishman Who Wrote Dracula.'* The People's Journal, January 5th 1963.

18 Horace Wyndam, 1922. *The Nineteen Hundreds.* London: G. Allen & Unwin Ltd.

19 Bram Stoker, 1895. *The Shoulder of Shasta.* Archibald Constable and Co, Westminster.

20 Bram Stoker, 1895. *The Shoulder of Shasta.* Archibald Constable and Co, Westminster.

21 Bram Stoker. 'An Interview with Winston Churchill' *The World,* New York. October 5, 1907. http://www.bramstoker.org/nonfic/churchill.html

22 *Acting-Manager and Author: Bram Stoker Finds Recreation in Writing Romances.* Boston Sunday Herald April 6th 1902. Reprinted in *The Forgotten Writings of Bram Stoker*, edited by John Edgar Browning, 2012, Palgrave MacMillan.

23 H.G. Hibbert, 1916. *Fifty Years of a Londoner's Life.* Grant Richards Ltd, London.

24 Bram Stoker, 1907. *Personal Reminiscences of Henry Irving.* William Heinemann, London.

25 Terry, Ellen, 1908. The *Story of My Life: Recollections and Reflections.* London: Hutchinson.

26 Jane Stoddard. *A Chat with the Author of "Dracula".* The British Weekly, July 1897.

27 *Bram Stoker's Notes for Dracula A Facsimile Edition* Bram Stoker, Annotated and Transcribed by Robert Eighteen-Bisang and Elizabeth Miller. McFarland & Company. Jefferson, North Carolina and London.

28 Emily Gerard, 1885. *Transylvanian Superstitions.* Nineteenth Century (Vol. 18), London, July-December 1885, pp. 130-150.

29 Lokke Heiss, 1999. *Madame Dracula: The Life of Emily Gerard.* Journal of the Fantastic in the Arts, Vol. 10, No. 2 (38), P.174-186.

30 *A Chat with the Author of "Dracula".* The British Weekly, July 1897.

31 Sabine Baring-Gold, 1865. *The Book of Were-Wolves.* Smith, Elder & Co., London.

32 *Bram Stoker's Notes for Dracula A Facsimile Edition* Bram Stoker, annotated and Transcribed by Robert Eighteen-Bisang and Elizabeth Miller. McFarland & Company. Jefferson, North Carolina and London.

33 Joseph Sheridan le Fanu, 1872. *Carmilla.*

34 Henry Rider Haggard, 1886. *She.* Longmans, Green & Co., London.

35 Bram Stoker, 1907. *Personal Reminiscences of Henry Irving.* William Heinemann, London.

36 Jane Stoddard. *A Chat with the Author of "Dracula"*. The British Weekly, July 1897.

37 *Bram Stoker's Notes for Dracula A Facsimile Edition* Bram Stoker, annotated and Transcribed by Robert Eighteen-Bisang and Elizabeth Miller. McFarland & Company. Jefferson, North Carolina and London.

38 Bram Stoker, 1907. *Personal Reminiscences of Henry Irving*. William Heinemann, London.

39 Kat Long, 2017. The Charming English Fishing Village That Inspired Dracula. Mental Floss: http://mentalfloss.com/article/506367/charming-english-fishing-village-inspired-dracula#
See also the Facebook Page: Bram-Stokers-holiday-in-Whitby
https://www.facebook.com/Bram-Stokers-holiday-in-Whitby-676450659053817/

40 *Bram Stoker's Notes for Dracula A Facsimile Edition* Bram Stoker, annotated and Transcribed by Robert Eighteen-Bisang and Elizabeth Miller. McFarland & Company. Jefferson, North Carolina and London.

41 William Wilkinson, 1820. *An Account of the Principalities of Wallachia and Moldavia with Various Political Observations Relating to Them*. Longman, Hurst, Rees, Orme and Brown, London.

42 *Bram Stoker's Notes for Dracula A Facsimile Edition* Bram Stoker, annotated and Transcribed by Robert Eighteen-Bisang and Elizabeth Miller. McFarland & Company. Jefferson, North Carolina and London.

43 F.K. Robinson, 1876. *A Glossary of Words Used in the Neighbourhood of Whitby*. Trubner, London.

44 Horace Wyndam, 1922. *The Nineteen Hundreds*. G. Allen & Unwin Ltd, London.

45 Harry Ludlam, 1977. *A Biography of Bram Stoker Creator of Dracula*. New English Library.

46 Bram Stoker, 1902. *The Mystery of the Sea,* William Heinemann, London.

47 Rev. Adam Mackay, 1912. *Cruden and its Ministers*. 1912. Printed by P. Scrogie, 'Buchan Observer' Works, Peterhead.

48 Samuel Johnson, 1775. *A Journey to the Western Isles of Scotland.*

49 Bram Stoker, 1902. *The Mystery of the Sea,* William Heinemann, London.

50 Bram Stoker, 1902. *The Mystery of the Sea,* William Heinemann, London.

51 Bram Stoker, *The Crooken Sands,* in *Dracula's Guest.* 1914, George Routledge and Sons.

52 Gordon Casely interviewed 4/10/2017

54 *'She Remembers the Cheery Irishman Who Wrote Dracula.'* The People's Journal, January 5th 1963.

55 Gordon Casely interviewed 4/10/2017

56 Daniel Farson, 1975. *The Man Who Wrote Dracula. A Biography of Bram Stoker.* Michael Joseph, London.

57 Harry Ludlam, 1977. A Biography of Bram Stoker Creator of Dracula. New English Library.

58 *Acting-Manager and Author: Bram Stoker Finds Recreation in Writing Romances.* Boston Sunday Herald April 6th 1902 Reprinted in *The Forgotten Writings of Bram Stoker,* edited by John Edgar Browning, 2012, Palgrave MacMillan.

59 James Drummond, *Bram Stoker's Cruden Bay,* Scots Magazine April 1976

60 Rev. John B. Pratt, 1901. *Buchan.* Fourth Edition Revised By Robert Anderson. Lewis Smith & Son Aberdeen.

61 Ewen Carmichael, personal communication 2017. 'My memories go back to the fifties. Being brought up in the hotel gave me deep insight into the gossip, being among the local women who worked for my father. They were like surrogate mothers. It was common knowledge of his stay in the Killie. As it was tee-total at the time, Mr Cruickshank being a 'temperance mannie', Bram Stoker always had his replenishment with him. A case full. He was known to like a tipple.'

62 SP Duncan / JJ Waterman 1989 *Postal Histories* – The Postal Service in the Parish of Cruden. Unpublished document in the files of Jim Gentle.

227

63 J. A. Lillie, 1970. *Tradition and Environment*, Aberdeen University Press

64 J. A. Lillie, 1970. *Tradition and Environment*, Aberdeen University Press

65 Lord Boyd Orr, 1966. *As I Recall* MacGibbon and Kee, London

66 Gordon Casely interviewed 4/10/2017

67 *Interesting discovery of Human Remains at Port Erroll.* Buchan Observer, 17/7/1894.

68 William Ferguson, 1886. *Notes on the Seaboard of Aberdeenshire*, Scottish Geographical Magazine, 2:7

70 Bram Stoker, 1902. *The Mystery of the Sea,* William Heinemann, London.

71 Bram Stoker, 1895. *The Watter's Mou'*, A. Constable & Co., Westminster.

72 Harry Ludlam, 1977. *A Biography of Bram Stoker Creator of Dracula.* New English Library.

73 Bram Stoker, 1895. *The Watter's Mou'*, A. Constable & Co., Westminster.

74 Bram Stoker, 1902. *The Mystery of the Sea,* William Heinemann, London.

75 Bram Stoker, *The Crooken Sands*, in *Dracula's Guest.* 1914, George Routledge and Sons.

76 James Miller, 1999. *Salt in the Blood.* Canongate, Edinburgh.

77 Bram Stoker, 1902. *The Mystery of the Sea,* William Heinemann, London.

78 James Miller, 1999. *Salt in the Blood.* Canongate, Edinburgh.

79 James Miller, 1999. *Salt in the Blood.* Canongate, Edinburgh.

80 Bram Stoker, 1902. *The Mystery of the Sea,* William Heinemann, London.

81 James Miller, 1999. *Salt in the Blood.* Canongate, Edinburgh.

82 Alex. Inkson McConnochie, *Cruden Bay.* In *The Book Of Ellon*, Edited By Alex. Inkson McConnochie, Ellon, The Victoria Hall Committee, 1901.

83 J. A. Lillie, 1970. *Tradition and Environment*, Aberdeen University Press.

84 William Leslie Low, 1904. *Vignettes From A Parson's Album*. Printed and Published by Robert G, Mann at the Courier and Herald Press, Dumfries.1904.

85 James Leatham, 1937. *Fisherfolk of the North-East* Second edition. Deveron Press.

86 RF Mackenzie, 1989. *A Search for Scotland*. Collins, London.

87 *Tales of Grandfather. The Memoirs of Alexander Smith*. Edited by Dr. Alistair Smith. Leopard Magazine. June / July 1985, p.34-37.

88 Bram Stoker, *The Crooken Sands*, in *Dracula's Guest*. 1914 George Routledge and Sons.

89 Bram Stoker, 1895. *The Watter's Mou'*, A. Constable & Co., Westminster.

90 Bram Stoker, 1895. *The Watter's Mou'*, A. Constable & Co., Westminster.

91 *The Dublin Years The Lost Journal of Bram Stoker*. Edited by Elizabeth Miller and Dacre Stoker. The Robson Press, 2012.

92 Dacre Stoker, pers. comm.

93 Although not the Mrs Cruickshank quoted elsewhere.

94 *Dracula: Bram Stoker's Local Links Confirmed*. The Buchan Observer, 9th March, 1993.

96 *Minutes of the Port Erroll Hall Committee*. Copies held in Cruden Bay Public Library.

97 Buchan Observer, August 28th 1894.

98 RF Mackenzie, 1989. *A Search for Scotland*. Collins, London.

99 Henry Gray Graham, 1909. *The Social Life of Scotland in the 18th Century*. Adam and Charles Black, London.

100 Bram Stoker, 1895. *The Watter's Mou'*, A. Constable & Co., Westminster.

101 Rev. John B. Pratt , 1901. *Buchan*. Fourth Edition Revised By Robert Anderson. Lewis Smith & Son Aberdeen.

102 William Leslie Low, 1904. *Vignettes From A Parson's Album*. Printed And Published By Robert G. Mann At The Courier And Herald Press, Dumfries.

103 William Leslie Low, 1904. *Vignettes From A Parson's Album*. Printed And Published By Robert G. Mann At The Courier And Herald Press, Dumfries.

104 Quoted in: *The Critical Response to Bram Stoker*, edited by Carol. A. Senf, Greenwood press, Westport, Connecticut, London, 1993.

105 Quoted in: Harry Ludlam, 1977. *A Biography of Bram Stoker Creator of Dracula*. New English Library.

106 Bram Stoker, 1895. *The Shoulder of Shasta*. Archibald Constable and Co, Westminster.

107 Walt Whitman 1855, preface to *Leaves of Grass*. Brooklyn, New York.

108 Review of *The Shoulder of Shasta*, Athenaeum, November 1895.

110 Henry Gray Graham, 1909. *The Social Life of Scotland in the 18th Century*. Adam and Charles Black, London .

111 Ian Shepherd. The Early Peoples. In *The Grampian Book*, edited by Donald Omand, 1987. The Northern Times limited, Golspie. Richard Bradley, 2005. *The Moon and the Bonfire: An Investigation of Three Stone Circles in North-east Scotland*. Society of Antiquaries of Scotland, Edinburgh.

112 James, Rust, 1871. *Druidism Exhumed*. Edmonston & Douglas, Edinburgh.

113 John Allardyce, 1913. *Byegone Days in Aberdeenshire, Being A History of the County From a Standpoint Different From That of Previously Published Works*. The Central Press Aberdeen.

114 Henry Gray Graham, 1909. *The Social Life of Scotland in the 18th Century*. Adam and Charles Black, London.

115 Thomas Mair, 1898. *Narratives and Extracts from the Records of the Presbytery of Ellon.* W. Jolly and sons, Aberdeen.

116 James Rust, 1871. *Druidism Exhumed.* Edmonston & Douglas, Edinburgh.

117 J. M. McPherson, 1929. *Primitive Beliefs in the North-East of Scotland.* Longmans, Green And Co., London, New York, Toronto.

118 Peter F. Anson, 1965. *Fisher Folklore, Old Customs, Taboos and Superstitions Among Fisher Folk, Especially in Brittany and Normandy, and on the East Coast Of Scotland.* The Faith Press London.

119 Thomas Pennant, 1769. *A Tour in Scotland.*

120 Henry Gray Graham, 1909. *The Social Life of Scotland in the 18th Century.* Adam and Charles Black, London.

121 Rev. John B. Pratt, 1901. *Buchan.* Fourth Edition Revised By Robert Anderson. Lewis Smith & Son Aberdeen.

122 Ronald Hutton, 2013. *Pagan Britain.* Yale University Press, New Haven and London.

123 J. M. McPherson, 1929. *Primitive Beliefs in the North-East of Scotland.* Longmans, Green And Co., London, New York, Toronto.

124 J. M. McPherson, 1929. *Primitive Beliefs in the North-East of Scotland.* Longmans, Green And Co., London, New York, Toronto.

125 Thomas Mair, 1898. *Narratives and Extracts from the Records of the Presbytery of Ellon.* W. Jolly and sons, Aberdeen.

126 James Rust, 1871. *Druidism Exhumed.* Edmonston & Douglas, Edinburgh.

127 J. M. McPherson, 1929. *Primitive Beliefs in the North-East of Scotland.* Longmans, Green And Co., London, New York, Toronto.

128 J. M. McPherson, 1929. *Primitive Beliefs in the North-East of Scotland.* Longmans, Green And Co., London, New York, Toronto.

129 J. M. McPherson, 1929. *Primitive Beliefs in the North-East of Scotland.* Longmans, Green And Co., London, New York, Toronto.

130 Emily Gerard, 1885. *Transylvanian Superstitions*. The Nineteenth Century (Vol. 18), London, July-December 1885, p. 130-150.

131 Julian Goodare, Lauren Martin, Joyce Miller and Louise Yeoman, *'The Survey of Scottish Witchcraft'*, http://www.shca.ed.ac.uk/witches/ (archived January 2003, accessed November 2017.

132 Julian Goodare, Lauren Martin, Joyce Miller and Louise Yeoman, *'The Survey of Scottish Witchcraft'*, http://www.shca.ed.ac.uk/witches/ (archived January 2003, accessed November 2017.

133 Christine Larner, 1981. *Enemies of God. The Witch-hunt in Scotland.* John Hopkins University Press.

134 The reader may find this confusing. The original Slains Castle was constructed to the south of Port Erroll and the surrounding area became Slains Parish. The new Slains Castle came later, and was built near Port Erroll in the Cruden Parish.

135 Julian Goodare, 2001. *The Aberdeenshire Witchcraft Panic of 1597*. Northern Scotland. Volume 21, P.17-37.

136 Miscellany of the Spalding Club, Vol. 1. Spalding Club, Aberdeen 1841.

137 Thomas Mair, 1898. *Narratives and Extracts from the Records of the Presbytery of Ellon.* W. Jolly and sons, Aberdeen.

138 Thomas Mair, 1898. *Narratives and Extracts from the Records of the Presbytery of Ellon.* W. Jolly and sons, Aberdeen. P.360.

139 Julian Goodare, Lauren Martin, Joyce Miller and Louise Yeoman, *'The Survey of Scottish Witchcraft'*, http://www.shca.ed.ac.uk/witches/ (archived January 2003, accessed 'June 2017').

140 Barbara Belford writes that Bram Stoker was present on this journey, and he was said to have caught his first sight of Port Erroll while en route. This is unlikely, not the least because the Aberdeen Evening Express for 3/8/1887 mentions the guest list at the Marine Hotel in Nairn. These were Henry Irving, Ellen Terry and a Mrs Stirling, presumably a chaperone for Ellen Terry.

141 George Bain, 1893. *History of Nairnshire.* Publisher: Nairn Telegraph Office.

142 Henry Gray Graham, 1909. *The Social Life of Scotland in the 18th Century.* Adam and Charles Black, London.

143 Emily Gerard, 1885. *Transylvanian Superstitions.* The Nineteenth Century (Vol. 18), London, July-December 1885, pp. 130-150.

144 Bram Stoker, 1910. *Famous Imposters.* London, Sidgwick & Jackson.

145 Peter F. Anson, 1965. *Fisher Folklore, Old Customs, Taboos and Superstitions Among Fisher Folk, Especially in Brittany and Normandy, and on the East Coast Of Scotland.* The Faith Press London.

146 Peter F. Anson, 1965. *Fisher Folklore, Old Customs, Taboos and Superstitions Among Fisher Folk, Especially in Brittany and Normandy, and on the East Coast Of Scotland.* The Faith Press London.

147 Peter F. Anson, 1965. *Fisher Folklore, Old Customs, Taboos and Superstitions Among Fisher Folk, Especially in Brittany and Normandy, and on the East Coast Of Scotland.* The Faith Press London. See also Duncan Harley, 2017. *The A-Z of Curious Aberdeenshire: Strange Stories of Mysteries, Crimes and Eccentrics.* The History Press.

148 Christian Watt, David Fraser. *The Christian Watt Papers* edited by David Fraser 2004, Birlinn Edinburgh.

149 Fiona-Jane Brown, 2015. *'A Superstitious Lot': Belief and Identity in Scottish Fishing Communities*, Hub for the Study of British Identities, Research Network, Journal and Blog.
https://britishidentities.wordpress.com/2016/03/02/a-superstitious-lot-belief-and-identity-in-scottish-fishing-communities/

150 Ronald Hutton, 2013. *Pagan Britain.* Yale University Press, New Haven and London.

151 John Gregorson Campbell, 1902. *Witchcraft and Second Sight in the Highlands and Islands of Scotland - Tales and Traditions collected entirely from Original Sources.* James MacLehose and Sons, Glasgow.

152 Bram Stoker, 1897. *Dracula.* Hutchinson & Co, London. The tradition that blue flames mark the site of hidden treasure was sourced from Emily Gerard's article on Transylvanian superstitions.

153 Walter Gregor, 1881. *Notes on the Folk-Lore of the North-East of Scotland.* Elliot Stock, London.

154 Walter Gregor, 1881. *Notes on the Folk-Lore of the North-East of Scotland.* Elliot Stock, London.

155 J. M. McPherson, 1929. *Primitive Beliefs in the North-East of Scotland.* Longmans, Green And Co., London, New York, Toronto.

156 John Ramsay, 1888. *Scotland and Scotsmen in the 18th Century.* Scott, London.

157 J. M. McPherson, 1929. *Primitive Beliefs in the North-East of Scotland.* Longmans, Green And Co., London, New York, Toronto.

158 Walter Gregor, 1881. *Notes on the Folk-Lore of the North-East of Scotland.* Elliot Stock, London.

159 Walter Gregor, 1881. *Notes on the Folk-Lore of the North-East of Scotland.* Elliot Stock, London.

160 Bram Stoker, 1897. *Dracula.* A. Constable & Co, London.

161 Walter Gregor, 1881. *Notes on the Folk-Lore of the North-East of Scotland.* Elliot Stock, London.

162 John Allardyce, 1913. *Byegone Days in Aberdeenshire, Being A History of the County From a Standpoint Different From That of Previously Published Works.* The Central Press (John Milne) 61-63 Belmont Street Aberdeen.

163 J. M. McPherson, 1929. *Primitive Beliefs in the North-East of Scotland.* Longmans, Green And Co., London, New York, Toronto.

164 Bram Stoker, 1903. *The Jewel of Seven Stars.* William Heinemann, London.

165 Jane Stoddard. *A Chat with the Author of "Dracula".* The British Weekly, July 1897.

166 Harry Ludlam, 1977. *A Biography of Bram Stoker Creator of Dracula.* New English Library.

167 Bram Stoker, 1897. *Dracula.* Hutchinson & Co, London.

168 Peter Haining and Peter Tremayne, 1997: *The Un-Dead - The Legend of Bram Stoker and Dracula,* Constable, London.

169 *Dracula's Guest.* In Bram Stoker 1914, *Dracula's Guest and Other Stories.* George Routledge & Sons, Ltd., London.

170 *Slains and the Errolls.* P. Scrogie, Peterhead. 1973. Author not named, but believed to be Iain Moncreiffe former husband of Diana, Countess of Erroll.

171 John Mackintosh, 1898. *Historic Earls and Earldoms of Scotland.* W. Jolly & Sons, Aberdeen.

172 JFK Johnstone, *Notes on the Library of the Earl of Erroll, Slains Castle.* Aberdeen University Library Bulletin, April 1917.

173 Mike Salter, 1995. *The Castles of Grampian and Angus.* Folly Publications.

174 Samuel Johnson, 1775. *A Journey to the Western Isles of Scotland.*

175 James Boswell, 1785. *The Journal of a Tour to the Hebrides.*

176 www.thepeerage.com

177 Rev. John B. Pratt , 1901. *Buchan.* Fourth Edition Revised By Robert Anderson. Lewis Smith & Son Aberdeen.

178 Margaret Aitken 2004, *Six Buchan Villages Re-visited.* Scottish Cultural Press, Dalkeith.

179 Margaret Aitken 2004, *Six Buchan Villages Re-visited.* Scottish Cultural Press, Dalkeith.

180 Angus Hay, *pers. comm.*

181 Angus Hay, *pers. comm.*

182 Bram Stoker, 1897. *Dracula.* Hutchinson & Co, London.

183 The Cincinnati Enquirer Saturday, April 30, 1927.

184 David J. Skal, 2016. *Something in the Blood – The Untold Story of Bram Stoker, The Man Who Wrote Dracula.* Liveright Publishing Corporation New York, London.

185 Norval Scrymgeour. *"Dracula" and Dundee.* Dundee Evening Telegraph, February 17th 1937.

186 Bram Stoker, 1907. *Personal Reminiscences of Henry Irving.* William Heinemann, London.

187 Daniel Farson, 1975. *The Man Who Wrote Dracula. A Biography of Bram Stoker.* Michael Joseph, London.

188 Georges Simenon in *The Paris Review Interviews.* Volume 3. Canongate Books, Edinburgh. 2007.

189 Anna Margrét Björnsson , 2017. Icelandic version of Dracula, Makt myrkranna, turns out to be Swedish in origin. Iceland Monitor: https://icelandmonitor.mbl.is/news/culture_and_living/2017/03/06/icelandic_v ersion_of_dracula_makt_myrkranna_turns_o/

190 Walter Gregor, 1881. *Notes on the Folk-Lore of the North-East of Scotland.* Elliot Stock, London.

191 *Bram Stoker's Notes for Dracula A Facsimile Edition* Bram Stoker, annotated and Transcribed by Robert Eighteen-Bisang and Elizabeth Miller. McFarland & Company. Jefferson, North Carolina and London.

192 I have found no record of a Marine Hotel in Banff, although there is a Marine Hotel in the nearby village of Buckie.

193 Adrian Smith *pers. comm.* Adrian's grandmother Isabella Smith was the housekeeper of Roselea Cottage.

194 Jim Gentle, *The Street Names Of Cruden Bay.* Copy held in Cruden Bay Public Library.

195 Morag Ledingham, *Tourist Board bites back at Whitby over Dracula Origins*. Buchan Observer 27th March 2001.

196 Bram Stoker, 1897. *Dracula.* Hutchinson & Co, London.

197 John McGibbon, 1922. *The Fisher-Folk of Buchan - A True Story of Peterhead.* Marshall Brothers, Limited, London, Edinburgh, New York.

198 James McBey. *The Early Life of James McBey An Autobiography 1883-1911,* Edited by Nicolas Barker Oxford University Press 1977.

199 James Leatham, 1937. *Fisherfolk of the North-East* . Second edition. Deveron Press.

200 John McGibbon, 1922. The *Fisher-Folk of Buchan - A True Story of Peterhead.* Marshall Brothers, Limited, London, Edinburgh, New York.

201 D.M. Ferguson, 1991. *Shipwrecks of North East Scotland, 1444-1990.* Aberdeen University Press.

202 http://myweb.tiscali.co.uk/xenia1

203 *Bravery of Whinnyfold Fishermen Acknowledged.* Scotsman, June 30th, 1903.

204 *Wreck of the Wistow Hall.* Scotsman, January 19th, 1912. *Wreck Report for 'Frederick Snowdon',* 1912, Board of Trade.

205 I've used the name Temptin' Rock as written on the Ordnance Survey maps of the time; Tempion Rock is the spelling on most reports of the disaster.

206 Liz and James Taylor, 1988. *Our Forgotten Heroes.* http://www.fraserburghheritage.com/default.asp?page=604

207 Bram Stoker, 1897. *Dracula.* Hutchinson & Co, London.

208 James M. Cain in *The Paris Review Interviews*, Volume 1. Canongate Books, Edinburgh. 2007.

209 "Review of *Dracula,"* *Spectator* July 31, 1897.

210 *Shades of Dracula. The Uncollected Stories of Bram Stoker.* Edited by Peter Haining. William Kimber, London, 1982.

211 *Bram Stoker's Notes for Dracula A Facsimile Edition* Bram Stoker, annotated and Transcribed by Robert Eighteen-Bisang and Elizabeth Miller. McFarland & Company. Jefferson, North Carolina and London.

212 Harry Bingham, 2012. *Writers' & Artists' Guide to How to Write.* Bloomsbury Publishing Inc., London.

213 Peter Haining and Peter Tremayne, 1997: *The Un-Dead The Legend of Bram Stoker and Dracula*, Constable, London.

214 Harry Ludlam, 1977. *A Biography of Bram Stoker Creator of Dracula.* New English Library.

215 Peter Haining and Peter Tremayne, 1997: *The Un-Dead The Legend of Bram Stoker and Dracula*, Constable, London.

216 Buchan Observer, 29th June 1897.

217 J. A. Lillie, 1970. *Tradition and Environment*, Aberdeen University Press.

218 *The Cruden Railway*. Scotsman. September 10th 1894.

219 James Dalgarno, 1896. *From The Brig O' Balgownie To The Bullers O' Buchan: With The Golf Courses*. W. Jolly & Sons, Albany Press, Aberdeen.

220 *The Cruden Railway*. Scotsman. September 10th 1894.

221 Rev. R. Ross, *Cruden*, in: *The Vale of Ythan: Book of the Bazaar for the Logie Buchan Bridge Scheme.* Reverend WM Frank Scott (editor), Free Press, Aberdeen, 1895.

222 *Guide to Cruden Bay and Neighbourhood.* The Rosemount Press, Aberdeen. 1908.

223 *A Visit to Cruden Bay*, The Aberdeen Journal. October 22d, 1897.

224 *Pers. comm.* Steven Davie, Scottish Land Registry.

225 Cruden Bay Golf Club, 1998. *A Century of Golf at Cruden Bay 1899-1999 Including a Local History* P. Scrogie, Peterhead.

226 Cruden Bay Golf Club, 1998. *A Century of Golf at Cruden Bay 1899-1999 Including a Local History* P. Scrogie, Peterhead.

227 Margaret Aitken 2004, *Six Buchan Villages Re-visited.* Scottish Cultural Press, Dalkeith.

228 Alex. Inkson McConnochie, *Cruden Bay.* In *The Book Of Ellon*, Edited By Alex. Inkson McConnochie, Ellon The Victoria Hall Committee, 1901.

229 Alex. Inkson McConnochie, *Cruden Bay.* In *The Book Of Ellon*, Edited By Alex. Inkson McConnochie, Ellon The Victoria Hall Committee, 1901.

230 Bram Stoker, 1902. *The Mystery of the Sea.* William Heinemann, London.

231 Rev. Adam Mackay, 1912. *Cruden and its Ministers.* Printed by P. Scrogie, 'Buchan Observer' Works.

232 www.henryirving.co.uk/correspondence

233 Bram Stoker, 1902. *The Mystery of the Sea.* William Heinemann, London.

234 Bram Stoker, *The Crooken Sands*, in *Dracula's Guest.* 1914 George Routledge and Sons.

235 Harry Ludlam, 1977. *A Biography of Bram Stoker Creator of Dracula.* New English Library.

236 Bram Stoker, 1907. *Personal Reminiscences of Henry Irving.* William Heinemann, London.

237 *Dracula: Bram Stoker's Local Links Confirmed.* The Buchan Observer, 9th March, 1993.

238 Press and Journal, 6/9/1899.

239 Bram Stoker, 1902. *The Mystery of the Sea.* William Heinemann, London.

240 The cigarette case is engraved A.F., and it is not clear if this is a gift from Bram Stoker.

241 *Dracula: Bram Stoker's Local Links Confirmed.* The Buchan Observer, 9th March, 1993.

242 J. A. Lillie, 1970. *Tradition and Environment*, Aberdeen University Press.

243 Harry Ludlam, 1977. *A Biography of Bram Stoker Creator of Dracula.* New English Library.

244 Arthur Conan Doyle, 1892. *Lot No. 249.* Harper's Monthly Magazine.

245 Bram Stoker, 1903. *The Jewel of Seven Stars.* William Heinemann, London.

246 Lord Kilmarnock (Victor Hay), 1903. *Ferelith.* Hutchinson.

247 *Shot by the King.* West Coast Times (New Zealand). Sep 18 1910.

248 Angus Hay, *pers. comm.*

249 Margaret Aitken 2004, *Six Buchan Villages Re-visited.* Scottish Cultural Press, Dalkeith.

250 Jim Buchan 2007; *Old Cruden Bay and Port Erroll Whinnyfold*, Boddam, Buchanhaven. Stenlake Publishing Ltd.

251 Tom Scott Sutherland, 1957. *Life on One Leg.* Christopher Johnson.

252 *Peterhead Flower Show, Speech by Mr. Bram Stoker.* Buchan Observer August 10th 1904.

253 Norval Scrymgeour *"Dracula" and Dundee.* The Evening Telegraph, February 17th, 1937.

254 Horace Wyndam, 1922. *The Nineteen Hundreds.* G. Allen & Unwin Ltd., London.

255 Michael Shelden, 2013. *Young Titan - The Making of Winston Churchill.* Simon and Schuster, UK.

256 Bram Stoker. 'An Interview with Winston Churchill' *The World*, New York. October 5, 1907.

257 Buchan Observer, 1/9/1908.

258 *Alarming Incident at Cruden Bay*. Buchan Observer. 22/9/1908.

259 Sylvia Munro, *pers. comm.*

260 Michael Shelden, 2013. *Young Titan - The Making of Winston Churchill.* Simon and Schuster, UK.

261 One of the biographers, Daniel Farson, refers to Bram's lodging in Whinnyfold as 'Isy-Leay's'. He obviously couldn't read his hand-written notes because the fisherman's cottage he refers to is 'Isy Cay's'.

262 Interview with Elsie Watt, 22/05/17.

263 As told to Elsie Watt by her mother whose aunt was Isy Cay. This was on a visit by myself and Dacre Stoker to see Elsie in 2017. It was a poignant occasion, and I took a photo of the two of them together, the grand-niece of Isy Cay and the great-grandnephew of Bram Stoker.

264 The Isy Cay photograph is on page 118 of Donald Anderson's self-published book, *Fae Rosehearty tae Fittie : history of boats and fishing villages of North East Scotland.* Peterhead, 2011.

265 Margaret Aitken 2004, *Six Buchan Villages Re-visited.* Scottish Cultural Press, Dalkeith.

266 Barbara Belford, 1996. *Bram Stoker: A Biography of the Author of Dracula.* Phoenix Giant, London.

267 *'She remembers the cheery Irishman who wrote Dracula.'* The People's Journal, January 5th 1963.

268 Daniel Farson, 1975. *The Man Who Wrote Dracula. A Biography of Bram Stoker.* Michael Joseph, London.

269 Harry Ludlam, 1977. *A Biography of Bram Stoker Creator of Dracula.* New English Library.

270 Cruden Parish Church. *Cruden Recipes and Wrinkles. A Souvenir Bazaar Book.* P Scrogie, Peterhead, 1912.

271 Perry, Dennis R., 1986. *Whitman's Influence on Stoker's Dracula*. *Walt Whitman Quarterly Review* 3 p.29-35.

272 Bram Stoker, 1897. *Dracula*. William Heinemann, London.

273 Edward Carpenter, *Days with Walt Whitman* (London, 1906) quoted in Gay Wilson Allen, 1955. *The Solitary Singer: A Critical Biography of Walt Whitman*. The Macmillan Company, New York.

274 Gay Wilson Allen, 1955. *The Solitary Singer: A Critical Biography of Walt Whitman*. The Macmillan Company, New York.

275 Frances Wright, 1822. *A Few Days in Athens: Being the Translation of a Greek Manuscript Discovered in Herculaneum*. London: Longman, Hurst, Rees, Orme, and Brown.

276 Walt Whitman, *Song of Myself*. Boston: Thayer and Eldridge, 1860.

277 Gay Wilson Allen, 1955. *The Solitary Singer: A Critical Biography of Walt Whitman*. The Macmillan Company, New York.

278 Hugh I'anson Fausset, 1942. *Walt Whitman: Poet of Democracy*. Jonathan Cape, London.

279 Quoted in Hugh I'anson Fausset, 1942. *Walt Whitman: Poet of Democracy*. Jonathan Cape, London.

280 Bram Stoker, 1907. *Personal Reminiscences of Henry Irving*. William Heinemann, London.

281 Bram Stoker, 1907. *Personal Reminiscences of Henry Irving*. William Heinemann, London.

282 Bram Stoker, 1907. *Personal Reminiscences of Henry Irving*. William Heinemann, London.

283 James Dalgarno, 1896. *From The Brig O' Balgownie To The Bullers O' Buchan: With The Golf Courses*. W. Jolly & Sons, Albany Press, Aberdeen.

284 Henry Gray Graham, 1909. *The Social Life of Scotland in the 18th Century*. Adam and Charles Black, London.

285 Morag Ledingham, *Tourist Board bites back at Whitby over Dracula Origins*. Buchan Observer 27th March 2001.

286 James Drummond, *Bram Stoker's Cruden Bay*, Scots Magazine April 1976.

287 Bram Stoker, 1911. *The Lair of the White Worm*. William Rider and Son, Ltd., London.

288 Bram Stoker, 1897. *Dracula*. William Heinemann, London.

289 Walt Whitman, *Song of Myself*. Boston: Thayer and Eldridge, 1860. Bram Stoker was so impressed with this episode from the poem he used it again for his novel *The Man*. In the later novel the episode takes place amongst sea reefs called The Skyres.

290 Bram Stoker, 1902. *The Mystery of the Sea*. William Heinemann, London.

291 Robert Smith 1997 *One Foot in the Sea*: Fishing Villages of North East Scotland. John Donald Publishers Ltd.

292 Walt Whitman, *Song of Myself*. Boston: Thayer and Eldridge, 1860.

293 John Gregorson Campbell, 1902. *Witchcraft and Second Sight in the Highlands and Islands of Scotland - Tales and Traditions collected entirely from Original Sources*. James MacLehose and Sons, Glasgow.

294 John Gregorson Campbell, 1902. *Witchcraft and Second Sight in the Highlands and Islands of Scotland - Tales and Traditions collected entirely from Original Sources*. James MacLehose and Sons, Glasgow.

295 Norval Scrymgeour. *"Dracula" and Dundee*. Dundee Evening Telegraph, February 17th 1937.

296 Quoted in Harry Ludlam, 1977. *A Biography of Bram Stoker Creator of Dracula*. New English Library.

297 Walt Whitman, *Leaves of Grass*.

298 Bram Stoker, 1902. *The Mystery of the Sea*. William Heinemann, London.

299 *The Dublin Years The Lost Journal of Bram Stoker.* Edited by Elizabeth Miller and Dacre Stoker. The Robson Press, 2012.

300 Bram Stoker, 1902. *The Mystery of the Sea.* William Heinemann, London.

301 Bram Stoker, 1902. *The Mystery of the Sea.* William Heinemann, London.

302 James E Miller Jr, 1966. *A Critical Guide to Leaves of Grass* Phoenix Books, University of Chicago Press.

303 Bram Stoker, 1907. *Personal Reminiscences of Henry Irving.* William Heinemann, London.

304 Bram Stoker, 1902. *The Mystery of the Sea.* William Heinemann, London.

305 Bram Stoker,1885. *The One Thing Needful.* In *The Youth's Companion,* Perry Mason & Co., Publishers, Boston, Massachusetts.

306 Bram Stoker, 1902. *The Mystery of the Sea.* William Heinemann, London.

307 *Peterhead Flower Show, Speech by Mr. Bram Stoker.* Buchan Observer August 10th 1904.

308 Bram Stoker, 1902. *The Mystery of the Sea.* William Heinemann, London.

309 Bram Stoker, 1907. *Personal Reminiscences of Henry Irving.* William Heinemann, London.

310 Bram Stoker, 1907. *Personal Reminiscences of Henry Irving.* William Heinemann, London.

311 Bram Stoker, 1903. *The Jewel of Seven Stars.* William Heinemann, London.

312 Bram Stoker, 1903. *The Jewel of Seven Stars.* William Heinemann, London.